# 익혀먹는 레알 AP 용어사전

임해용 저

해외 유학생을 위한
# 익혀먹는 레알 AP 경제 용어사전

| 만든 사람들 |

**기획** 실용기획부 | **진행** 신지나 | **집필** 임해용 | **편집 디자인** design86 | **표지 디자인** 전민경

| 책 내용 문의 |

도서 내용에 대해 궁금한 사항이 있으시면 아이생각(디지털북스) 홈페이지의 게시판을 통해 해결하실 수 있습니다.
**아이생각(디지털북스) 홈페이지** : www.ithinkbook.co.kr (www.digitalbooks.co.kr)
**디지털북스 이메일** : digital@digitalbooks.co.kr

| 각종 문의 |

**영업 관련** hi@digitalbooks.co.kr
**기획 관련** dgbookplan@digitalbooks.co.kr, digital@digitalbooks.co.kr
**전화 번호** (02) 447-3157~8

※ 이 책의 일부 혹은 전체 내용에 대한 무단 복사, 복제, 전재는 저작권법에 의해 금합니다.
※ 잘못 만들어진 책은 구입하신 서점에서 교환해 드립니다.

# 익혀먹는 리얼 AP 용어사전

## 저자의 말

　이 책은 경제학입문자, 특별히 기초적인 경제개념 이해를 하고자 하는 학생들을 위해 쓰였습니다. 어떤 분야의 공부를 하든지 기본적인 용어에 대한 명확한 이해를 통해서 접근해야 시간과 에너지를 절약할 수 있습니다. 대한민국에서 가르치는 경제학은 기본적으로 영미의 경제학을 모체로 하기 때문에, 경제학 공부는 원서를 통해 하는 것이 바람직하다고 할 수 있습니다. 하지만 한국어를 모국어로 사용하고 있는 우리에게는 번역을 통해 원어에 다가가는 것이 필요하기도 합니다.

　우선, 경제학원론 수준에서 단어나 어구들을 중심으로 정리하였는데, 앞부분에서는 내용별로, 뒤 부분 APPENDIX에서는 사전식으로 정리를 수록하였습니다. 이 책의 장점이라면 각 PART의 앞부분에 개념 지도를 그려 놓아, 경제학 전체 지도와 각 CHAPTER의 내용에서 다루는 경제개념들이 어떻게 연결되어 있는지를 한 눈에 파악할 수 있게 해서 입문자들에게 경제학에 대한 그림을 그려주었다는데도 있고, 사전식 배열을 통해 개념이 명확하지 않을 때 바로 찾아볼 수 있도록 한 것입니다.

　마지막으로는 저의 강의 경험을 살려 학생들이 이해하기 어려워하는 부분에 대해서는 가급적 명쾌하고 상세하게 해설하려고 노력했습니다. 또한 문제를 통해 공부한 내용을 확인할 수 있도록 각 CHAPTER마다 문제를 제시하였고, 전체 내용을 포괄하는 실전문제와 정답해설을 수록하였습니다. 무엇보다 AP Economics 시험 대비를 하거나 경제기본용어의 개념을 영어로 익히는 데에 도움을 얻으시기를 바랍니다.

임해용

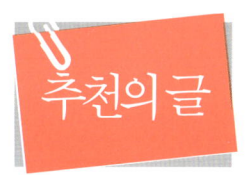

## 추천의 글

고등학교에서 AP 경제학 시험을 준비할 때 해롤드 선생님의 자료와 강의는 다른 어떤 자료보다 큰 도움이 됐습니다. 경제학 특성상 각종 용어와 그래프가 가지는 의미와 서로 어떻게 연관돼있는지를 아는 것이 중요한데 이 책은 그런 면에서 설명이 매우 잘 돼 있다고 생각합니다. 또한 해설이 심플하면서도 필요한 내용만을 담아 이해하는데 별다른 어려움이 없고 풀 수 있는 문제도 포함돼 있어 AP 경제학 시험을 준비하시는 분이나 경제학을 독학하실 분께 꼭 추천하고 싶은 책입니다.

한영외고 졸업, 2013 Cal Tech 입학 예정, 김재빈

요즘은 다들 공부를 할 때 시험에 나오는 요점만 알고 빨리 넘어가려고 하는 경향이 있는데, 선생님은 경제학의 정석대로 학생에게 가능한 한 많은 지식을 전해주려고 애쓰시는 분입니다. 시험의 유형보다는 아주 기초적인 핵심을 위주로 다루고 있는 이 책은, 대부분이 지름길로 바쁘게 가로질러갈 때, 경제학의 기본 개념부터 탄탄히 다지며 나아가지는 선생님의 가치관이 그대로 담겨있는 책입니다.

한영외고 졸업, 2013 Cornell University 입학 예정, 문희정

경제라는 학문을 공부함으로서 우리는 시장에서의 인간활동을 이론적으로 이해하고 더 나은 자원분배를 위한 실용적인 방안을 추구하는 것이 가능합니다. 해롤드 선생님의 강의는 미래의 경제 구성원으로서 갖춰야 할 경제적인 소양을 제공합니다. 〈익혀먹는 AP 경제 용어사전〉을 통해 두 마리 토끼를 모두 잡으시길 바랍니다.

한영외고 졸업, 2013 University of Chicago 입학 예정, 홍지우

저는 학교 수업을 통하여 해롤드 선생님의 경제학 강의를 듣게 되었습니다. 〈익혀먹는 AP 경제 용어사전〉은 해롤드 선생님의 강의와 같이 개념정리, 그래프의 이해, 문제풀이에 중점을 두어 경제학을 처음 배우는 모든 이에게 접근하기 쉽게 쓰였습니다. 독자 여러분들도 해롤드 선생님의 강의가 담겨있는 이 책을 통하여 탄탄한 경제학 기초를 다지시길 바랍니다.

한영외고 졸업, 2013 Dartmouth University 입학 예정, 성태호

해롤드 샘의 수업을 듣고 AP Economics Micro와 Macro를 준비했었습니다. 이번 책은 경제 용어와 그래프를 잘 정리해 놓아서 AP를 준비할 때 보다 쉽고 명료하게 접근하게 해줄 것입니다. 이에 더하여 언어적 측면에서도 기존의 원서가 부담되었던 국내학생들에게 도움이 되리라 생각합니다.

용인외고 졸업, 서울대학교 경제학부 재학, 이은도

저자의 말

미시경제학 개념지도

**Chapter 1** | Basic Concepts
Lesson 1  What is Economics ······20
Lesson 2  Economic System ······22
Lesson 3  Production Possibilities Curve ······25
Lesson 4  Circular Flow Diagram ······27
Lesson 5  Trade ······29
**Problem Set** ······32

**Chapter 2** | Demand, Supply and Market
Lesson 1  Demand ······40
Lesson 2  Supply ······43
Lesson 3  Elasticity ······47
Lesson 4  Market Equilibrium ······52
Lesson 5  Government Policy to Regulate Markets ······55
Lesson 6  Tax ······57
Lesson 7  The Theory of Consumer Choice ······62
**Problem Set** ······68

## Chapter 3 | Production and Cost
Lesson1  Production ······80
Lesson2  Cost ······82
Lesson3  Short run vs Long run ······85
**Problem Set** ······88


## Chapter 4 | Market Structures
Lesson 1  Perfect Competition ······98
Lesson 2  Monopoly ······105
Lesson 3  Oligopoly ······110
Lesson 4  Monopolistic Competition ······114
**Problem Set** ······117


## Chapter 5 | Factor Market and Income Distribution
Lesson 1  Factor Market ······128
Lesson 2  Income Distribution ······134
**Problem Set** ······136


## Chapter 6 | Market Failure
Lesson1  Externalities ······144
Lesson2  Common Resources and Public Good ······147
Lesson3  Information Asymmetry ······149
**Problem Set** ······151
**Practice Exam Microeconomics** ······158

# Part1 02 Macroeconomics

거시경제학 개념지도

### Chapter 1 | Measuring Economic Performance
Lesson 1 Macroeconomics ······192
Lesson 2 Real GDP and Nominal GDP ······195
Lesson 3 Price Level ······196
Lesson 4 Inflation and Unemployment ······198
**Problem Set** ······203

### Chapter 2 | Income-Expenditure and AD-AS model
Lesson 1 Consumption ······216
Lesson 2 Aggregate Expenditure Model ······219
**Problem Set** ······226

### Chapter 3 | Money, Banking and Financial Market
Lesson 1 Saving, Investment and Loanable Fund Market ······234
Lesson 2 Money Market ······236
Lesson 3 Tools of Monetary Policy ······240
**Problem Set** ······246

### Chapter 4 | Economic Stabilization Policy and Economic Growth
Lesson1 Economic Stabilization Policy ······258
Lesson2 Philips Curve ······266
Lesson3 Economic Growth ······270
**Problem Set** ······272

**Chapter 5** | Open Economy

Lesson1 Free Trade ······288

Lesson2 Balance of Payments ······291

Lesson3 Determining International Value of a Country's Currency ······293

**Problem Set** ······298

**Practice Exam Macroeconomics** ······306

**Appendix**

ABC순 정리 ······326

미국경제학회가 제시하는 20가지 경제 법칙 ······358

# Part 01

## Microeconomics
## 미시경제

희소한 자원의 배분 allocations of scarce resources 에 관해 연구하는 경제학은 미시경제학 microeconomics 과 거시경제학 macroeconomics 으로 이루어집니다. 미시경제학은 가계 household 와 기업 firm 의 행동에 대해 주로 초점을 두며, 거시경제학 macroeconomics 은 국가 경제 전체의 활동에 중심을 둡니다. 미시경제학은 수요 demand 와 공급 supply, 소비자이론 consumer theory 과 생산자이론 producer theory, 시장의 유형 market type, 요소시장 factor market, 소득분배 income distribution, 시장실패 market failures 를 다룹니다.

**Chapter 01** **Basic Concepts**
기본 개념

**Chapter 02** **Demand, Supply and Markets**
수요, 공급과 시장

**Chapter 03** **Production and Cost**
생산과 비용

**Chapter 04** **Market Structures**
시장구조

**Chapter 05** **Factor Market and Income Distribution**
요소시장과 소득분배

**Chapter 06** **Market Failure**
시장실패

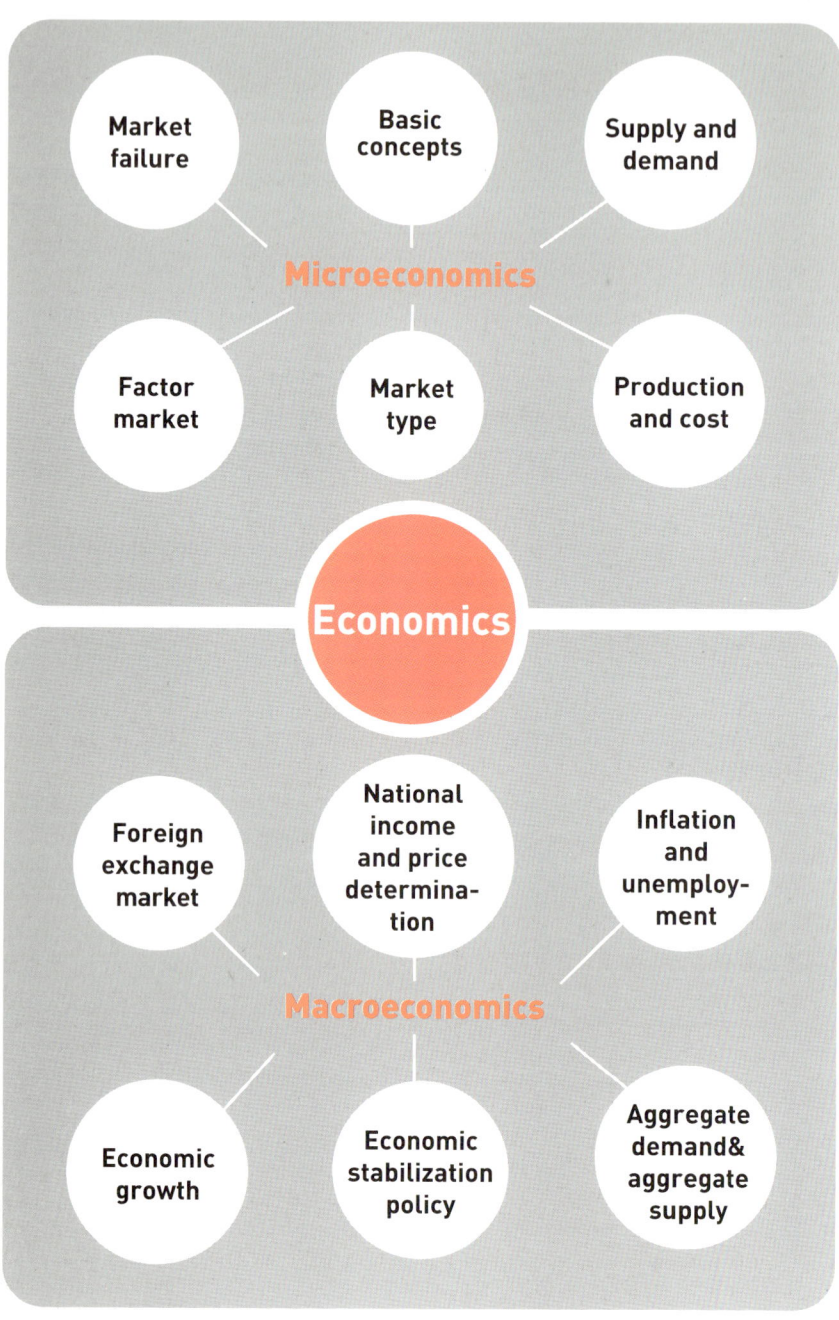

개념지도

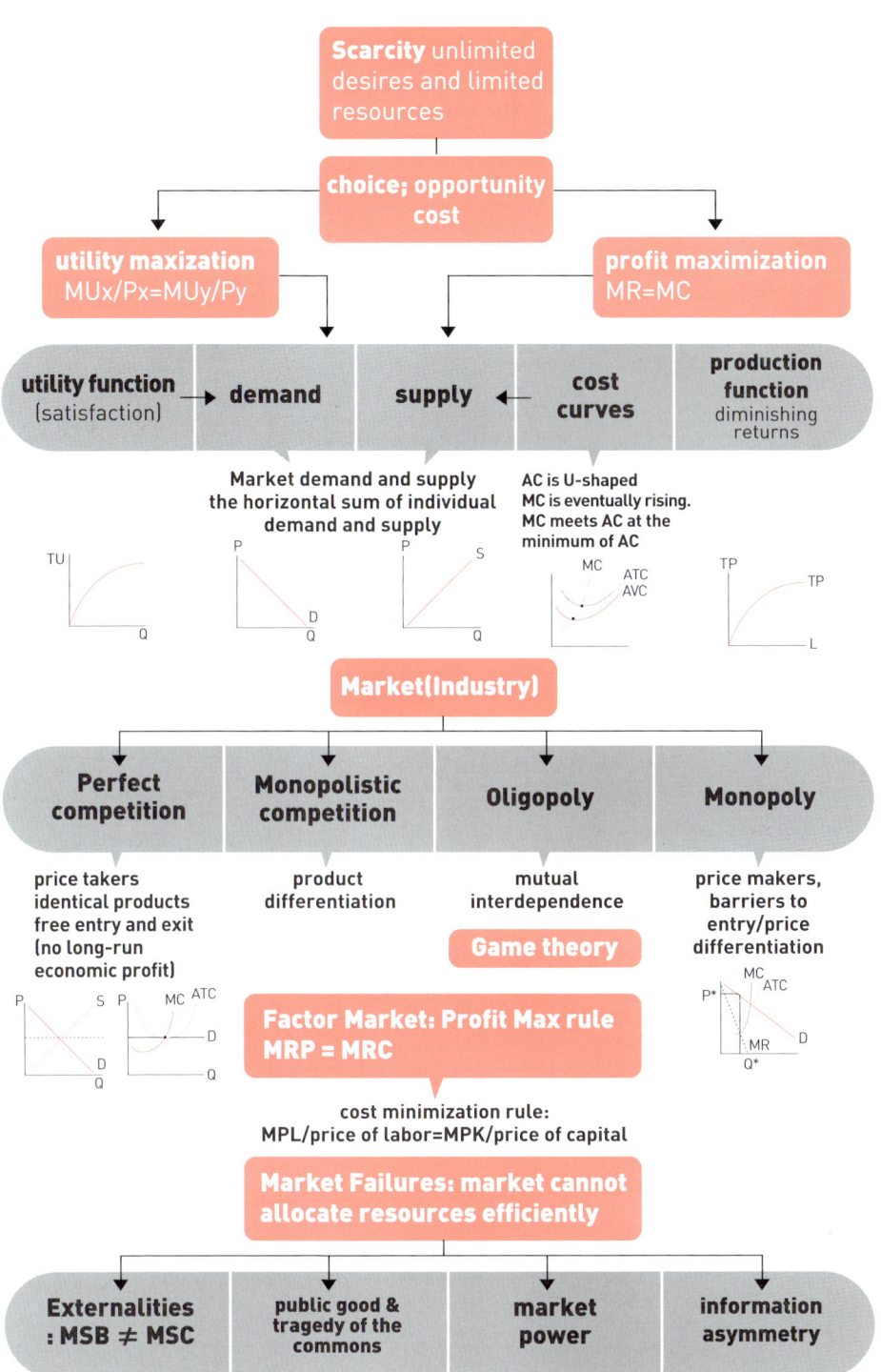

Microeconomics Map for AP Microeconomics

## 개념지도 설명

경제학은 희소한 자원을 어떻게 배분할 것인가 하는 문제를 다루는 학문입니다. 경제문제가 발생하는 가장 근본적인 원인은 바로 자원의 희소성 scarcity 입니다. 즉, 자원은 유한하지만 사람들의 욕구는 무한하기 때문입니다. 그래서 선택의 문제가 발생합니다. 선택은 비용과 편익을 발생시킵니다. 대부분 선택은 전부 아니면 전무 all or nothing 식의 선택이라기보다는 주어진 상황에서 추가적인 선택을 해야 하는 경우가 많습니다. 따라서 한계비용 marginal cost 과 한계편익 marginal benefit 을 비교하여 결정을 내립니다.

희소한 자원이 분배되는 장소는 시장이므로 바로 시장에서 선택이 이루어집니다. 시장은 수요와 공급이 존재하는 곳으로 백화점이나 전통시장처럼 눈에 보이는 시장도 있지만 과외시장처럼 눈에 보이지 않는 시장도 존재합니다. 시장에서는 소비자와 공급자가 만납니다. 수요를 결정하고 생산자는 공급을 결정합니다. 수요곡선은 효용극대화 utility maximization 를 추구하는 소비자의 선택에서, 공급곡선은 이윤극대화 profit maximization 를 추구하는 생산자의 선택에서 도출됩니다.

시장에는 여러 가지 유형이 있습니다. 크게 시장은 거래 대상에 따라 재화와 서비스가 거래되는 생산물시장 product market 과 생산요소가 거래되는 생산요소시장 factor market 으로 나뉩니다. 생산물시장은 가장 효율적인 모델인 완전경쟁시장 perfect competition, 한 개의 기업이 한 산업을 구성하는 독점시장 monopoly, 소수의 기업이 전략적인 상황에서 상호작용하는 과점시장 oligopoly, 제품의 차별화를 특징으로 하는 독점적경쟁시장 monopolistic competition 이 바로 그것입니다. 각각의 시장에서 자원이 어떻게 배분되는가에 초점을 두고 공부를 해야 합니다. 자원의 배분은 가격과 수량을 통해 파악됩니다. 생산요소시장에서는 시장의 유형으로는 완전경쟁노동시장 perfectly competitive labor market 과 수요독점시장 monopsony 이 있습니다. 이 시장에서의 자원배분은 임금과 고용량으로 통해 결정됩니다.

마지막으로 외부효과 externalities, 공공재 public good, 시장지배력 information asymmetry, 정보비대칭 information asymmetry 의 문제로 자원이 효율적으로 배분되지 못하는 시장실패 market failure 현상이 발생합니다.

# Chapter 01

## Basic Concept

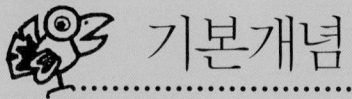 기본개념

"Basically, economics is all about choices."

희소한scarce 자원의 분배에 관한 연구인 경제학은 결국 선택에 대한 문제로 귀결되고, 선택에는 편익benefit과 비용cost이 수반됩니다. 이 선택은 하나를 얻으려면 다른 어떤 것을 포기해야 하는 상충관계trade-off를 의미하지요. 한 경제가 생산가능한 상품의 조합을 나타내는 생산가능곡선Production Possibilities Curve 에서도 선택의 문제는 발생합니다. 일반적인 생산가능곡선은 원점에 대해 볼록concave하고, 이 경우에 X재화 생산을 늘려 나갈 때, Y재화의 생산량이 점점 더 크게 줄어드는데, 이는 기회비용이 증가하는 것increasing opportunity cost을 의미합니다. 교역trade을 통해 각 개인과 국가는 더 큰 소비를 경험하게 됩니다. 이는 절대우위absolute advantage가 아니라 비교우위comparative advantage에 기초하여 교열을 합니다. 국가의 경제체제는 크게 전통경제체제traditional economy, 시장경제체제market economy, 계획경제체제planned economy, 혼합경제체제mixed economy로 나눌 수 있습니다.

# Lesson 1: What is Economics?
## 경제학이란?

### economics
### 경제학

**The study of how the limited resources are allocated to satisfy our unlimited human wants**
우리의 유한한 자원이 인간의 무한한 욕망과 욕구를 만족시키기 위하여 어떻게 배분되는지에 대해 연구하는 학문

- **A good understanding of economics would allow you to answer the question about why we study economics.**
  경제학을 잘 이해하면 우리가 왜 경제학을 공부하는지에 대해 대답할 수 있다.

### scarcity
### 희소성

**Fundamental economic situation in which men have unlimited wants and needs in a world of limited resources**
욕망은 무한한데 그것을 충족시켜줄 수 있는 자원은 유한한 상태

- **All the economic problems are fundamentally caused by scarcity.**
  모든 경제적인 문제는 근본적으로 희소성에 기인한다.
- **All economic systems face the problems of allocating scarce resources how to allocate scarce resources**
  모든 경제체제는 희소한 자원의 배분 방식에 대한 문제를 가지고 있다.

### trade-off
### 상충관계

**The situation in which to get one thing, one must give up something else. You have to sleep less in order to study more**
하나를 얻으려면 다른 것을 포기해야 하는 상황

- **There is no trade-off between inflation and unemployment in the long run.**
  장기에는 인플레이션과 실업 사이에 상충관계가 없다.
- **The trade-off between income and leisure is closely related to the individual decision about how many hours he would work.**
  소득과 여가사이의 상충관계는 한 개인이 얼마나 일할 것인지를 결정하는 것과 밀접하게 연관되어 있다.

## opportunity cost
### 기회비용

**The cost of any choice measured in terms of the value of the best alternative that is foregone**
어떤 선택을 했을 때 포기해버린 최선의 대안의 가치, 또는 그것을 기준으로 측정된 비용

- **No opportunity cost would be incurred when you go on a date with her.**
  네가 그 여자와 만날 때 어떤 기회비용도 발생하지 않을 거야.

## marginal thinking
### 한계적 사고

**Thinking about the changes brought by additional choices**
추가적인 선택이 주는 변화에 대해 생각하는 것

> **Tip** 여기서 '한계적marginal'은 '추가additional'의 의미

- **If you understand marginal thinking, you are ready to be a good student of economics.**
  네가 한계적 사고를 이해한다면 경제학을 잘 배울 준비가 된 거야.

## marginal cost vs. marginal benefit
### 한계비용 vs. 한계편익

**The increase in total cost from producing an additional unit of good vs. the increase in total benefit from consuming additional unit of good**
한 단위 더 생산할 때 총비용의 증가분 vs. 한 단위 더 소비할 때 총편익의 증가분

- **When Steve decided to buy another book, his marginal benefit from the choice must have been greater than the marginal cost.**
  스티브가 책을 한권 더 사기로 결정했을 때 그의 한계편익이 한계비용보다 컸음이 분명하다.

# Lesson 2: Economic System
## 경제 체제

### traditional economy
### 전통경제체제

An economy is based on custom and tradition. The decisions are based on tradition of the community or family such as Native Americans in the U.S.
관습과 전통에 기초한 경제. 의사결정은 공동체나 가족의 전통에 기반을 둔다. 미국의 원주민이 예이다.

### market economy
### 시장경제

An economy in which the resources are allocated through markets
자원이 시장을 통하여 배분되는 경제

### planned economy
### 계획경제

An economy in which the resources are allocated through government plan and command(former USSR, North Korea, Cuba)
구소련, 북한, 쿠바처럼 자원이 정부의 계획이나 명령에 의해 배분되는 경제

### mixed economy
### 혼합경제

The combination of market economy and planned economy
시장경제와 계획경제의 결합, 현대국가의 일반적인 형태

**The Three Questions all economic systems face**
모든 경제체제가 직면하는 세 가지 질문

What goods and services will be produced?(what to produce)
어떤 상품과 서비스를 생산할 것인가?

How will the goods and services be produced?(how to produce)
그 상품과 서비스를 어떤 방법으로 생산할 것인가?

For whom will the goods and services be produced?(for whom to produce)
누구를 위해 그 상품과 서비스를 생산할 것인가?

## positive economics and normative economics
실증경제학과 규범경제학

Economics can be divided to positive economics, which describes how the economy works, and normative economics, which prescribes how the economy should work. Positive economics often involves making forecasts. Economists can determine correct answers for positive questions, but typically not for normative questions, which involve value judgments.

경제학은 경제가 어떻게 작동하는가를 서술하는 실증경제학과 경제가 어떻게 작동해야 하는가를 처방하는 규범경제학으로 나누어질 수 있다. 실증경제학은 종종 예측하는 것을 포함하기도 한다. 경제학자들은 실증적인 질문에 대해서는 정확한 답을 확정할 수 있지만, 보통 가치판단을 포함하는 규범적인 질문에 대해서는 그렇게 하지 못한다.

## positive(descriptive) statement(analysis)
실증적(서술적) 진술(분석)

**An objective, testable statement about how the economy works**
경제가 어떻게 작동하는가에 대한 객관적이고 검증 가능한 진술

- **A minimum wage increases unemployment among the young and unskilled workers.**
  최저임금제는 청년과 미숙련 노동자들의 실업률을 증가시킨다.

- **A control on rents reduces the quantity and quality of rental housing available.**
  임대료 통제는 임대주택의 양과 질을 감소시킨다.

## normative(prescriptive) statement(analysis)
규범적(처방적) 진술(분석)

**A subjective, contestable statement about how the economy should be**
경제가 어떠해야 하는 가에 대한 주관적이고 논쟁적인 진술

- **The government should raise the minimum wage.**
  정부는 최저임금을 높여야 한다.
- **The central bank ought to increase the money supply to fight recession.**
  중앙은행은 통화량을 증가시켜 경기침체에 대응해야 한다.

# Lesson 3: Production Possibilities Curve
생산가능곡선

## production possibilities curve(PPC)
생산가능곡선

**A curve showing the maximum combinations of output of two goods given the available resources and technology**
주어진 자원과 기술 하에서, 두 상품의 최대 조합을 보여주는 곡선

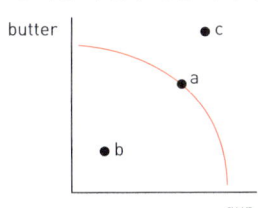

**a**점 : efficient production(production on the PPC)
**b**점 : inefficient production(production below PPC)
**c**점 : unattainable production(production above PPC)

**Tip**
A curve showing the maximum combinations of output of two goods given the available resources and technology.
생산가능곡선이 오른쪽으로 이동하는 것은 경제성장을 의미한다.

## different kinds of PPC relating to opportunity cost
기회비용과 생산가능곡선

**The phenomenon that opportunity cost rises when producing additional unit of a good(the graph, above)**
생산을 늘릴 때 기회비용이 커지는 상황

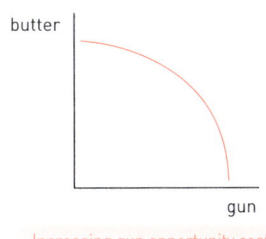
Increasing gun opportunity cost
기회비용이 증가하는 경우

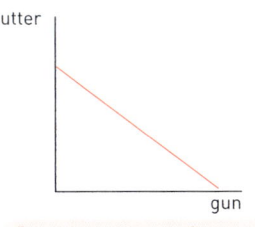
Constant opportunity cost
기회비용이 변함없는 경우

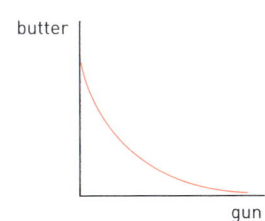
Decreasing opportunity cost
기회비용이 감소하는 경우

## outward shift of PPC
생산가능곡선의 바깥쪽 이동

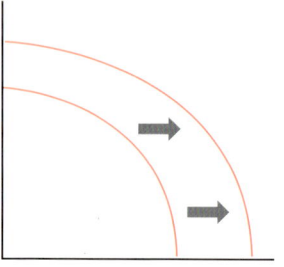

economic growth: the increase in real GDP
경제성장 : 실질GDP의 증가

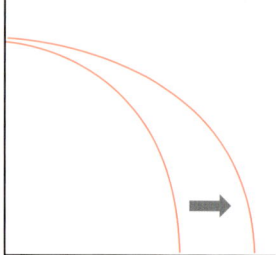

technological advance in the gun industry
총 산업의 기술 진보

## factors of economic growth
경제성장의 원인

**Increase in labor(L), capital(K), and natural resources(N) and technological advance**
노동력 증가, 자본의 증가, 천연자원의 증가, 기술의 진보

### 기본 단어 익히기

**labor** 노동력

**capital** 자본

**natural resources** 천연자원

# Lesson 4

# Circular Flow Diagram
## 경제순환모형

## circular flow diagram
### 경제순환모형

**A model that shows how households and firms circulate goods, services, resources, revenues, and incomes through markets**
시장을 통해 상품, 서비스, 자원, 매출, 소득이 순환되는 것을 보여주는 모형

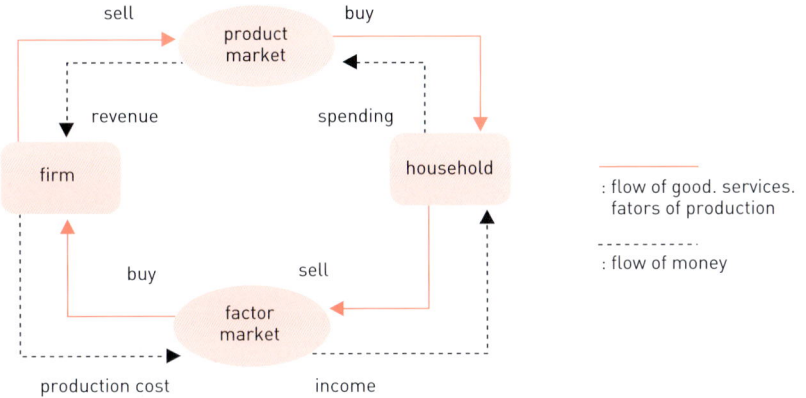

## product market
### 상품시장

**The market in which firms sell and households buy goods and services**
상품과 서비스를 사고파는 시장

## factor market
### 요소시장

**The market in which households sell and firms buy factors of production**
생산요소를 사고파는 시장

## factors of production (factor, resource)
생산요소

**Inputs or resources used to produce goods and services**
상품과 서비스를 생산하는 과정에 투입·결합되는 경제자원

### 기본 단어 익히기

**land(N):** natural resources used to produce goods and services
천연자원 : 상품과 서비스 생산에 사용되는 천연자원

**labor(L):** human efforts used to produce goods and services
노동 : 상품과 서비스 생산에 사용되는 사람의 노력

**capital(K):** the equipment, machinery, and structures used to produce goods and services
자본 : 상품과 서비스 생산에 들어가는 장비, 기계, 구조물

**entrepreneurial efforts(entrepreneurship):** the ability of business management such as innovation and risk-taking.
기업가적 노력 : 혁신이나 위험 감수 등의 기업경영 능력

# Lesson 5 | Trade
## 교역

### trade
### 교역

**The activity of buying, selling, or exchanging goods or services between people, firms, or countries**
개인, 기업, 국가 사이에 상품이나 서비스를 사고팔거나 교환하는 활동

- **Trade is based on the differences in relative costs of production.**
  교역은 생산의 상대적 비용의 차이에 기초한다.

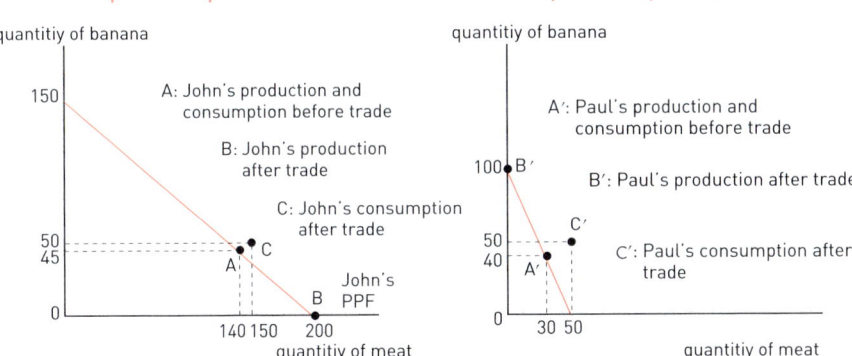

In the side-by-side production possibilities curves above, John has the absolute advantage, which means the ability to produce more with the same amount of resources, in the production of meat and bananas. But remember the question which good is specialized by a country specializes in is determined by comparative advantage, not by absolute advantage. Comparative advantage means the ability to produce a good or service with the lower opportunity cost. In the case above, in the production of meat, John has comparative advantage, because John's opportunity cost of producing one unit of meat, 3/4 bananas is less than Paul's, 2 bananas. In the production of bananas, Paul has comparative advantage, because, Paul's opportunity cost, 1/2 meat, is less than John's, 4/3 meat. Therefore John specializes in meat, and Paul specializes in banana. Then comes the question of terms of trade, the rate of exchange in trading with each other. Terms of trade depends on the domestic rate of exchange before trade. Before trade, 1 meat can be traded for 3/4 banana for

John. For Paul, 1 meat can be traded for 2 bananas. The terms of trade is determined between the two domestic rates of exchange. For example, If 1 meat could be traded with 1 bananas, both could be better off. Through trade, both can consume more of meat and bananas than before trade.

위의 두 개의 생산가능곡선에서 존은 고기와 바나나 생산에 같은 양의 자원으로 더 많은 생산을 할 수 있는 능력을 뜻하는 절대우위를 모두 가졌다. 하지만 어느 나라가 무엇을 전문화할 것인가를 결정하는 것은 절대우위가 아니라 비교우위이다. 비교우위는 더 적은 기회비용으로 상품하나를 생산하는 것이다. 위의 문제에서 고기 생산에는 존이 비교우위를 갖는다. 존의 고기 생산의 기회비용은 바나나 3/4개로 폴의 2개 보다 작기 때문이다. 바나나 생산의 비교우위는 폴이 갖는다. 폴의 바나나 생산의 기회비용은 고기 1/2개로, 존의 경우 바나나 4/3개 보다 작기 때문이다. 따라서 존은 고기에 폴은 바나나에 전문화한다. 그리고 나면 상품교역시 재화의 교환비율인 교역조건의 문제가 온다. 교역조건은 거래시작 전의 국내교환비율에 달려있다. 교역 전에 존은 고기 한 개와 바나나 3/4개를 거래했고, 폴은 고기 한 개를 바나나 2개와 거래했다. 고역 조건은 이 두 개의 국내교환비율 사이에서 결정된다. 예를 들면, 고기 한 개가 바나나 한 개와 거래된다면 둘 다 더 잘살게 될 것이다. 교역을 통해 둘 다 교역 전보다 고기와 바나나를 더 많이 소비할 수 있게 된다.

## comparative advantage
### 비교우위

**Ability to produce a good with lower opportunity cost**
낮은 기회비용으로 상품을 생산할 수 있는 능력

- **South Korea had comparative advantage in light industries such as textiles in the 1960s.**
  한국은 1960년대에는 섬유 같은 경공업에 비교우위가 있었다.

## absolute advantage
### 절대우위

**Ability to produce a good with fewer resources (higher productivity)**
적은 자원으로 상품을 생산할 수 있는 능력(높은 생산성)

- **Any country will benefit from trade even if it has absolute advantage on all the goods it produces.**
  어느 국가가 생산하는 모든 상품에 절대우위가 있더라도 교역으로부터 이득을 얻게 될 것이다.

## specialization
### 전문화(특화)

**Focusing on the production of one good**

한 가지 생산에 집중하는 것

- **Trade occurs between countries through specialization.**

  교역은 전문화를 통하여 국가사이에 일어난다.

## terms of trade
### 교역조건

**The rate at which two goods are exchanged**

두 상품이 교환되는 비율

- **Terms of trade is closely related to the prices of exported and imported goods.**

  교역조건은 수출상품과 수입상품의 가격과 밀접하게 연관되어 있다.

## Problem Set A — Short Answer Question

Write down a proper word for the definition

1. the study of how the limited resources are allocated to satisfy our unlimited human wants and desires

2. ability to produce a good with fewer resources

3. a model that shows how households and firms circulate goods, services, resources, revenues, and incomes through markets

4. the market in which firms sell and households buy goods and services

5. a subjective, contestable statement about how the economy should be

6. the fundamental economic situation in which men have unlimited wants and needs in a world of limited resources

7. the situation in which to get one thing one must give up something else

8. a curve showing the maximum combinations of output of two goods given the available resources and technology

**9** the market in which households sell and firms buy factors of production

**10** inputs or resources used to produce goods and services

**11** an objective, testable statement about how the economy works

## Define these words

**12** comparative advantage ?

**13** opportunity cost ?

---

### Answer

1 economics  2 absolute advantage  3 circular flow diagram  4 product market
5 normative(prescriptive) statement(analysis)  6 scarcity  7 trade-off
8 production possibility curve  9 factor market  10 factors of production
11 positive(descriptive) statement(analysis)

12 ability to produce a good with lower opportunity cost
13 the cost of any choice measured in terms of the value of the best alternative that is foregone.

## Problem Set B: multiple questions

**1** Economics is the study of _____.

A) how to make much money
B) how one manages a firm
C) how to control the resources of a country
D) how society manages its scarce resources

**2** Scarcity means that _____.

A) a society's consumption is greater than its production
B) resources are unlimited, and desires are limited
C) a society's wants are greater than what it can produce with its limited resources
D) governments must make up for shortages in resources

**3** The three major economic questions all economics systems face?

A) What?, How?, and For Whom?
B) What?, How?, and Why?
C) Why?, How much?, and where?
D) When?, What?, and Why?

**4** The opportunity cost of a decision is measured in terms of _____.

A) time and money
B) the choice you make
C) the next best alternative
D) the price of a chosen good or service

**5** In economics, the benefit you get when making a choice refers to _____.

A) the difference between what you get and what you pay for
B) the gain you could get from the highest-valued alternative forgone
C) the return for providing factors of production
D) the gain or pleasure brought by your choice

**6** The marginal cost of an activity is _____.

A) the increase in total cost from producing an additional unit of good
B) the increase in average cost
C) the opportunity cost of a choice
D) time and money given up for the activity

## 7

Decision making on the margin means _____.

A) comparing the average cost and the average benefit
B) comparing the total cost and the total benefit
C) comparing the marginal cost and marginal benefit
D) determining the total benefits of a decision

## 8

Instead of studying math, Harold decided to study economics for additional two hours. Harold is making a(n) _____.

A) decision that does not incur an opportunity cost
B) rational decision if his marginal cost from studying economics is greater than his marginal benefit
C) rational decision if his marginal benefit from studying economics is greater than his marginal cost
D) irrational decision because studying math is more important than studying economics

## 9

Microeconomics includes the study of the _____.

A) aggregate impacts on the world economy
B) recessions and expansion in the mational economy
C) choices made by firms and households
D) reasons why the government lowers interest rates in recessions

**10** The statement that "As output falls, unemployment rises" is an example of a _____.

A) hypothetical statement
B) microeconomic statement
C) normative statement
D) positive statement

**11** Which of the following correctly lists the factors of production?

A) land, labor, capital, and entrepreneurship
B) land, equipment, capital, and entrepreneurship
C) natural resources, buildings, capital, and entrepreneurship
D) money, bond and mutual fund

**12** A production possibilities curve illustrates _____.

A) the limits to a nation's future economic growth
B) how good and services can be allocated among members of society
C) maximum combinations of goods and services that can be produced given its available factors of production and technology
D) that if price of one good decreases, the quantity demanded of the good increases

**1** D **2** C **3** A **4** C **5** D **6** A **7** C **8** C **9** C **10** D **11** A **12** C

# Chapter 02

# Demand, Supply and Markets
## 수요와 공급 그리고 시장

Chapter2에서는 본격적으로 수요demand와 공급supply, 시장의 균형equilibrium에 대해서 배웁니다. 경제학은 수요와 공급에 관한 것이라는 말이 있을 정도로 수요와 공급에 대한 이해는 경제학 공부의 가장 중요한 기초를 이룹니다. 수요와 수요량quantity demanded의 차이, 수요의 변동요인, 공급과 공급량quantity supplied의 차이, 공급의 변동요인, 네 가지 탄력성elasticity, 가격상한제price ceiling, 가격하한제price floor, 세금tax 등의 정부 규제, 그리고 마지막으로 소비자선택이론theory of consumer choice에 대해 충분히 학습하도록 합시다.

# Lesson 1: Demand 수요

## market 시장

**A group of buyers and sellers of a good or services**
상품과 서비스의 구매자와 판매자의 그룹

## law of demand 수요의 법칙

**All other things being constant, when the price of a good falls, the quantity demanded increases.**
다른 모든 것이 일정하다고 가정할 때ceteris paribus, 가격이 떨어지면 수요량이 증가한다.

- **According to the law of demand, people will buy less if the price of a good rises.**
  수요의 법칙에 따르면, 사람들은 가격이 오르면 덜 사게 될 것이다.

## quantity demanded 수요량

**the quantity of a good which is demanded at any given price**
주어진 가격에서 구매하고자 하는 수량

- **Quantity demanded of a good varies inversely with its price.**
  수요량은 가격과 반비례하며 변화한다.

| | Change in Quantity demanded | Change in Demand |
|---|---|---|
| display on graph | price P0, P1, quantity demanded(q0), Q1, D1, quantity | price, D1, D0, D2, quantity<br>$D_0 \rightarrow D_1$: increase in demand<br>$D_0 \rightarrow D_2$: decrease in demand |
| meaning | quantity demanded: the quantity of a good which is demanded at any given price | demand: the relationship between the price of a good and the quantity demanded |
| style of change | movement along a given demand curve | shift in the demand curve |
| causes of movement or shift | change in price | change in non-price determinants |

## non-price determinants shifting demand curve
수요곡선을 이동시키는 비가격요인

### ❶ consumer income 소비자 소득
- **normal good** 정상재

  When consumer income increases, the demand for normal goods increases too.
  소득이 증가하면 정상재에 대한 수요는 증가한다.

- **inferior good** 열등재

  When consumer income increases, the demand for inferior goods decreases.
  소득이 증가하면 열등재에 대한 수요는 감소한다.

### ❷ prices of related goods 관련 상품의 가격
- **substitutes** 대체재

  Goods that can be replaced by each other because they give the similar satifaction to the consumer. If the price of one good rises, the demand for the substitutes also rises. For example, 'coffee and tea', 'butter and margarine', and 'Coca-cola and Pepsi-cola'.

  소비자에게 유사한 만족감을 주기 때문에 대신 사용할 수 있는 재화. 어느 재화의 가격이 올라갔을 때, 대체재에 대한 수요가 증가한다. 커피나 차, 버터와 마가린, 코카콜라와 펩시콜라의 예가 있다.

- **complements** 보완재

  Two goods that tend to be used together, therefore a rise in the price of one leads to a decrease in the demand for the other. For example, 'DVDs and DVD players', 'bread and butter', 'printer and toner'.

  함께 사용되는 두 재화. 한 재화의 가격이 상승하면 다른 재화에 대한 수요가 감소한다. 예를 들면, DVD와 DVD 플레이어, 빵과 버터, 프린터와 토너, MP3와 이어폰

❸ **Tastes, preferences** 기호

If a good becomes more attractive, the demand for the good increases.

어떤 재화가 더 매력적이 되면, 그 재화에 대한 수요는 증가한다.

❹ **Expectations** 기대

If people expect the price of a good to rise in the near future, the demand for the good increases.

사람들이 어떤 재화의 가격이 가까운 미래에 상승할 것이라고 예상하면 그 재화에 대한 수요는 증가한다.

If people expect the price of a good to fall in the near future, the demand for the good decreases.

사람들이 어떤 재화의 가격이 가까운 미래에 떨어질 것이라고 예상하면 그 재화에 대한 수요는 감소한다.

❺ **Number of buyers, or population** 구매자의 수

If the number of buyers increases, the demand for the good increases.

구매자의 수가 증가한다면 그 재화에 대한 수요는 증가한다.

## individual demand vs. market demand
### 개인수요 vs. 시장수요

- **Market demand is the horizontal summation of individual demands.**
  시장수요는 개인수요의 수평 합이다.
- **Market demand curve is flatter than individual demand curve.**
  시장수요곡선은 개인수요곡선보다 더 평평하다.

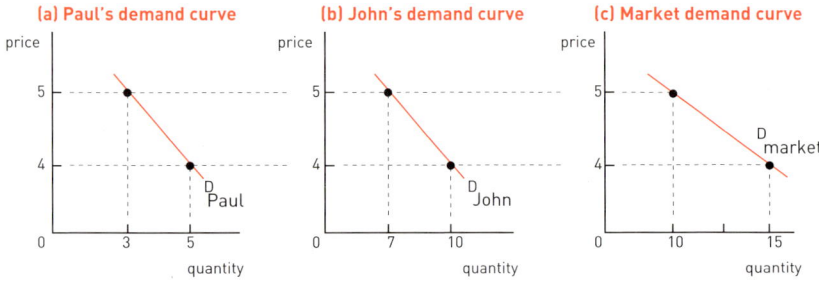

# Lesson 2 | Supply
## 공급

### supply
### 공급

The relationship between the price of a good and the quantity supplied
상품의 가격과 공급량의 관계

### law of supply
### 공급의 법칙

All other things being constant, when the price of a good rises, the quantity supplied increases.
다른 모든 것이 일정할 때, 상품의 가격이 오르면, 공급량이 증가한다.

### quantity supplied
### 공급량

The quantity of a good which is supplied at any given price
주어진 가격에 공급되는 물량

| | Change in Quantity supplied | Change in Supply |
|---|---|---|
| display on graph | P1, P0 on Supply curve with P: Price, Qs: Quantity Supplied | $S_2$, $S_0$, $S_1$ curves; $S_0 \to S_1$: increase in supply; $S_0 \to S_2$: decrease in demand |
| meaning | quantity supplied: the quantity of a good which is demanded at any given price | supply: the relationship between the price of a good and the quantity demanded |
| style of change | movement along a given supply curve | shift in the supply curve |
| causes of movement or shift | change in price | change in non-price determinants |

## non-price determinants shifting supply curve
공급곡선을 이동시키는 비가격요인

**❶ input prices, production cost** 투입요소 가격
- If input price of a good rises, supply curve of the good shifts to the left. On the other hand, if input price of a good falls, supply curve of the good shifts to the right.

투입요소 가격이 상승하면 공급곡선은 왼쪽으로 이동한다. 반면에, 투입요소 가격이 하락하면 공급곡선은 오른쪽으로 이동한다.

**❷ technology** 기술
- If technological advances in the production of a good occur, the supply curve of the good shifts to the right.

상품생산에 기술이 발전이하면 공급곡선으로 오른쪽으로 이동한다.

**❸ prices of alternative goods** 다른 상품의 가격
- If price of an alternative good rises, the supply of the currently produced good decreases.

다른 상품의 가격이 오르면 현재 생산되는 상품의 공급은 감소한다.
- If price of an alternative good falls, the supply of the currently produced good increases.

다른 상품의 가격이 떨어지면, 현재 생산되는 상품의 공급은 증가한다.

### ❹ expectations 기대
- If expected price of a good rises, the supply curve of the good shifts to the left.

상품의 기대가격이 상승하면, 공급곡선은 왼쪽으로 이동한다.
- If expected price of a good falls, the supply curve of the good shifts to the right.

상품의 기대가격(현시점에서 예상한 가격)이 하락하면 공급곡선은 오른쪽으로 이동한다.

### ❺ number of firms(sellers) 판매자의 수
- If the number of firms producing a good increases, the supply curve of the good shifts to the right.

기업의 수가 증가하면 공급곡선은 오른쪽으로 이동한다.
- If the number of firms producing a good decreases, the supply curve of the good shifts to the left.

기업의 수가 감소하면 공급곡선은 왼쪽으로 이동한다.

### ❻ taxes/subsidies 세금/보조금
- If government levies tax on the producers of a good, supply curve of the good shifts to the left

정부가 상품 생산자에게 세금을 부과하면 그 상품의 공급곡선은 왼쪽으로 이동한다.
- If government gives a subsidy to the producers of a good, supply curve of the good shifts to the right.

정부가 상품 생산자에게 보조금을 지급하면 그 상품의 공급곡선은 오른쪽으로 이동한다.

# individual supply vs. market supply
## 개별공급 vs. 시장공급

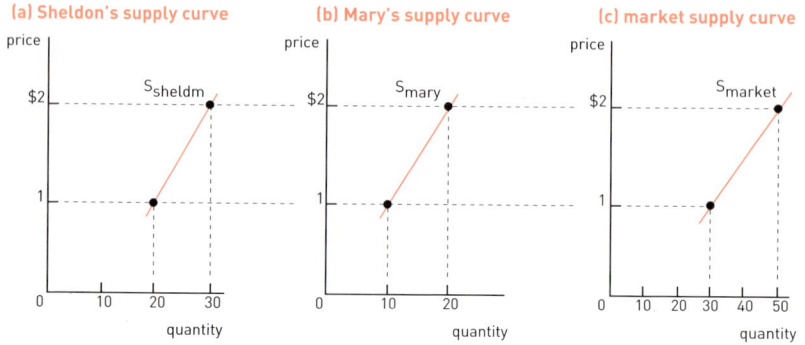

- **Market supply curve is the horizontal sum of the individual supply curves.**
  시장공급은 개별공급의 수평 합이다.
- **Market supply curve is flatter than individual supply curves.**
  시장공급곡선은 개별공급곡선보다 더 평평하다.

# Lesson 3

# Elasticity
## 탄력성

## elasticity
### 탄력성

**The responsiveness or sensitivity to a change in other variables**
다른 변수의 변화에 대한 반응도, 민감도

- **A elasticities of B: the responsiveness of B to the percentage change in A**
  B의 A 탄력성 : A의 변화에 대한 B의 반응도

## price elasticity of demand
### 수요의 가격탄력성

**A measure of how responsive the quantity demanded of a good is to a change in the price of that good**
상품 가격의 변화율에 대하여 수요량이 반응하는 정도

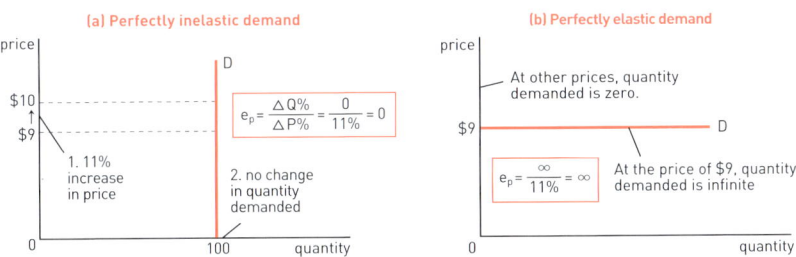

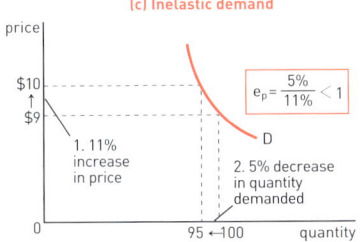

Chapter 2 Demand, Supply and Market

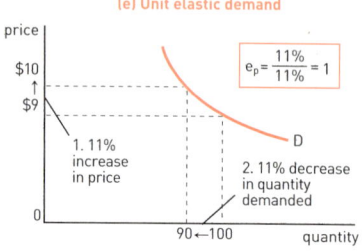

## the determinants of price elasticities of demand
### 수요의 가격탄력성의 결정요인

❶ **the substitutability of a good** 상품의 대체성
❷ **luxuries vs. necessities** 사치재 vs. 필수재
❸ **the proportion of expenditure spent on the product** 상품에 지출한 비중
❹ **market definition** 시장에 대한 정의
❺ **time horizon** 시간의 길이

**Tip** 대체제가 많을수록, 사치재일수록, 지출에서 차지하는 비중이 클수록, 시장을 좁게 정의할수록, 장기일수록 수요의 가격탄력성은 탄력적이다.

## price elasticity of demand and total revenue
### 수요의 가격탄력성과 총수입

| | |
|---|---|
| elastic demand<br>탄력적인 수요의 경우 | When price of a good rises, total revenue falls<br>가격이 상승하면 총수입은 하락한다.<br>When price of a good falls, total revenue rises.<br>가격이 하락하면 총수입은 증가한다. |
| inelastic demand<br>비탄력적인 수요의 경우 | When price of a good rises, total revenue rises.<br>가격이 상승하면 총수입은 증가한다.<br>When price of a good falls, total revenue falls.<br>가격이 하락하면 총수입은 감소한다. |
| unit-elastic demand<br>단위탄력적인 수요의 경우 | Whether price of a good rises or falls, total revenue stays constant.<br>가격이 상승하든지 하락하든지, 총수입은 변화가 없다. |

> **Tip** Change in Total Revenue(TR) 총수입의 변화

**+: increase in TR** 총수입의 증가
**0: no change** 변화 없음
**-: decrease in** 총수입 감소

|  | price increase | price decrease |
|---|---|---|
| elastic | − | + |
| unit-elastic | 0 | 0 |
| inelastic | + | − |

## income elasticitiy of demand
### 소득탄력성

**A measure of how responsive consumption of a good is to a change in consumer's income**
소비자의 소득의 변화에 대해 상품 소비가 반응하는 정도

- **Income elasticities of demand for normal good is positive**
  정상재에 대한 소득탄력성은 양(+)이다.
- **Income elasticities of demand for inferior good is negative**
  열등재에 대한 소득탄력성은 음(−)이다.

## necessities
### 필수재

**A good whose consumption rises less than in proportion to increases in income. Income elasticity of demand for necessities is less than one.**
소비량의 증가율이 소득의 증가율보다 작은 재화. 소득탄력성이 1보다 작음.

## luxuries
### 사치재

**A good whose consumption rises more than in proportion to increases in income. Income elasticity of demand for luxuries is greater than one.**
소비량의 증가율이 소득의 증가율보다 큰 재화. 소득탄력성이 1보다 큼.

## cross-price elasticity of demand
교차탄력성

**A measure of how responsive the quantity demanded of one good responds to a change in the price of another good**
한 상품의 수요량이 다른 상품의 가격 변화에 얼마나 반응하는가 하는 정도

- **cross-price elasticity of demand for substitutes is positive**
  대체제에 대한 교차탄력성은 양(+)이다.
- **cross-price elasticity of demand for complements is negative**
  보완재에 대한 교차탄력성은 음(-)이다.

## price, marginal revenue and total revenue
가격, 한계수입 그리고 총수입

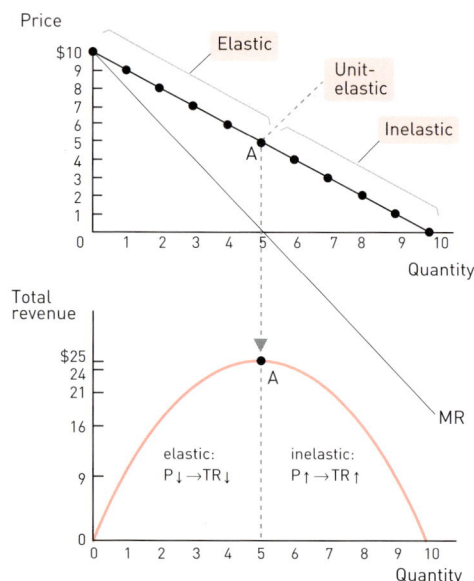

Why is marginal revenue less than price? Because price must be lowered to sell one more good.
왜 한계수입은 가격보다 작은가? 한 단위 더 팔려면 가격이 낮아져야하기 때문이다.

# price elasticity of supply
## 공급탄력성

**A measure of how responsive the quantity supplied of a good is to a change in the price of that good**
상품의 공급량이 가격의 변화에 얼마나 반응하는가 하는 정도

The Five Types of Price Elasticity of Supply.

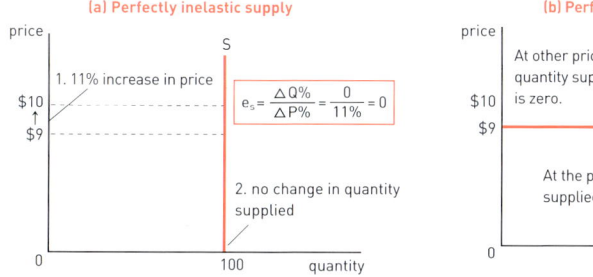

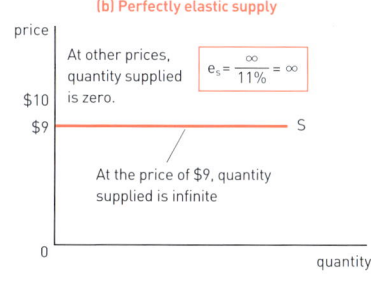

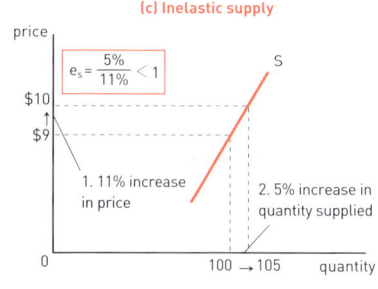

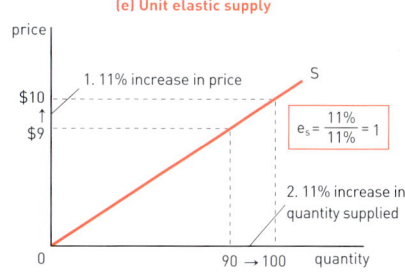

**Tip** 공급탄력성의 결정요인은?
1. flexibility of production 생산의 유연성
2. time horizon 시간의 길이

# Lesson 4: Market Equilibrium
## 균형

### equilibrium
### 균형

**A situation in which quantity demanded equals quantity supplied**
수요량과 공급량이 같은 상황

### surplus(excess supply)
### 과잉(초과 공급)

**A situation in which quantity supplied is greater than quantity demanded**
공급량이 수요량보다 큰 상황

### shortage(excess demand)
### 부족(초과 수요)

**A situation in which quantity demanded is greater than quantity supplied.**
수요량이 공급량보다 큰 상황

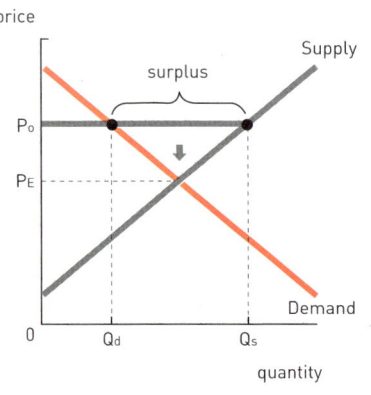

Surplus(Excess Supply)

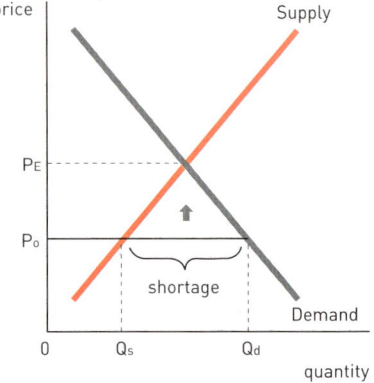

Shortage(Excess Demand)

## equilibrium price
### 균형가격

**Price at which quantity demanded equals quantity supplied**
수요량과 공급량이 같아지는 가격

## equilibrium quantity
### 균형수량

**Quantity at which quantity demanded equals quantity supplied**
수요량과 공급량이 같아지는 수량

## change in equilibrium
### 균형의 변화

|  | no change in supply | an increase in supply | a decrease in supply |
|---|---|---|---|
| No change in demand | P same<br>Q same | P down<br>Q up | P up<br>Q down |
| An increase in demand | P up<br>Q up | P uncertain<br>Q up | P up<br>Q uncertain |
| A decrease in demand | P down<br>Q down | P down<br>Q uncertain | P uncertain<br>Q down |

**Tip** 수요와 공급이 모두 변하는 경우는 가격과 수량 둘 중의 하나의 변화는 불확실하다.

**How to find new equilibrium**
1 decide whether the event given shifts the demand or demand curve.
2 decide whether the curve shifts to the right or to the left
3 find new equilibrium at the new intersection.

# the efficiency of the market
## 시장의 효율성

• **Allocative Efficiency** 배분 효율성

P가격 = Marginal Cost한계비용, or Marginal Benefit(MB)한계편익 = Marginal Cost(MC)한계비용

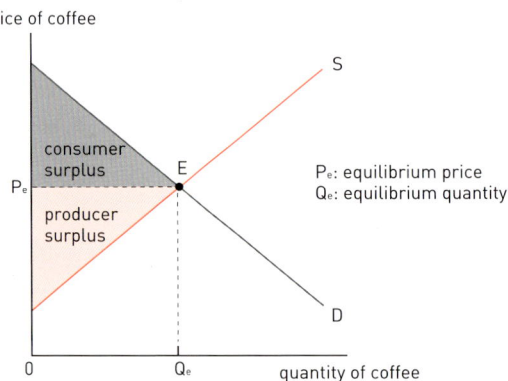

$P_e$: equilibrium price
$Q_e$: equilibrium quantity

## 기본 단어 익히기

**consumer surplus:** the difference between a consumer's willingness to pay and the amount the buyer actually pays
소비자잉여: 소비자의 지불 용의 금액과 실제 지불 가격의 차이

**producer surplus:** the difference between price and the seller's cost
생산자잉여: 가격과 생산자의 비용의 차이

**total surplus:** the sum of consumer surplus and producer surplus
총잉여금: 소비자잉여와 생산자잉여의 합

# Lesson 5 | Government Policy to regulate markets
## 시장규제정책

### price ceiling
### 가격상한제

**Maximum price set for a product by government (for the protection of consumers)**

정부가 부과한 한 상품의 최고 가격(소비자 보호 목적)

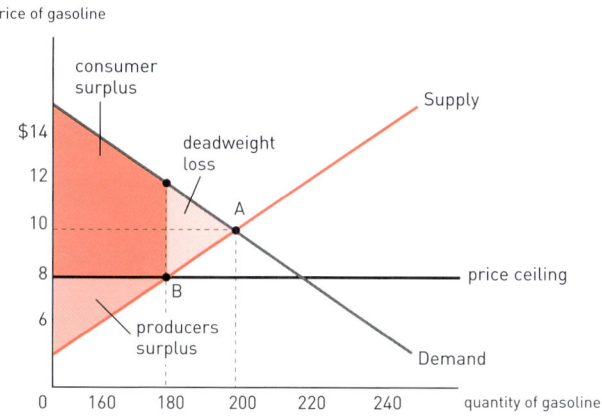

When government imposes binding price ceiling on the gasoline, ceiling price will be $8 in the graph above. This incur excess demand, shortage, resulting in change in consumer surplus and producer surplus, and deadweight loss.

정부가 가솔린에 구속력있는 가격상한을 부과할 때 위 그래프에서 상한가격은 8달러가 될 것이다. 이로 인해 초과수요가 초래되고, 소비자잉여와 생산자잉여에 변화가 생기고 자중손실이 발생한다.

Chapter 2 Demand, Supply and Market

## deadweight loss
### 자중손실

**The loss in total surplus caused by market failures, government intervention, and tax**
시장실패, 정부 간섭, 세금 등에 의해 발생하는 총잉여의 손실분

## price floor
### 가격하한제

**Minimum price set for a product by government (for the protection of prooducers)**
정부가 부과한 한 상품의 최소 가격(생산자 보호 목적)

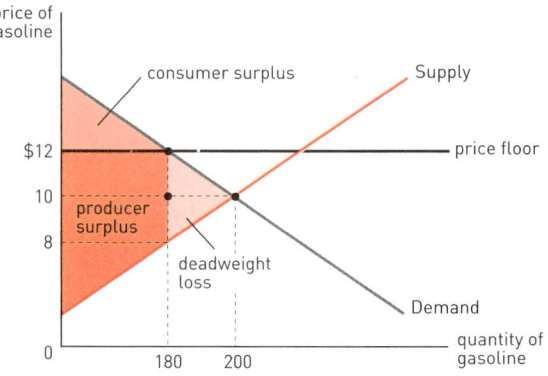

When government imposes binding price floor on the gasoiline market, floor price will be $1.2 in the graph above. This incur excess supply, surplus, resulting in change in consumer surplus and producer surplus, and deadweight loss.
정부가 가솔린시장에 구속력 있는 가격하한을 부과할 때 위 그래프에서 상한가격은 1.2달러가 될 것이다. 이로 인해 초과공급이 초래되고, 소비자잉여와 생산자잉여에 변화가 생기고 자중손실이 발생하게 된다.

## price support
### 가격지지

**A policy by which the government sets the price of a good, usually an agricultural product, above the free-market level and buys up whatever output is needed to maintain that price**
보통 농산물시장에서 정부가 시장균형 이상으로 가격을 정하여 그 가격을 유지하기에 필요한 생산량만큼 사들이는 정책

# Lesson 6 | Tax
## 세금

### tax
### 세금

**Payment compulsorily collected from individuals or firms by the government**
개인이나 기업에게서 정부가 강제로 거두어들인 납입금

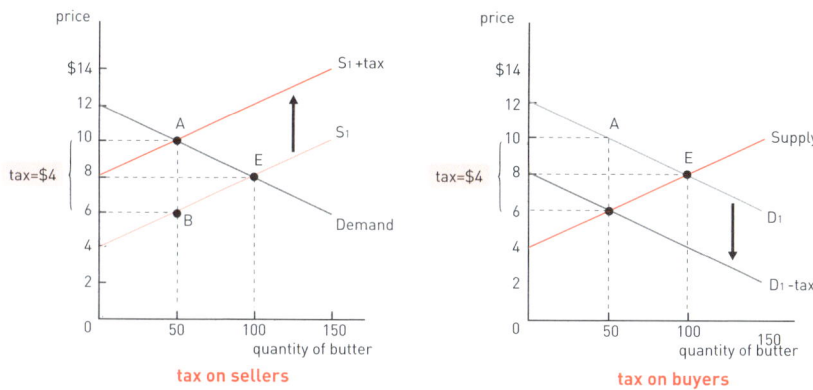

tax on sellers    tax on buyers

- **The burden of the tax is divided between consumers and sellers. Tax burden does not depend on who officially pays the tax.**
  세금부담은 소비자와 판매자에게 나누어진다. 세금부담은 누가 공식적으로 세금을 내느냐에 달려있지 않다.

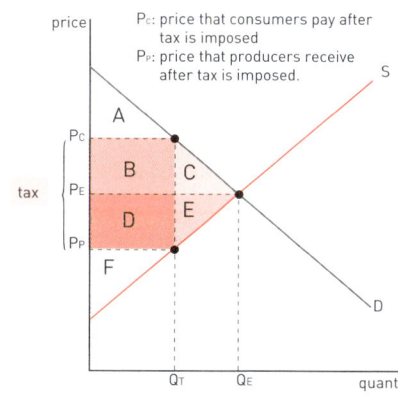

changes in social welfare

|  | Without Tax | With Tax |
|---|---|---|
| consumer surplus | A+B+C | A |
| producer surplus | D+E+F | F |
| Government Revenue | 0 | B+D |
| Total Surplus | A+B+C+D+E+F | A+B+D+F |

*C+E=deadweight loss

# tax burden
조세부담

**Tax is heavily burdened with the participant that is less elastic.**
세금은 덜 탄력적인 경제주체에 무겁게 부과된다.

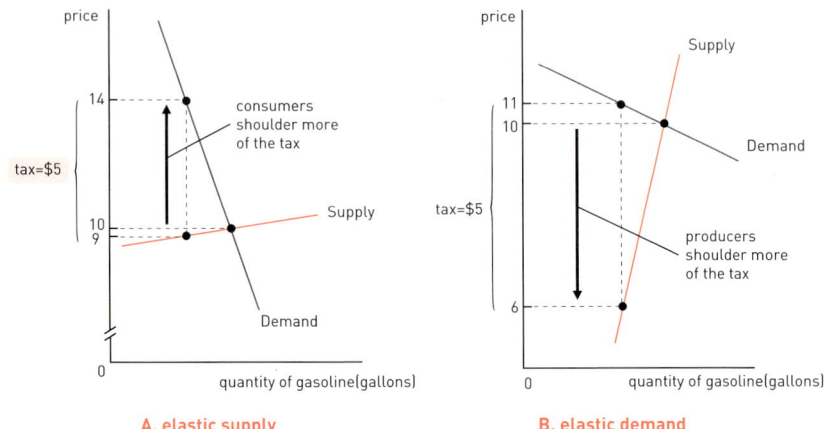

A. elastic supply

B. elastic demand

Graph A shows relatively inelastic demand and elastic supply, in which case the consumer is heavily burdened with tax. Graph B represents relatively inelastic supply and elastic demand, in which case the producer has heavier burden of tax.
그래프 A는 상대적으로 비탄력적인 수요와 탄력적인 공급을 보여준다. 이런 경우에는 소비자에게 더 조세부담이 크다. 그래프 B는 상대적으로 비탄력적인 공급과 탄력적인 수요를 보여준다. 이런 경우에는 생산자가 더 큰 조세부담을 안는다.

# how to measure tax burden
어떻게 조세부담을 측정하는가

**Comparing the change on the part of consumers vs. the change on the part of producers**
소비자 측 변화와 생산자 측 변화 비교하기

### ❶ The change on the part of consumers
소비자 측 변화
The price paid after taxation minus the price paid before taxation
(세금부과 후 지불가격) – (세금부과 전 지불가격)

### ❷ The change on the part of producers
생산자 측 변화
The price received before tax minus price received after tax
(세금부과 전 받던 가격) − (세금부과 후 받던 가격)

- **The party with a heavier tax burden is the one incurred a larger change in price due to taxation.**
  과세로 인해 더 큰 변화가 초래된 쪽이 조세부담을 더 크게 짊어지고 있는 것이다.

## different types of tax[1)]
### 세금의 종류

### ❶ income tax 소득세
A tax on the income of an individual or a family from wages and investments
임금이나 투자 등 개인과 가계의 소득에 부과되는 세금

### ❷ payroll tax 급여세
A tax the earnings a firm pays to a worker
기업이 노동자에게 지급하는 소득에 부과되는 세금

### ❸ sales tax 판매세
Tax on the value of goods sold
상품 판매에 부과되는 세금

### ❹ profits tax 이윤세
A tax on a firm's profits
기업의 이윤에 부과되는 세금

### ❺ property tax 재산세
A tax on the value of property, such as the value of a home
주택 가격처럼 재산 가치에 부과되는 세금

### ❻ lump-sum tax 정액세
The same amount of tax for everyone.
모두에게 똑같은 액수의 세금

> **Tip** Remember that lump-sum taxes do not affect economic actors' marginal behaviors.
> 정액세는 경제행위자의 추가적인 행동에 영향을 미치지 않는다.

## three kinds of tax according to tax rate related to income
소득관련 세율에 따른 세금 세 종류

**❶ progressive tax** 누진세
A tax by which tax rate increases as income increases
소득이 증가할 때 세율이 증가하는 세금

**❷ proportional tax(flat tax)** 비례세
A tax by which tax rate stays the same as income increases
소득이 증가할 때 세율이 동일한 세금

**❸ regressive tax** 역진세
A tax by which tax rate decreases as income increases
소득이 증가할 때 세율이 감소하는 세금

## taxation principle
조세 제도

**According to ability-to-pay principle, those with greater ability to pay a tax should pay more tax.**
능력과세 원칙에 따르면 세금 낼 능력이 더 큰 사람이 더 많은 세금을 내야 한다.

**According to benefit principle, those who benefit from public spending should bear the burden of the tax that pays for that spending**
수익자부담 원칙에 따르면 공공지출을 통해 이익을 보는 사람들이 그 지출에 대한 세금을 부담해야 한다.

# special cases of tax burden
## 조세부담의 특수사례

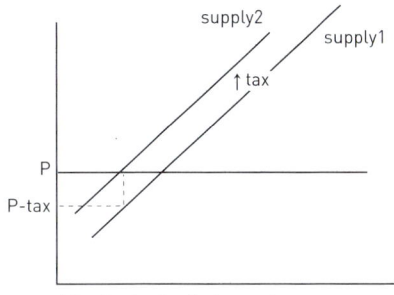

A. Perfectly elastic demand

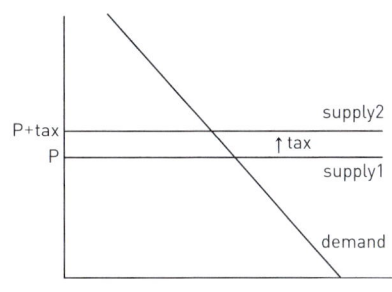

B. Perfectly elastic supply

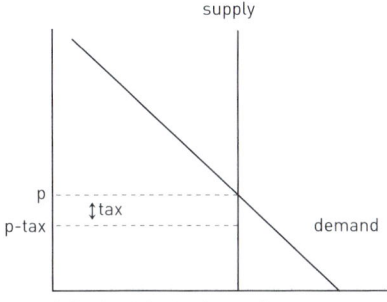

C. Perfectly inelastic supply

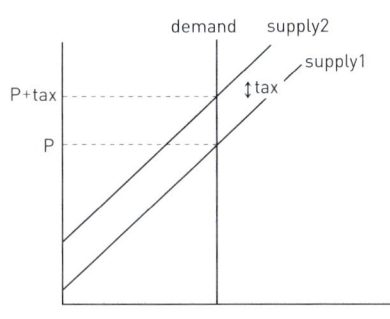

D. Perfectly inelastic demand

| | | | |
|---|---|---|---|
| **A** | Perfectly Elastic Demand: tax on producers<br>　tax burden of consumers: 0<br>　tax burden of producers: tax | **B** | Perfectly Elastic Supply: tax on producers<br>　tax burden of consumers: tax<br>　tax burden of producers: 0 |
| **C** | Perfectly Inelasic Supply: tax on producers<br>　tax burden of consumers: 0<br>　tax burden of producers: tax | **D** | Perfectly Inelatic Demand: tax on producers.<br>　tax burden of consumers: tax<br>　tax burden of producers: 0 |

**Tip** The Conclusion of Special cases of Complete Burden
세금 전적 부담의 특수 사례의 결론

- Tax is completely burdened with the participants that are perfectly inelastic
  세금은 전적으로 완전 비탄력적인 참가자에게 부담된다.
- Tax is completely burdened with the part the opposite participants of the one that is perfectly elastic.
  세금은 전적으로 완전 탄력적인 참가자의 상대방에게 완전히 부담된다.

# Lesson 7
# The Theory of Consumer Choice
## 소비자 선택 이론

### the theory of consumer choice
소비자 선택 이론

**A theory of microeconomics that shows that an individual consumes in order to optimize his or her satisfaction, linking preferences for the goods or services to budget constraint and finally to consumer demand curves.**

만족을 최적화하기 위해 소비자가 자신의 선호를 예산제약과 연결하여 소비하는 것을 보여주며, 최종적으로는 소비자 수요곡선과 연결되는 미시경제의 이론 중 하나.

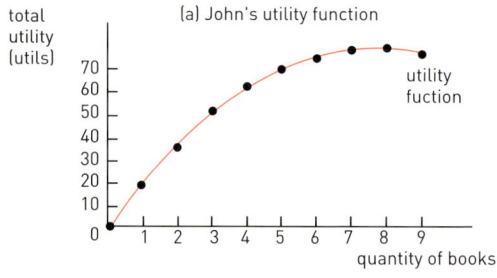

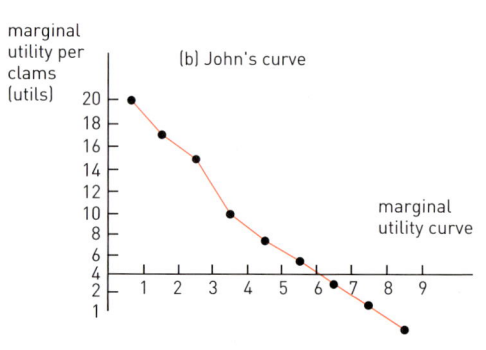

| Quantity of clams | Total utility (utils) | Marginal utility per book(utils) |
|---|---|---|
| 0 | 0 | |
| 1 | 20 | 20 |
| 2 | 37 | 17 |
| 3 | 52 | 15 |
| 4 | 62 | 10 |
| 5 | 69 | 7 |
| 6 | 74 | 5 |
| 7 | 77 | 3 |
| 8 | 78 | 1 |
| 9 | 75 | −3 |

- **The graph shows the law of diminishing marginal utility, which means that additional increase in total utility when John buys one more book decreases.**

위의 그래프는 한계효용체감의 법칙을 보여준다. 이는 존이 책을 하나 더 살 때 총효용의 증가분이 감소한다는 것을 의미한다.

## 기 본 단 어 익 히 기

**utility** 효용
The level of satisfaction, happiness, pleasure, enjoyment that a person gets from consuming goods and services
한 개인이 재화와 서비스를 소비할 때 얻는 만족감, 행복감, 기쁨, 즐거움의 수준

**total utility** 총효용
The total satisfaction, happiness, pleasure, enjoyment that a person gets from consumption of a number of units of a good.
한 개인이 많은 재화를 소비함으로써 얻는 만족감, 행복감, 기쁨, 즐거움의 총량

**marginal utility** 한계효용
The additional satisfaction from consuming one more unit of a good or service.
한 단위의 재화나 서비스를 더 소비함으로서 느끼는 추가적 만족감

**law of diminishing marginal utility** 한계효용체감의 법칙
The phenomenon that the additional increase in total satisfaction from a good falls as consumption increases.
소비를 증가시킬 때 재화로부터 얻는 전체 만족감의 증가분이 줄어드는 현상

**Tip**
In economics, 'marginal' means 'additional' or 'extra'. Not the peripheral or limited or something else.
경제학에서 '한계'의 의미는 '하나 더', '추가적'인을 뜻한다. '주변적', '제한적인'의 의미가 아니다.

## budget constraints
### 예산제약

**All combinations of goods that can be purchased with a consumer's income**
소비자의 소득으로 구입할 수 있는 상품의 조합

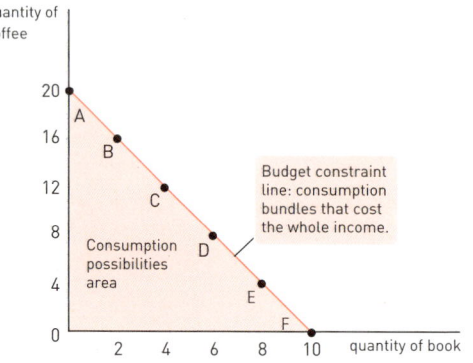

| Consumption bundle | Quantity of book | Quantity of coffee |
|---|---|---|
| A | 0 | 20 |
| B | 2 | 16 |
| C | 4 | 12 |
| D | 6 | 8 |
| E | 8 | 4 |
| F | 10 | 0 |

## income effect
### 소득효과

**The change in consumption caused by the change in consumer's purchasing power(real income) when the price of good changes**
상품의 가격이 변화할 때 소비자의 구매력(실질소득)의 변화로 인해 발생하는 소비량의 크기를 의미

## substitution effect
### 대체효과

**The change in consumption causes by the change in its price because the good has become relatively cheaper or more expensive.**
상품이 상대적으로 싸졌거나 비싸졌기 때문에 변화하는 소비량의 크기를 말한다.

## income effect and substitution effect
### 소득효과와 대체효과

**Giffen good is a special case. In case of giffen good the income effect as a inferior good dominates the substitution effect. When price rises, the positive income effect of giffen good is greater than negative substitution effect. So the quantity demanded increases when price rises. This phenomenon violates of law of demand. This kind of good that quantity demanded increases when price rises is called a giffen good, named after economist Robert Giffen who first proposed such possibility.**

기펜재는 특별한 경우이다. 기펜재의 경우는 열등재로서의 소득효과가 대체효과보다 크다. 가격이 상승할 때 기펜재의 양의 소득효과가 음의 대체효과보다 크게 나타난다. 따라서 가격이 상승할 때 수요량이 증가한다. 이러한 현상은 수요의 법칙을 위배한다. 이렇게 가격이 상승할 때 수요량이 증가하는 재화를 그러한 가능성을 처음 제기한 경제학자 로버트 기펜의 이름을 따라서 기펜재라고 부른다.

**Suppose that price of a good rises.**

Change in Quantity demanded = income effect + substitution effect
```
        (-10)    =  (-3)   +  (-7)  ← normal good
        (-5)     =  (2)    +  (-7)  ← inferior good but still
                                       follow law of demand
        (3)      =  (10)   +  (-7)  ← giffen good
```

*Remember that giffen good belongs to inferior good, not vice versa.

## utility maximization rule
## 효용극대화 공식
$$\frac{MU_x}{P_x} = \frac{MU_y}{P_y}$$

The formula means that marginal utility of $1 spent on good X equals marginal utility of $1 spent on good Y. If marginal utility of $1 spent on good X is greater than that of good Y, the buyer must consume good X one more and consume good Y one less in order to increase total utility. By the same logic, If marginal utility of $1 spent on good Y is greater than that of good X, the buyer ought to buy good Y one more decreasing consumption of good X. In short, the formula means equalizing marginal utility of each good per dollar.

이 공식은 X재에 지출한 1달러가 주는 한계효용과 Y재에 지출한 1달러가 주는 한계효용을 같게 한다는 의미이다. X재에 사용한 1달러가 주는 한계효용이 Y재보다 크다면 효용극대화를 위해 Y재 소비를 한 단위 줄이고, X재 소비를 한 단위 늘려야 한다. 같은 논리로 Y재에 사용한 1달러가 주는 한계효용이 X재보다 크다면 효용극대화를 위해 Y재 소비를 한 단위 늘리고 X재 소비를 줄인다. 요약하자면 이 공식은 각 재화의 달러당 한계효용을 동일하게 한다는 것을 의미한다.

Paul has $8. The price of Pizza is $2 and price of hamburger is $1
What is Paul's utility maximizing combination of consumption?

| Pizza($2) | | | | Hamburger($1) | | | |
| --- | --- | --- | --- | --- | --- | --- | --- |
| Quantity | Total utility | Marginal Utility | $\frac{MU_x}{P_x}$ | Quantity | Total utility | Marginal Utility | $\frac{MU_y}{P_y}$ |
| 0 | 0 | | | 0 | 0 | | |
| 1 | 30 | 30 | 15 | 1 | 20 | 20 | 20 |
| 2 | 55 | 25 | 12.5 | 2 | 30 | 10 | 10 |
| 3 | 75 | 20 | 10 | 3 | 35 | 5 | 5 |
| 4 | 90 | 15 | 2.5 | 4 | 38 | 3 | 3 |
| 5 | 100 | 10 | 5 | 5 | 40 | 2 | 2 |

The answer is three pizzas and two hamburgers, equalizing marginal utility per dollar of each good. Total utility is 105.

답은 피자 세 개와 햄버거 두 개로 각 재화의 달러당 한계효용이 최대화되는 소비이다. 총 효용은 105이다.

# paradox of value(water-diamond paradox)
## 가치의 역설(물-다이아몬드역설)

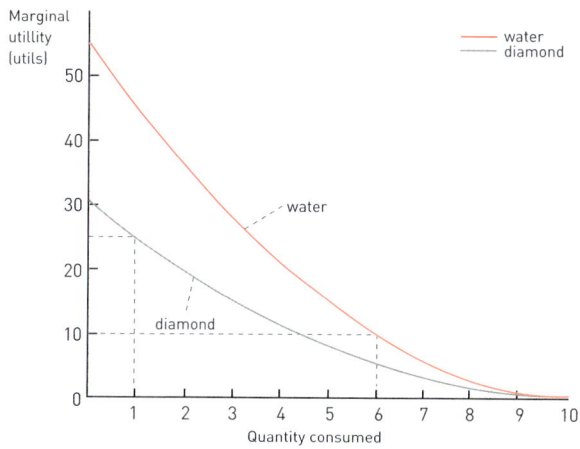

### Phenomenon

The paradox of value(also known as the diamond-water paradox) is the apparent contradiction that, although water is more useful in terms of survival than diamonds, diamonds command a higher price in the market.

물과 다이아몬드의 역설이라고도 알려진 가치의 역설은 물이 생존의 측면에서 다이아몬드보다 전반적으로 더 유용하지만 다이아몬드가 시장에서 훨씬 더 높은 가격을 받고 있는 걸으로 보기엔 모순되어 보이는 현상을 말한다.

### Reasoning

At low levels of consumption, water has a much higher marginal utility than diamonds and thus is more valuable. People usually consume water at much higher levels than they do diamonds and thus the marginal utility and price of water are lower than those of diamonds.

낮은 소비 수준에서는 물이 다이아몬드보다 훨씬 더 한계효용도 높고 더 귀중하다. 하지만 사람들은 물을 매우 높은 수준에서 소비하고 있기 때문에 물의 한계효용과 가격은 다이아몬드보다 낮은 것이다.

# Problem Set A: Short Answer Question

Write down a proper word for the definition

**1** the responsiveness or sensitivity to a change in other variables

**2** two goods that tend to be used together, therefore a rise in the price of one leads to a decrease in the demand for the other

**3** all other things being constant, when the price of a good rises, the quantity supplied increases

**4** the quantity of a good which is demanded at any given price

**5** the change in consumption causes by the change in its price because the good has become relatively cheaper or more expensive

**6** goods that can be replaced by each other because they give the similar satisfaction to the consumer

**7** the quantity of a good which is supplied at any given price

**8**    a measure of how responsive consumption of a good is to a change in consumer's income

**9**    a good whose consumption rises less than in proportion to increases in income

**10**    a good whose consumption rises more than in proportion to increases in income

**11**    a measure of how responsive the quantity demanded of one good responds to a change in the price of another good

**12**    the change in consumption caused by the change in consumer's purchasing power(real income) when the price of good changes

**13**    a situation in which quantity demanded equals quantity supplied

**14**    minimum price set for a product by government (for the protection of producers)

**15**    the same amount of tax for everyone

**16**    maximum price charged for a product by government

# Define these words

**17** law of demand?

**18** normal good?

**1** elasticities  **2** complements  **3** law of supply  **4** quantity demanded
**5** substitution effect  **6** substitutes  **7** quantity supplied  **8** income elasticities of demand
**9** necessities  **10** luxuries  **11** cross-price elasticities of demand  **12** income effect
**13** equilibrium  **14** price floor  **15** lump-sum tax  **16** price ceiling

**17** all other things being constant, when the price of a good falls, the quantity demanded increases
**18** when consumer income increases, the demand for normal goods increases too

# Problem Set B: multiple questions

**1.** A market is best defined as _____.

A) a visible place where people buy goods and services
B) a place where one good is exchanged for another
C) a store where people can buy goods
D) a collection of buyers and sellers of a good or a service

**2.** The 'law of demand' means that, when the price of a good decreases, other things being constant, _____.

A) the demand curve shifts to the right
B) the quantity demanded of the good rises
C) the quantity demanded of the good falls
D) the demand curve shifts to the right there is a movement up along the demand curve

**3.** If the price of a good rises, and other things being constant, quantity demanded decreases because _____.

A) the good gives less utility than before
B) people are able and willing to buy less of it
C) people might buy substitutes
D) both answers B and C are correct

## 4

The market demand curve _____.

A) cannot show how demand for a good changes in response to a change in income
B) cannot show how quantity demanded of a good changes in response to a change in price
C) is the horizontal sum of individual demand curves
D) is the vertical sum of individual demand curves

## 5

The law of supply states that, if the price of a good rises, other things being constant, _____.

A) demand for the good increases
B) the supply of the good increases
C) the quantity supplied of the good increases
D) the supply of the good decreases

## 6

Which of the following is true about supply?

i) Supply curves slopes upward
ii) Supply is the relationship between quantity supplied and the price of the good
iii) Supply curves change when the price of a good changes

A) i
B) i, ii
C) ii, iii
D) i, ii, iii

## 7

**Which of the following shifts the supply curve of icecream leftward?**

A) a decrease in the price of icecream
B) a increase in the cost of producing icecream
C) a technological development in the production of icecream
D) a decrease in the number of icecream suppliers

## 8

**When there is a shortage of chocolates, _____.**

A) the demand for chocolates is greater than the supply of chocolates
B) the supply of chocolates is greater than the demand for chocolates
C) the quantity of chocolates demanded is greater than the quantity of chocolates supplied
D) the quantity of chocolates supplied is greater than the quantity of chocolates demanded

## 9

**Suppose that the equilibrium price and quantity of snowboards both increase. Which of the following could cause this change?**

A) Both the supply and the demand for snowboards increased and the supply increased by more than the demand
B) The demand for snowboards increased and the supply did not change
C) Both the supply and demand for snowboards decreased
D) The supply of snowboards decreased and the demand for new houses did not change

**10** Smart phones are a normal good. When the economy slips into recession, the demand for smart phones _____ so that the price of smart phones _____.

A) increases; rises
B) increases; falls
C) decreases; rises
D) decreases; falls

**11** Bread and butter are complementary goods. Suppose that the price for flour, the input to bake bread, increases. The equilibrium price of butter _____ and the equilibrium quantity of butter _____.

A) rises; decreases
B) rises; increases
C) falls; decreases
D) falls; increases

**12** The price elasticity of demand is a measures _____.

A) buyers' purchasing power of a product
B) buyers' sensitivity to changes in the price of a product
C) how much a change in price affects the equilibrium price
D) whether a product is a normal good or a substitute

## 13 The demand for a good is more elastic if _____.

i) the good is a necessity
ii) the good has many substitutes
iii) the good is narrowly defined
iv) the good is very cheap relative to other goods

A) i), ii)
B) i), iii)
C) ii), iii)
D) iii), iv)

## 14 The price elasticity of supply measures _____.

A) how the equilibrium price changes in response to a change in the equilibrium quantity supplied
B) how much the quantity supplied of a good changes when the price of a good changes, other things being constant
C) percentage change in supply from a percentage change in demand
D) the slope of the supply curve

## 15. Total revenue equals _____.

A) price × cost
B) price × quantity sold
C) price × profit
D) quantity sold − cost.

## 16. The figure above shows the demand curve for a good with a _____.

A) perfectly elastic demand
B) perfectly inelastic demand
C) elastic demand
D) inelastic demand
E) unit elastic demand

**17** The cross price elasticity of demand measures how _____.

A) the quantity sold of one good responds to a change in the price of another good
B) the demand for one good responds to a change in the price of a factor used to make it
C) the quantity demanded of one good responds to a change in the price of another good
D) the quantity demanded of a good responds to a change in income

**18** If a price ceiling for a good is set effectively, then _____.

A) there will be a surplus of the good
B) there will be a shortage of the good
C) there will be neither a shortage nor a surplus of the good
D) the government will get revenue from the price ceiling

**19** If a price floor for a good is set effectively, then _____.

A) there will be a surplus of the good
B) there will be a shortage of the good
C) there will be neither a shortage nor a surplus of the good
D) the government will get revenue from the price ceiling

**20** In the figure below, suppose that the government levies a tax of $4 per butter. All of the following are true except _____.

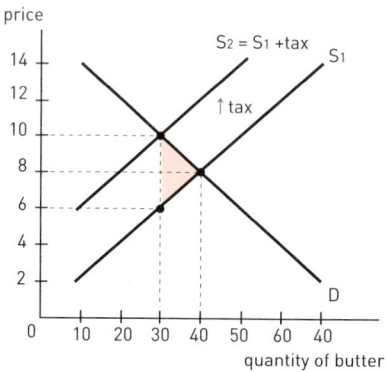

A) buyers and sellers equally share the tax burden
B) shaded area is the deadweight loss from the tax
C) tax revenue is equal to $120
D) Only A and B are correct

1 D  2 B  3 D  4 C  5 C  6 B  7 D  8 C  9 B  10 D
11 C  12 B  13 C  14 B  15 B  16 A  17 C  18 B  19 A  20 D

# Chapter 03

# Production and Cost

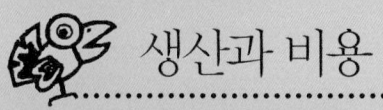
생산과 비용

---

**"Why firms produce and what happens to production cost in the process of production?"**

앞에서 배운 공급곡선의 주체는 기업 firm 입니다. 기업은 이윤극대화 profit maximization 를 위해 생산하지요. 기업이 생산을 할 때 생산함수 production function 와 비용 cost 이 함께 변화합니다. 생산할 때 그 비용이 발생하는 것은 당연하므로, 생산과 비용은 동전의 양면과 같습니다. 생산함수와 여러 가지의 비용곡선 cost curves 이 어떤 모양을 갖게 되는지, 왜 그렇게 되는지에 대해서 이해하는 것이 시장구조 market structures 를 이해하는데 매우 중요합니다. 시장구조에 따라 시장유형이 달라지기 때문에 우리는 완전경쟁 perfect competition, 독점 monopoly, 과점 oligopoly, 독점적 경쟁 monopolistic competition 시장에 대해 알아볼 것입니다. 덧붙여서 생산요소가 교환되는 요소시장 Factor Market 과 소득분배 income distribution 에 대해서도 기본 개념을 학습하겠습니다.

# Lesson 1

# Production
생산

## production function[2)]
생산함수

**The relationship between the quantity of inputs and the quantity of output**
투입요소와 산출량 사이의 관계

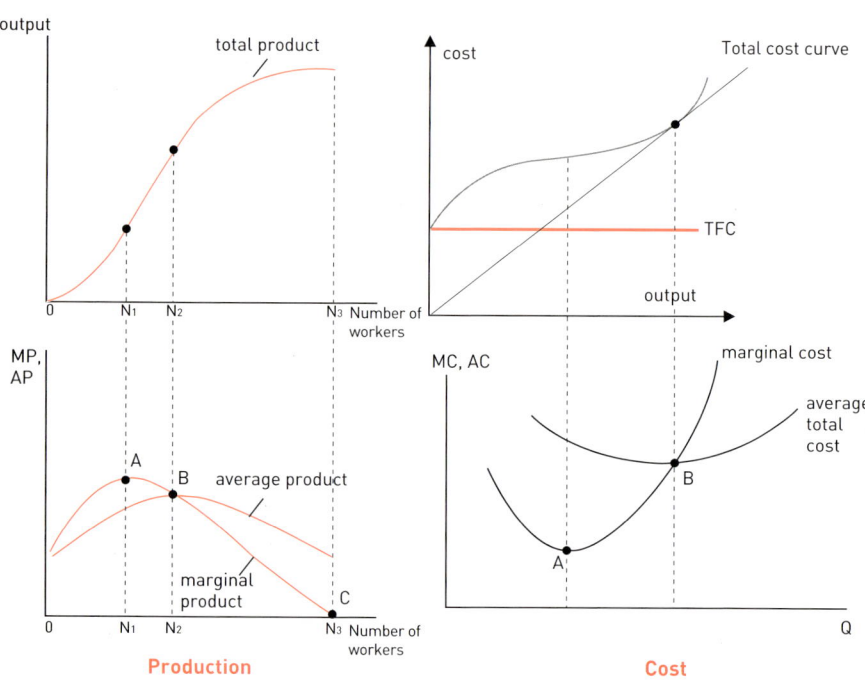

Production

Cost

The four graphs above show the relationship between production and cost. The upper-left graph represents production function, which is the relationship between total product and quantity of labor. The production function shows diminishing marginal product of labor, which means that the change in total product resulting from hiring additional worker decreases. Diminishing marginal product of labor is so called diminishing returns. The lower-left graph is derived from the production function. It shows marginal product curve and average product curve. Marginal product eventually decreases because the fixed input per person such as capital falls. The upper-right graph shows total cost curve. Total cost is the sum of total factor cost(TFC) and total variable cost(TVC). The lower-right graph is derived from the total cost curve. It shows marginal cost(MC) curve and average total cost(ATC) curve. average total cost(ATC) is the sum of average fixed cost(AFC) and average variable cost(AVC). Marginal cost finally rises due to diminishing returns. average total cost curve is U-shaped, because at initial production average fixed cost decreases, but finally average variable cost increases because marginal cost increases. Marginal cost curve meets average cost curve at the minimum of average total cost curve. Point A and Point B on the lower-left and lower-right graph corresponds with each other, respectively.

## total product(TP)
### 총생산

**The level of output corresponding to level of inputs**
투입수준에 상응하는 산출수준

## average product(AP)
### 평균생산

**Total product divided by the number of inputs employed**
총생산을 고용된 투입량으로 나눈 값

## marginal product(MP)
### 한계생산

**The increase in total output from using an additional unit of input**
한 단위 투입요소를 더 사용했을 때 총생산의 증가분

## diminishing marginal product(diminishing returns)
### 한계생산의 체감

**The property that the marginal product decreases as the number of inputs increases**
투입요소를 증가시킬 때 한계생산이 줄어드는 성질

# Lesson 2 | Cost
## 비용

## economic cost
### 경제적 비용

**economic cost = opportunity cost = explicit cost + implicit cost (in terms of choice)**
경제적 비용 = 기회비용 = 명시적 비용 + 암묵적 비용

- **explicit cost: the direct outlay of money from your wallet and bank account**
  **명시적 비용:** 지갑이나 은행 계좌에서 돈이 직접 인출되는 비용
- **implicit cost: the cost that a firm must give up without direct payments or the value of the benefits that are foregone.**
  **암묵적 비용:** 직접인출은 없지만 기업이 포기해야 하는 비용, 지나가버린 편익의 가치

## total cost(TC)
### 총비용

**total cost = Total Fixed cost(TFC or FC) + Total Variable Cost(TVC or VC) (in terms of production)**
총비용 = 총고정비용 + 총가변비용

- **Total cost: the total cost of production, the sum of total fixed and total variable costs**
  **총비용:** 생산의 전체비용, 총고정비용과 총가변비용의 합
- **Average cost: total cost divided by quantity of output**
  **평균비용:** 총비용을 생산량으로 나눈 값
- **Marginal cost: the increase in total cost from producing additional unit of output**
  **한계비용:** 한 단위 더 생산할 때 총비용의 증가분

### 기본 단어 익히기

**ATC:** TC devided by quantity of output
**AFC:** TFC devided by quantity of output
**AVC:** TVC devided by quantity of output

## three properties of cost curves
비용곡선의 세 가지 특성

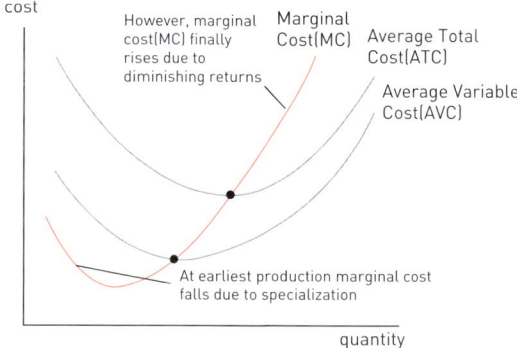

1. **Average total cost is U-shaped** 평균 총비용곡선은 U자모양이다.

2. **Marginal cost curve intersects the average total cost(ATC) curve at the minimum of ATC**
한계비용곡선은 평균 총비용곡선의 최저점에서 평균 총비용곡선과 만난다.

3. **Marginal cost finally rises due to diminishing marginal product (diminishing returns)**
한계비용은 한계생산 체감으로 인해 결국에는 상승한다.

## relationship between average cost and marginal cost
평균비용과 한계비용의 관계

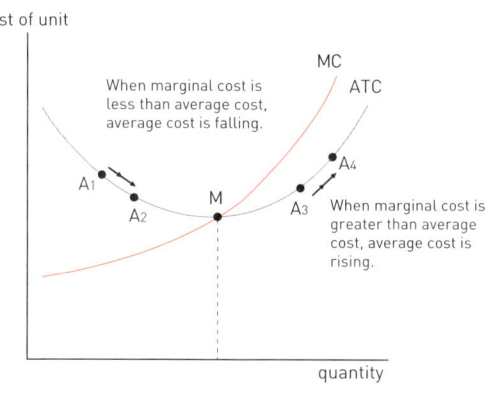

Chapter 3 Production and Cost

- **When marginal cost is less than average cost, average cost falls.**
  한계비용이 평균비용보다 작으면, 평균비용은 하락한다.
- **When marginal cost is greater than average cost, average cost rises.**
  한계비용이 평균비용보다 크면, 평균비용은 상승한다.

중간고사가 끝나고 과목성적이 하나씩marginally 나오고 있다고 생각을 해보자.
총 여덟 과목 중에서 세 과목점수가 발표되었다. 다음 과목점수Marginal Cost가 평균Average Cost보다 낮으면 평균은 떨어질 것이다. 반면에 다음 과목 점수가 평균보다 높으면 평균은 상승할 것이다.
이 원리를 적용해 보자. Average Cost는 U-shape이라는 점을 전제하면, 처음에는 MC가 AC보다 낮아야 AC가 하락할 것이고, 나중에는 MC가 AC보다 높아야 AC가 상승할 것이다. 그렇다면 전환국면(그림의 M점)에서 MC가 AC의 최저점을 통과해야 한다.

# Lesson 3

# Short run vs Long run
## 단기와 장기

## short run
### 단기

**The time span in which fixed costs exist, such as the plant, which does not vary with the quantity of output.**

공장설비 같은 고정비용이 존재하는 기간. 고정비용은 생산량이 증가(감소)해도 변화하지 않는다.

## long run
### 장기

**The time span in which no fixed costs exist. In the long run, all costs are variable.**

고정비용이 존재하지 않는 기간. 장기에는 모든 비용이 가변비용이다.

## long-run average total cost
### 장기 평균비용곡선

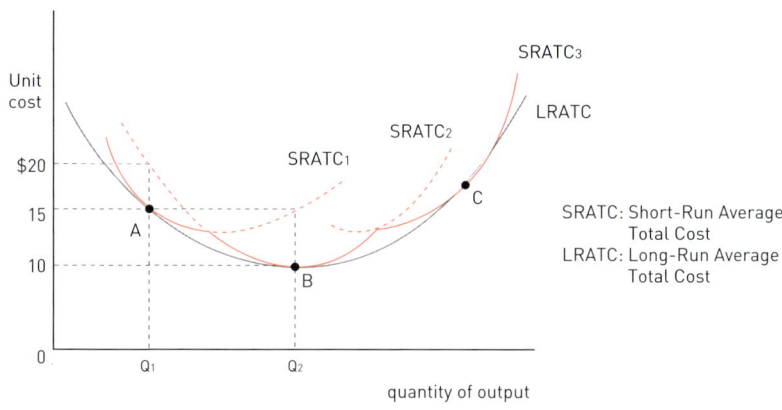

Long-run Average Total Cost Curve is the average total cost curve derived from the various short-run average total cost curves in the long run in which the size of facilities can be variable. Firms that maximizes profits try to minimize production cost. In the long run, a new average total cost curve can be derived from the different short-run average cost curves given. This newly derived cost curve is the long-run average cost curve. Long-run average cost curve shape envelopes the short-run average cost curves.

장기의 평균비용곡선이란 공장설비(단기에는 고정비용)의 크기를 선택할 수 있는 장기에, 여러 단기 평균비용곡선에서 도출되는 평균비용곡선을 말한다. 이윤극대화를 추구하는 기업은 장기에도 생산비용을 최소화하려고 할 것이다. 장기에는 개별 생산량에서 주어진 단기 비용곡선(SRATC1, SRATC2, SRATC3)의 최저점을 연결하는 새로운 평균비용곡선이 도출될 수 있다. 이 새로운 비용 곡선이 바로 장기 평균비용곡선LRATC이다. 장기 평균비용곡선은 단기 평균비용곡선들을 감싸는 모양envelope이 된다.

## three areas of long-run average total costs
### 장기 평균총비용곡선의 세 영역

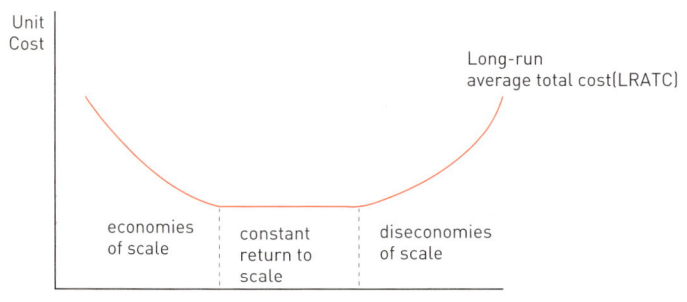

- **economies of scale** 규모의 경제

  The property that long-run average cost(unit cost) falls as the quantity of production increases

  생산량이 증가할 때 장기평균비용이 하락하는 현상

- **diseconomies of scale** 규모의 비경제

  The property that long-run average cost(unit cost) rises as the quantity of production increases

  생산량이 증가할 때 장기평균비용이 상승하는 현상

- **constant returns to scale** 규모의 불비경제

  The property that long-run average cost(unit cost) stays the same as the quantity of production increases.

  생산량이 증가할 때 장기평균비용에 변화가 없는 현상

## least cost rule $\frac{MP_L}{P_L} = \frac{MP_k}{P_k}$

**The cost-minimizing combination of labor and capital for a given production**
주어진 생산량에서 노동과 자본의 비용최소화 조합을 만들어 주는 공식을 말한다.

$\frac{MP_L}{P_L} = \frac{MP_k}{P_k}$ means equalizing marginal product of each good per dollar.
$\frac{MP_L}{P_L} = \frac{MP_k}{P_k}$ 은 달러당 각 재화의 한계생산을 똑같게 하는 공식이다.

# Problem Set A: Short Answer Question

## Write down a proper word for the definition

**1** the property that long-run average cost(unit cost) falls as the quantity of production increases

**2** the time span in which there exist fixed costs, such as the plant, which does not vary with the quantity of output

**3** the relationship between the quantity of inputs and the quantity of output

**4** the property that the marginal product decreases as the number of inputs increases

**5** total product divided by the number of inputs employed

**6** the property that long-run average cost(unit cost) stays the same as the quantity of production increases

**7** the increase in total cost from producing additional unit of output

**8** the time span in which there exists no fixed cost. In the long run, all costs are variable

**9** the property that long-run average cost(unit cost) rises as the quantity of production increases

**10** the increase in total output from using additional unit of input

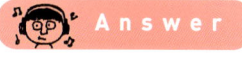

**1** economies of scale  **2** short run  **3** production function
**4** diminishing marginal product(diminishing returns)  **5** average product
**6** constant returns to scale
**7** marginal cost  **8** long run  **9** diseconomies of scale  **10** marginal product(MP)

## Problem Set B: multiple questions

**1.** The ultimate goal of a firm in economics is _____.

A) to minimize social cost
B) to make a good product
C) to maximize profit
D) maximize total revenue

**2.** When calculating cost, accountants consider _____.

A) economic recession as part of the firm's cost
B) the explicit cost of producing goods or services, which is the direct money payment
C) the opportunity cost of all the factors
D) all the firm's implicit costs

**3.** Which of the following is true?

A) Accounting profit and economic profit are usually equal
B) Accounting profit is always smaller than economic profit
C) Economic profit is always smaller than implicit costs
D) Economic profit is usually smaller than accounting profit

## 4

**Which of the following is true concerning the long-run time period?**

A) some of the firm's factors are fixed
B) all of the firm's factors are fixed
C) all of the firm's factors are variable
D) the firm can increase its output

## 5

**The production function shows the relationship between total product and _____.**

A) total cost
B) total revenue
C) the quantity of labor
D) the marginal cost

## 6

**Marginal product is _____.**

A) the total product divided by quantity of labor
B) defined as the change in total cost from employing one more worker
C) the total output divided by the change in cost from employing one more worker
D) the change in total product divided by the increase in the quantity of labor

## 7 Which of the following is true?

A) A firm undergoes the diminishing marginal returns when the marginal product of an additional worker is less than that of the previous worker
B) The slope of the total product curve is negative when the marginal product is falling
C) The slope of the average product curve must be negative when the marginal product exceeds the average product
D) The marginal product equals the average product when the marginal product is at its maximum

## 8 Average product is defined as _____.

A) total product minus marginal product
B) total product divided by price
C) total product divided by quantity of labor
D) total product multiplied by quantity of labor

## 9 Marginal cost equals _____.

A) total cost divided by total variable cost
B) the change in total variable cost resulting from producing one more unit of output
C) the change in total cost resulting from hiring one more worker
D) the change in total cost resulting from producing one more unit of output

# 10

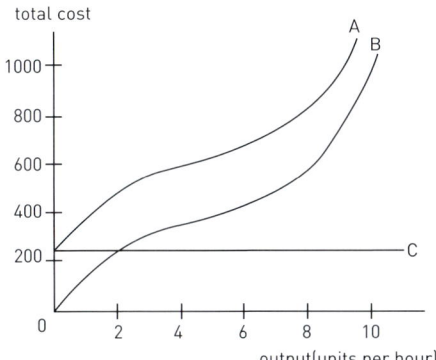

In the above graph, curve A is _____, curve B is _____, and curve C is _____.

A) average cost, variable cost, total fixed cost
B) total variable cost, total fixed cost, marginal cost
C) total cost, total fixed cost, total average cost
D) total cost, total variable cost, total fixed cost

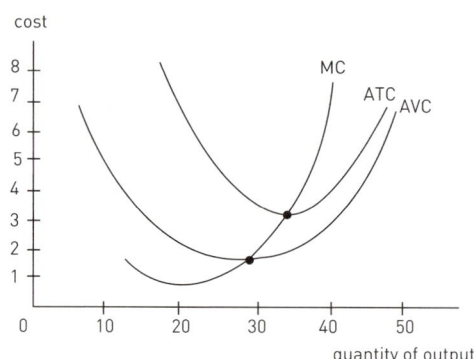

## 11

**The average total cost curve is U-shaped because _____ .**

A) firms desire to find the output level at its minimum average total cost
B) average total cost always increases as output increases
C) average fixed cost falls and marginal product of labor diminishes as output increases
D) marginal product increases

## 12

**Why is marginal cost curve rising?**

A) Because total cost is falling
B) Because total product is rising
C) Because marginal product is falling
D) Because marginal product is rising

**13** Marginal cost crosses the average cost curves at the minimum of average cost curves because _____.

   A) Average costs are U-shaped
   B) When marginal cost is less than average cost, average cost is falling
   C) When marginal cost is greater than average cost, average cost is rising
   D) B and C

**14** A firm has _____ when its average total cost of production _____ as quantity of output increases.

   A) diseconomies of scale; decreases
   B) economies of scale; does not change
   C) constant returns to scale; increase by the same percentage
   D) economies of scale; decreases

1 C  2 B  3 D  4 C  5 C  6 D  7 A
8 C  9 D  10 D  11 C  12 C  13 D  14 D

# Chapter 04

# Market Structures

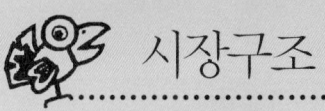 시장구조

"Resource allocation is all about price and quantity."

Chapter4는 미시경제의 꽃이라고 할 수 있는 시장의 유형에 대해서 학습합니다. 여기에서 다루는 시장은 기본적으로 생산물 시장 product market 으로 완전경쟁, 독점, 과점, 독점적 경쟁의 네 가지 유형입니다. 완전경쟁시장 perfect competition 을 먼저 학습하는데, 그 이유는 완전경쟁시장이 시장의 효율성의 기준이 되는 시장이기 때문입니다. 배분의 효율성 allocative efficiency 과 생산의 효율성 productive efficiency 을 달성하는 유일한 시장이 바로 완전경쟁시장으로, 다른 시장의 효율성을 평가하는 기준이 되지요. Chapter4에서는 각 시장의 발생원인, 배경, 자원배분의 특징에 대해 집중해서 배워야 합니다. 무엇보다 기억해야 할 것은, 자원배분은 가격과 수량에 관한 것이라는 사실입니다. 각 시장에서 가격과 수량이 어떻게 결정되는지를 잘 보아야 합니다. 그리고 단기와 장기를 구분하여 단기의 균형을 먼저 이해하고 장기의 균형으로 어떻게 변해가는지를 주의 깊게 들여다봅시다.

# Lesson 1
# Perfect competition
## 완전경쟁

### perfect competition
### 완전경쟁

**A market with many buyers and sellers who are all price takers, selling identical products, and with no barriers to entry and no information asymmetry**

구매자와 판매자가 많이 있으며 그들은 모두 가격순응자이다. 동질적인 상품을 판매하며 진입에 장벽이 없고 정보비대칭이 존재하지 않는 시장

### price taker
### 가격순응자

**In perfect competition, any firm has no market power to influence price, so it must act according to the price determined in the market.**

완전경쟁시장에서는 어떤 기업도 가격에 영향을 미치는 시장지배력을 가지고 있지 않다. 그래서 기업은 시장에서 결정된 가격에 따라 행동해야 한다.

### identical product
### 동질적인 상품

**The same, homogeneous product**

동일한, 동질적인 상품

### barrier to entry
### 진입장벽

**Anything that prevents new firms from entering a market. For example, exclusive rights such as copyright law, patent law, exclusive ownership of key resources, cost structure of production.**

새로운 기업이 시장에 진입하는 것을 막는 것. 예를 들면, 저작권이나 특허권 같은 배타적 권리, 핵심적인 자원에 대한 배타적 소유, 생산의 비용구조.

## information asymmetry
### 정보비대칭

**The situation in which one party has more or better information than the other in transaction**
거래 시에 한 쪽이 다른 쪽보다 더 많거나 더 나은 정보를 가지고 있는 상황

## profit, loss, normal profit
### 이윤, 손실, 정상이윤

- **Total Revenue(TR): the price of a good(P) times the quantity sold(Q)**
  총수입: 가격에 판매량을 곱한 값
- **Average Revenue(AR): total revenue divided by the quantity sold**
  평균수입: 총수입을 판매량으로 나눈 값
- **Marginal Revenue(MR): the increase in total revenue resulting from additional increase in sales**
  한계수입: 상품 한 단위를 더 팔 때 총수입의 증가분
- **Profit maximization: MR = MC**
  이익극대화: 한계수입 = 한계비용

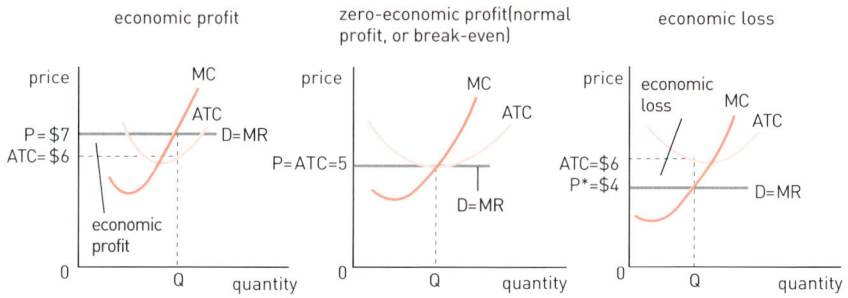

- **Profit = Total Revenue − Total Cost = P × Q − ATC × Q = (P − ATC) × Q**
  이윤은 총수입에서 총비용을 뺀 값이다.
  1. P > ATC  economic profit 경제적 이익을 보는 경우
  2. P < ATC  economic loss 경제적 손해를 보는 경우
  3. P = ATC  zero-economic profit(normal profit) 영의 경제적 이윤, 즉 정상이윤을 보는 경우

## a firm's short-run supply curve and firm's decision-making
기업의 단기 공급곡선과 의사결정

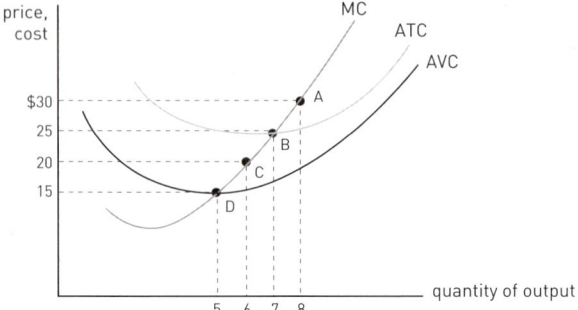

- **Marginal cost curve(MC) above average variable cost(AVC) is the firm's short-run supply curve.**
  총가변비용곡선 위에 있는 한계비용이 이 기업의 단기공급곡선이다.

  **A**(price = $30): The firm is making economic profits. 경제적 이윤상황

  **B**(price = $25): The firm is making zero economic profit. 영의 경제적 이윤상황

  **C**(price = $20): The firm is making economic loss but should keep producing.
  경제적 손해이지만 조업은 계속하는 상황

  **D**(price = $15): The firm should shut down if price would be lowered further.
  가격이 더 떨어지면 조업을 중단해야 함

**Tip** Profit maximizing rule : MR = MC
Whether a firm is making profits : P vs. ATC
Whether a firm should shut down : P vs. min AVC

## side-by-side graph of a firm and industry in perfect competition
## 완전경쟁에서 기업과 산업의 양편 그래프

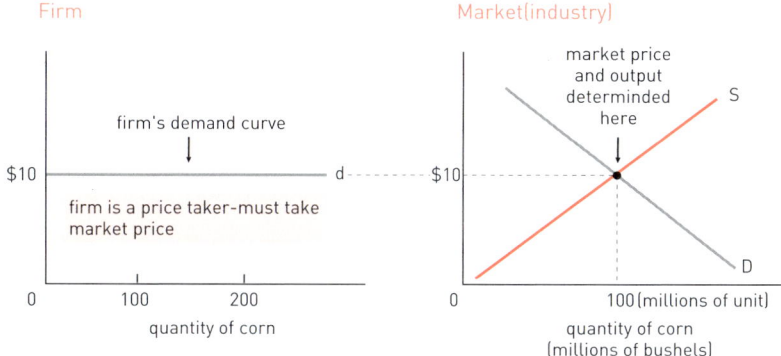

An individual firm in perfect competition has horizontal demand curve because the firm is a price taker. If the demand curve for a firm in perfect competition is downward sloping, it would mean that the firm could alter quantity of output and therefore could change price. This would violate the assumption that a firm in a perfectly competitive market is a price taker. Therefore, the demand curve for a firm in perfect competition is horizontal and perfectly elastic.

완전경쟁에서의 개별기업은 수평의 수요곡선을 갖는데, 이는 기업이 가격수용자이기 때문이다. 만약에 완전경쟁에 있는 기업의 수요곡선이 우하향한다면, 그것은 기업이 생산량을 변경해서 가격을 변화시킬 수 있다는 것을 의미한다. 이는 완전경쟁에서의 기업이 가격수용자라는 가정을 위배할 것이다. 그러므로 완전경쟁에서 개별기업의 수요곡선은 수평이고 완전탄력적이다.

# long-run equilibrium in perfect competition
## 완전경쟁에서의 장기 균형

### ❶ Initial Equilibrium 초기 균형

At initial condition, a market is in long-run equilibrium and a firm is making zero economic profit.

초기조건에서 시장은 장기균형에 있으며 기업은 경제적 이윤이 0이다.

### ❷ Short-run Profits 단기 이윤

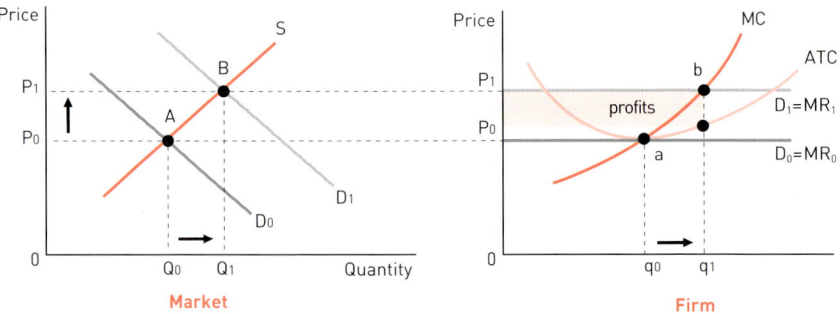

Suppose that the demand for a good increases. The equilibrium in the market goes from point A to point B, with price rising from P0 to P1 and quantity sold increasing from Q0 to Q1. Price for the firm is greater than average total cost, so the firm is making profits.

이 상품에 대한 수요가 증가했다고 가정하자. 시장에서의 균형은 A점에서 B점으로 이동하고 가격은 P0에서 P1으로 오르며 판매량도 Q0에서 Q1으로 증가한다. 기업은 가격이 평균비용보다 크므로 기업은 이윤을 얻고 있다.

### ❸ Long-Run Entry and Zero Economic Profits 장기 시장진입과 영의 경제적 이윤

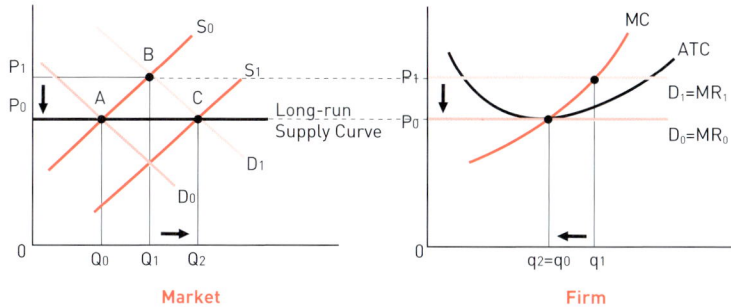

Market | Firm

Profits induce new firms to enter the market, so this entry increases supply curve from S0 to S1. In the long run equilibrium goes point B to point C. Therefore, the line connecting point C to point A is the long-run supply curve. Price goes back to P0 but the quantity sold increases from Q1 to Q2. The firm is now earning zero-economic profit(normal profit) again at the production of q0.

이윤이 발생하면 새로운 기업들이 시장으로 들어오고 이로 인해 공급곡선이 S0에서 S1으로 증가한다. 장기 균형은 B점에서 C점으로 이동한다. 그러므로 C점과 A점을 연결한 선이 장기공급곡선이 된다. 가격은 다시 P0로 돌아가지만 시장의 판매량은 Q1에서 Q2로 증가한다. 기업은 q0의 생산에서 다시 영의 경제적 이윤(정상이윤)을 얻게 된다.

# increasing-cost industry
## 비용 상승 산업

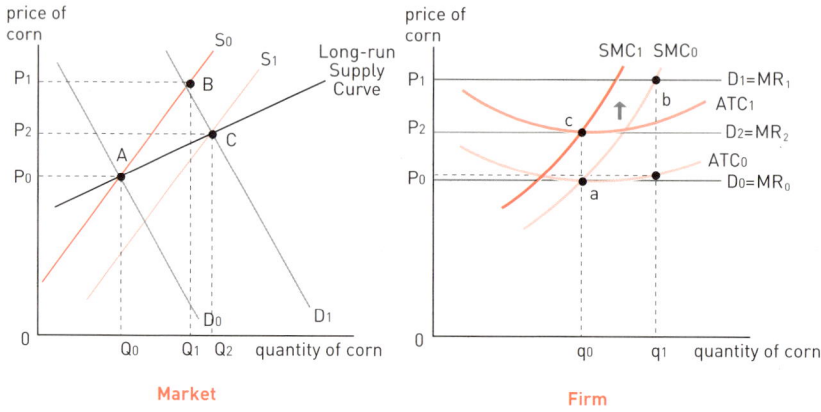

Market is in equilibrium at point A in graph A and at point a in graph B. Suppose that the demand for the good increases in the market, shifting the demand curve from D0 to D1. The equilibrium point in the market goes from point A to point B, and price rises from P0 to P1 in the graph A. Now price is greater than average total cost, so firms make profits, which induce other firms to enter the industry. In the graph B, the equilibrium point goes from point a to point b. Be careful that in this case the input prices rise as new firms enter and output increases. The rise in input prices leads to higer cost curves for the firm in graph B, shifting SMC0 to SMC1 and ATC0 to ATC1. The new long-run equilibrium goes from point B to point C in graph A and point b to point c in graph B. Then the line linking point A to point C is the long-run supply curve in the market.

시장은 그래프 A에서는 A점에서, 그래프 B에서는 a점에서 균형에 있다. 시장에서 상품에 대한 수요가 증가해서 수요곡선이 D0에서 D1으로 이동했다고 가정하자. 그래프 A에서 시장의 균형점은 A에서 B로 이동하고 가격은 P0에서 P1으로 상승한다. 이제 가격이 평균비용보다 커졌으므로 기업은 이익을 얻게 되고 이로 인해 다른 기업들이 시장으로 진입하게 된다. 그래프 B에서 균형점은 a에서 b로 이동하게 된다. 이 사례에서는 새로운 기업들이 진입하고 생산량이 증가하면서 투입요소가격이 상승한다는 것을 주의하라. 투입요소가격 상승은 그래프 B에서 기업의 비용곡선의 증가를 초래하여 SMC0가 SMC1으로, ATC0가 ATC1으로 이동한다. 새로운 장기균형점은 그래프 A에서는 B에서 C로, 그래프 B에서는 b에서 c로 이동한다. 그러면 점 A와 C를 연결하는 선이 시장에서의 장기공급곡선이 된다.

# Lesson 2 | Monopoly
## 독점

### monopoly
### 독점

**A market with a single firm in an industry**
산업 내에 기업이 하나만 존재하는 시장

### causes of monopoly
### 독점의 원인

❶ **ownership of key resources, natural or human resources**
   주요 자원, 천연 자원, 인적 자원의 배타적 소유
❷ **government policy**
   정부 정책
❸ **cost structures of production**
   생산의 비용구조

### perfect competition vs. monopoly
### 완전경쟁 vs 독점

demand curve faced by a firm in perfect competition

demand curve faced by a monopoly firm

A firm in perfect competition has horizontal demand curve. On the other hand, a firm in monopoly has downward sloping demand curve because the demand in the market becomes demand for the firm. In monopoly one industry consists of one firm.

완전경쟁의 기업은 수평의 수요곡선을 갖는다. 반면에, 독점의 기업은 우하향하는 수요곡선을 갖는데 이는 시장의 수요가 그 기업에 대한 수요가 되기 때문이다. 독점에서는 기업 하나가 산업 전체를 구성한다.

## demand and marginal revenue
### 수요와 한계수입

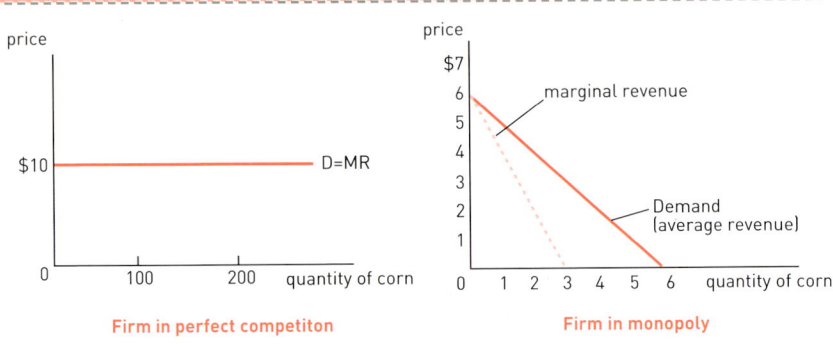

Firm in perfect competiton                Firm in monopoly

In perfect competition demand curve equals marginal revenue curve because the price is given to the firm and whenever the firm sells one more unit of output, the total revenue increases by the amount of price. Price equals marginal revenue in perfect competition. On the other hand, marginal revenue curve does not equal demand curve in monopoly. Marginal revenue is less than price because the firm must lower its price to sell one more unit of output.

완전경쟁에서는 수요곡선이 한계수입곡선이 된다. 왜냐하면 가격이 기업에게 주어지고 기업이 한 단위를 더 팔 때마다 총수입은 가격의 크기만큼 증가하기 때문이다. 완전경쟁에서 가격은 한계수입과 같다. 반면에 독점에서는 한계수입곡선은 수요곡선과 다르다. 한계수입은 가격보다 낮게 되는데, 이는 기업이 한 단위를 더 팔려면 가격을 낮춰야 하기 때문이다.

# determining price and quantity in monopoly (resource allocation)
## 독점에서 가격과 수량의 결정(자원배분)

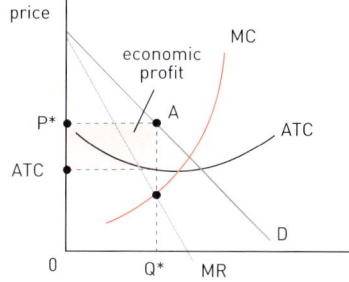

### Q* and P*

- **Profit-maximizing quantity(Q*) is determined at the quantity of output making MR equal MC**
  이윤극대화 생산량은 MR과 MC가 같아지는 곳에서 결정된다.
- **The firm sets the price on the demand curve, going straight to the demand curve from the quantity of output making MR equal MC**
  기업은 MR=MC인 생산량에서 곧바로 수요곡선으로 올라가서 해당되는 가격을 찾는다.

# price discrimination
## 가격차별

**Business practice of charging different prices to different customers for the same good or service**
동일한 상품이나 서비스를 다른 소비자에게 다른 가격을 부과하는 기업관행

- **Conditions of price discrimination** 가격차별의 조건
  1. Firms should be able to segment consumer groups according to their characteristics, especially price elasticity of demand.
     기업은 소비자의 특성, 특히 가격탄력성에 따라 소비자그룹을 분리시킬 수 있어야 한다.
  2. It is impossible to resell the good.
     재판매는 불가능하다.

# three types of price discrimination
## 가격차별의 세 종류

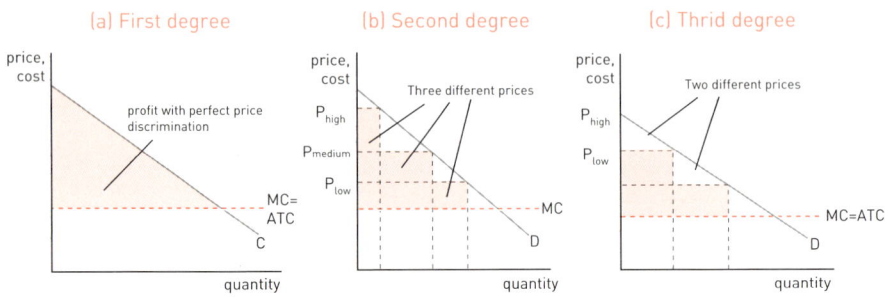

The First-degree price discrimination, in other words, perfect price discrimination is that monopoly firm imposes each customer different prices, so each consumer pays her willingness to pay as her prices. In this case the demand curve becomes marginal revenue curve for the monopoly firm. Second-degree price discrimination means dividing consumers into more than three different groups according to their willingness to pay, and third-degree price discrimination means dividing consumers into two different groups. In case of third-degree price discrimination, the firm raises its price for the consumers with inelastic demand, and lowers its price for consumers with elastic demand.

1급의 가격차별(완전가격차별)은 모든 소비자에게 각각 다른 가격을 부과하는 것으로 개별 소비자는 자신의 최대 지불용의금액을 가격으로 지불한다. 이 경우에 수요곡선은 한계수입곡선이 된다. 2급의 가격차별은 소비자를 지불용의금액에 따라 셋 이상의 여러 그룹으로 나누는 것을 말하고, 3급의 가격차별은 소비자를 두 그룹으로 나누는 것을 이야기한다. 3급의 가격차별의 경우에 기업은 비탄력적인 수요를 가진 소비자들에게는 가격을 올리고, 탄력적인 수요를 가진 소비자들에게는 가격을 내린다.

**How to price discriminate 가격차별 방법**
make price higher 높은 가격 -consumers with inelastic demand 비탄력적인 수요자
make price lower 낮은 가격 -consumers with elastic demand 탄력적인 수요자

## natural monopoly
## 자연독점

**A monopoly that arises because economies scale is so large that a single firm can provide goods to the entire market.**

규모의 경제가 매우 크게 나타나서 한 기업이 시장전체에 상품을 공급할 수 있기 때문에 발생하는 독점

## government policy to regulate natural monopoly
## 자연독점을 규제하기 위한 정부 정책

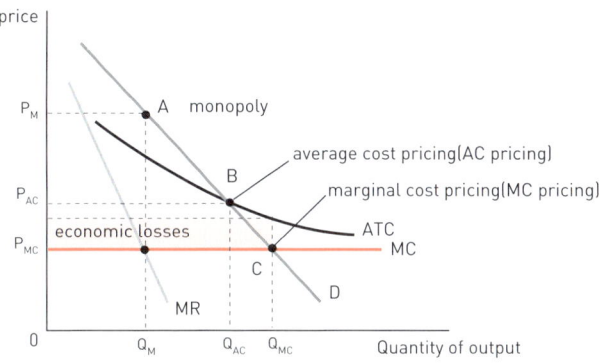

- **Point A:** Without any government interventions the firm will produce QM at PM. The firm could enjoy considerable monopoly profits.

  정부 개입이 없다면 기업은 PM의 가격에서 QM만큼 생산할 것이다. 기업은 상당한 독점 이윤을 누릴 수 있다.

- **Point B:** AC Pricing is called fair return price. With AC pricing, a firm have no incentives to exit the market

  평균비용 가격설정은 공정한 가격인데, 여기서는 기업이 이탈할 동기가 없다.

- **Point C:** MC pricing satisfies allocative efficiency but economic loss will cause firms to exit the industry unless the government gives a subsidy to the firm.

  한계비용 가격설정은 배분적 효율성을 만족시키지만 경제적 손실이 발생하여 정부가 보조금을 지급하지 않는다면 기업이 산업을 이탈하게 된다.

# Lesson 3

# Oligopoly
## 과점

## oligopoly
### 과점

**A market with a few interdependent firms offering similar or identical products. The firms compete in strategic situation.**

유사하거나 동일한 상품을 판매하는 소수의 상호의존적인 기업으로 구성된 시장. 과점기업들은 전략적인 상황에서 경쟁한다.

## game theory
### 게임 이론

**The theory that the output of one player's choice is based on the choices of the other's. a game is composed of players, strategies, and pay-offs.**

한 경기자의 선택의 결과가 다른 경기자의 선택에 달려있는 것에 대한 연구. 게임은 기본적으로 경기자, 전략, 보수로 이루어져 있다.

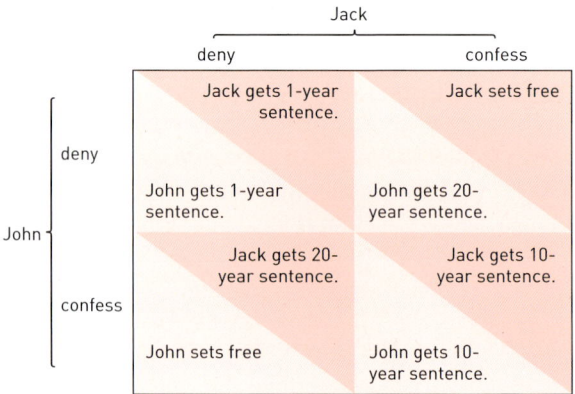

This game matrix shows a typical prisoners' dilemma. Let's think about the result of this game in terms of strategic situation. For John, if Jack deny, confess is a better choice for John and if Jack chooses to confess, confessing is a better choice for John, too. Regardless of Jack's choice, confessing is a better choice for John. This kind of choice is called dominant strategy. The same logic stands true for Jack. So both choose to confess and both get 10-year sentence. The result is more than when both players choose not to confess.

이 게임은 전형적인 죄수의 딜레마 게임을 보여준다. 이 게임의 해법을 전략적인 상황의 관점에서 생각해 보자. 존의 입장에서는 잭이 부인하면 자백하는 게 자신에게 더 좋은 선택이고, 잭이 자백해도 존에게는 자백이 역시 더 좋은 선택이다. 잭의 선택과 관계없이 자백이 존에게는 더 좋은 선택이다. 이런 종류의 선택을 우월전략이라고 한다. 같은 논리가 잭에게도 적용된다. 그래서 둘다 자백하게 되고, 모두 10년 형을 받는다. 이것은 둘 다 자백을 하지 않는 전략을 택하는 것보다 결과가 나쁘다.

### 기 본 단 어 익 히 기

**prisoners' dilemma** 죄수의 딜레마
A situation in which two individuals does not cooperate, even though the cooperation results in mutual profits
두 개인이 협력하는 것이 서로에게 이익이 됨에도 불구하고 협력하지 못하는 상황

**dominant strategy** 우월전략
A strategy that is best for a player regardless of what strategy a rival chooses
다른 경기자의 선택과 관계없이 한 경기자에게 최선인 전략

**dominant strategy equilibrium** 우월전략균형
The output when both players choose their own dominant strategies
두 경기자가 각자 자신의 우월전략을 선택했을 때의 결과

## Nash equilibrium
### 내쉬 균형

A situation in which two players choose their strategies on their own and no players can gain by changing one's current strategy. The current strategy is the best one to each player given the other's strategy.

두 경기자가 자신의 전략을 선택했을 때 발생하는 상황 중 하나로, 어느 한 경기자도 전략을 바꿔서 이득을 얻을 수 없는 상황이다. 상대편의 전략을 주어진 것으로 가정했을 때 현재의 전략이 각자에게 최선의 전략이다.

## collusion
### 담합

An agreement among firms about price and quantity of output to produce
기업 사이에서 일어나는 가격과 수량에 관한 합의

### cartel
카르텔

A group of firms that explicitly agree to set prices or control output, acting like a monopoly
명시적으로 가격을 설정하거나 생산량을 통제하며 독점기업처럼 행동하는 기업들의 집합

## business practice of oligopoly and anti-trust law
과점사업관행과 반트러스트법

- **Resale Price Maintenance** 재가격 유지판매
The business practice that a wholesaler or manufacturer require retailers to charge mandated price
도매업자나 제조업자가 소매업자에게 명령된 가격만을 부과하도록 요구하는 사업관행

- **Predatory Pricing** 약탈적 가격덤핑
The business practice that an oligopolistic firm slash its price in order to drive its competitors out of market and then regain its monopoly power and raise prices.
과점적 기업이 가격을 크게 내려서 경쟁자들을 시장에서 내쫓은 후 다시 독점력을 얻어 가격을 올리는 사업관행

- **Tying(bundling)** 묶어 팔기
Business practice that a firm requires the buyer of a product to also purchase a second product together.
기업이 물건 하나를 사는 사람에게 다른 물건도 함께 구매하도록 요구하는 사업관행

- **Anti-trust law** 반독점법(경쟁법)
Competition law
Known in the United States as antitrust law, is law that promotes or maintains market competition by regulating anti-competitive conduct by companies.
경쟁법
미국에서는 반트러스트법으로 알려져 있으며, 기업의 반경쟁적인 행동을 규제함으로써 시장경쟁을 촉진하거나 유지하는 법(US. Anti-trust law: 1894 Sherman Act, 1914 Clayton Act)

# kinked demand curve
## 굴절수요곡선

**A demand curve resulting from different responses to price changes in oligopoly**

과점에서 가격변화에 대한 다른 반응 때문에 도출되는 수요곡선

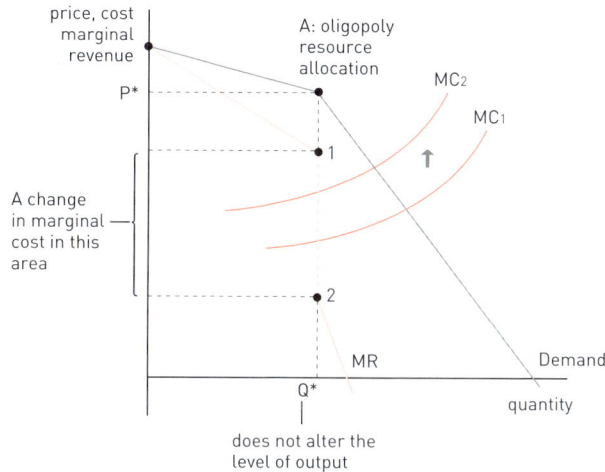

When one firm raises its price, the other firms do not follow the price increase because they are in price competition. On the other hand, when one firm lowers its price, the other firms follow the price decrease for the same reason. So, at the current price raising price means large decrease in quantity demanded because it is only the firm that raises price, and lowering price means small increase in quantity demanded because other firms follows the price decrease. The demand curve is kinked at the current price and quantity of output. In conclusion, current price becomes rigid, or sticky in oligopoly.

한 기업이 가격을 올리면 가격경쟁 중이기 때문에 다른 기업들은 그 가격상승을 따라가지 않는다. 다른 한편으로 한 기업이 가격을 내리면 같은 이유로 다른 기업들은 따라서 가격을 내린다. 그래서 현재 가격에서 가격을 올리면, 가격을 올린 기업은 그 기업뿐이기 때문에 수요량이 크게 감소하고, 가격을 내리면 다른 기업들도 따라서 내리기 때문에 수요량이 작게 증가하게 된다. 수요곡선은 현재 가격과 수량에서 꺾이게 된다. 결론적으로, 과점시장에서 현재 가격은 경직적이다.

# Lesson 4 | Monopolistic Competition
## 독점적 경쟁

### monopolistic competition
### 독점적 경쟁

**A market with many firms offering differentiated products**
차별화된 상품을 제공하는 여러 기업이 조업하는 시장

#### 기본 단어 익히기

- **monopolistic property** 독점적인 성격
  differentiated products
  차별화된 상품

- **competitive property** 경쟁적인 성격
  many buyers and sellers, easy entry or exit → there is no economic profit in the long run
  구매자와 판매자가 많고 진입과 이탈이 자유롭다. → 장기에 경제적 이윤이 없다.

### The short-run monopolistic competition is similar to short-run monopoly 단기 독점적 경쟁은 단기 독점과 유사하다

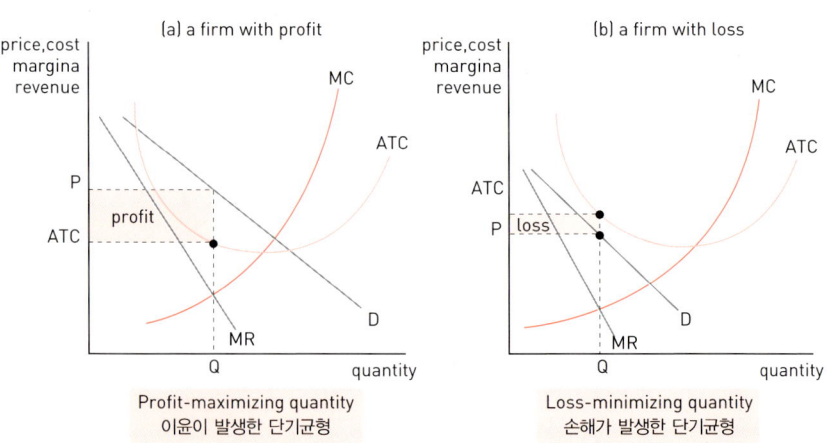

(a) a firm with profit — Profit-maximizing quantity / 이윤이 발생한 단기균형

(b) a firm with loss — Loss-minimizing quantity / 손해가 발생한 단기균형

## long-run equilibrium in monopolistic competition
### 독점적 경쟁에서 장기균형

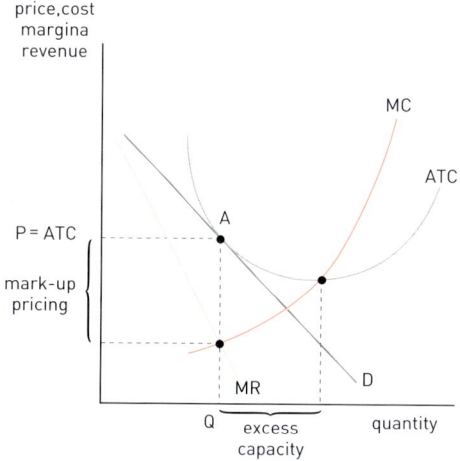

The graph shows the long-run equilibrium in a monopolistic competition. Because there are few barriers to entry in metropolitically competitive market, the short-run equilibrium changes over time. In case of profitable firms in the short run, the demand for the existing firms decreases because new firms enter the market, and in case of unprofitable firm in the short run, the demand for the existing firms increases because other firms exit the market. This process of entry and exit stops when the firms in the market are making no economic profits or loss. In long-run equilibrium the demand curve of a firm is tangent to the ATC.

이 그래프는 독점적 경쟁에서 장기균형을 보여준다. 독점적 경쟁시장에서는 진입장벽이 거의 없기 때문에 단기 균형은 시간이 지나면서 변하게 된다. 단기에 이익을 보는 기업의 경우는 새로운 기업들이 시장에 진입하기 때문에 기존 기업에 대한 수요는 줄어들게 되고, 단기에 손해를 보는 기업의 경우는 다른 기업들이 시장에서 이탈하므로 기존 기업들에 대한 수요는 증가하게 된다. 이 과정은 시장에서 기업들이 경제적 이익이나 손해가 없을 때 멈춘다. 장기 균형에서 기업의 수요곡선은 평균비용곡선에 접한다.

## excess capacity
### 초과설비

**The difference between the quantity of output in the long run and the quantity output at minimum average total cost, i.e. the efficient scale**

장기에서의 생산량과 최저평균비용(최소효율규모)에서의 생산량의 차이

## mark-up pricing
### 비용할증 가격설정

**Increasing the price of a good by a certain rate**
일정 비율만큼 상품 가격을 올리는 것

**Tip** Summary of Market Structures

|  | perfect competition | monopolistic competition | oligopoly | monopoly |
|---|---|---|---|---|
| Number of sellers | many | many | few | one |
| Price-setting power | none, price taker | somewhat | considerable | absolute, price maker |
| Long-run profits | 0 | 0 | positive | positive |
| Barriers to entry | no | few | considerable | absolute |
| Efficiency | allocatively and productively efficient | inefficient | inefficient | inefficient |
| Non-price competition | none | considerable (product differentiation) | considerable | none |
| Examples | rarely exist; agriculture | hospitals, books, CDs, retail stores, | car, steel, bed, mobile communication(SKT, KT, LGT), | electricity, water industry |

# Short Answer Question

Write down a proper word for the definition

**1** a monopoly that arises because economies scale are so remarkable that a single firm can provide goods to an entire market

**2** a market with many buyers and sellers who are all price takers, selling identical products, and with no barriers to entry and no information asymmetry

**3** in perfect competition, any firm has no market power to influence price, so it must act according to the price determined in the market

**4** a situation that two individuals might not cooperate, even though the cooperation appears mutually profitable

**5** anything that prevents new firms from entering a market. For example, exclusive rights such as copyright law, patent law, exclusive ownership of a key resources, cost structure of production

**6** the situation in which one party has more or better information than the other in transaction

**7** the increase in total revenue resulting from additional increase in sales

**8** the difference between total revenue and total cost

**9** a market with a single firm in an industry

**10** an agreement among firms about price and quantity of output to produce

**11** a market in which a few interdependent firms competing in strategic situation offer similar or identical products

**12** a market with many firms offering differentiated products

**13** the price of a good(P) times the quantity sold(Q)

**14** a group of firms that explicitly agree to set prices or control output, acting like a monopoly

# Define these words

**15** dominant strategy?

**16** price discrimination?

### Answer

**1** natural monopoly  **2** perfect competition  **3** price taker  **4** prisoners' dilemma
**5** barrier to entry  **6** information asymmetry  **7** marginal revenue(MR)  **8** profit
**9** monopoly  **10** collusion  **11** oligopoly  **12** monopolistic competition
**13** total revenue(TR)  **14** cartel

**15** a strategy that is best for a player regardless of what strategy a rival chooses
**16** business practice of charging different prices to different customers for the same good or service

## Problem Set B: multiple questions

**1.** A perfectly competitive firm _____.

A) is a price setter
B) produces differentiated products
C) has many competitors
D) face barriers to entry

**2.** A monopoly occurs when _____.

A) many firms produces differentiated products
B) one firm sells a good with no close substitutes
C) there are few firms producing the same product
D) one firm is larger than the many other firms that make an identical product

**3.** When a large number of firms compete by making similar but slightly different products, which market type is this?

A) Oligopolistic competition
B) Perfect competition
C) Monopsonitic competition
D) Monopolistic competition

**4** When a few firms compete interdependently, a market is classified as _____.

A) perfect competition
B) monopoly
C) oligopoly
D) monopolistic competition

**5** Total revenue minus total cost is _____.

A) normal profit
B) accounting profit
C) marginal profit
D) economic profit

**6** Which of the following is not true of monopoly?

A) can sell all of its output at the market price
B) can sell at a higher price to customers willing to pay more
C) can raise its price in order to increase its total revenue
D) can sell additional output by lowering its price

**7** For a perfectly competitive firm, the price of its good is equal to the firm's marginal revenue because _____.

A) there are only a small number of firms in the market
B) price does not change in perfect competition
C) the firm does not have any negligible impact on price, so it cannot change the price given
D) the firm's total revenue cannot be changed by anything the firms can do

## 8. Marginal revenue is _____.

A) the difference between total revenue and total cost
B) the change in total revenue from hiring an additional unit of input
C) the change in total cost from producing an additional unit of output
D) the change in total revenue from producing one additional unit of output

## 9. For a perfectly competitive firm profits will be maximized when _____.

A) the firm is able to earn economic profits
B) the firm can impose the highest price customers are willing to pay
C) the difference between total revenue and total cost is maximized
D) the difference between marginal revenue and marginal cost is maximized

## 10. The following figure illustrates the cost curves of a perfectly competitive firm. Choose the right combination

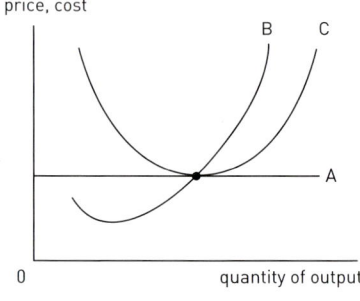

|   | curve A | curve B | curve C |
|---|---|---|---|
| A) | Marginal Revenue | Average Cost | Total cost |
| B) | Average Revenue | Marginal Cost | Fixed Cost |
| C) | Marginal Revenue | Total Cos | Average Cost |
| D) | Margnail Revenue | Marginal Cost | Average Cost |

**11** A perfectly competitive firm will shut down when the price is just below the minimum point on the _____.

A) average fixed cost curve
B) average total cost curve
C) average variable cost curve
D) average product curve

**12** A perfectly competitive firm's short-run supply curve is _____.

A) horizontal at the market price
B) its marginal cost curve below the marginal revenue curve
C) its marginal cost curve above the AVC curve
D) its marginal revenue curve below the ATC curve

**13** Which of the following is true of a perfectly competitive firm in the long run?

A) The firm earns a positive economic profit
B) The firm earns zero economic profit, that is, a normal profit
C) The firm earns zero accounting profit
D) The firm earns either a positive economic profit or a normal profit

## 14 A natural monopoly _____.

A) arises when no one firm can influence market price
B) arises when one firm controls a natural and human resource
C) arises as a result of the firm's production capacity to satisfy the entire market demand at a lower average total cost than two or more firms
D) arises as a result of government economic policy to grant one firm the exclusive right to produce social necessities

## 15 A price-discriminating monopoly is a firm that _____.

A) the firm sells the same product to the different customers at different prices
B) the firm sells its output at a single price to all of its customers
C) the firm has exclusive right to sell the product in the market
D) the firm controls over the resources used to produce the product

## 16 The demand curve for a monopoly is _____.

A) upward sloping
B) vertical
C) horizontal
D) downward sloping

**17** The relationship between total revenue and elasticity is _____.

A) when demand is elastic, total revenue increases as output increases
B) whenever the elasticity is positive, total revenue increases
C) whenever the elasticity is negative, total revenue decreases
D) that total revenue becomes zero at the quantity for which the demand is unit elastic

**18** Which of the following is the primary characteristic of monopolistic competition?

A) identical product
B) economies of scale
C) barriers to entry
D) product differentiation

**19** Which of the following is a general characteristic of oligopoly?

A) many differentiated product
B) many interdependent firms under leadership of one firm
C) few interdependent firms under strategic situation
D) few interdependent firms as price takers

**20** The prisoners' dilemma is an example of
_____.

A) perfect competition
B) monopoly
C) oligopoly
D) monopolistic competition

**21** The table below shows a game between two firms in pizza industry. The two firms have two strategy, price increase or price decrease. The number is economic profit, first one in the entry for Doomino, second one for Pizza Hoot.

|  |  | Pizza Hoot | |
|---|---|---|---|
|  |  | price increase | price decrease |
| Doomino | price increase | −250, −250 | −500, 500 |
|  | price decrease | 500, −500 | 0, 0 |

Choose the correct answer.
A) Doomino does not have dominant strategy
B) Pizza Hoot will choose price increase
C) No firm will earn economic profit
D) Neither of the firms will choose price decrease

A n s w e r

1 C  2 B  3 D  4 C  5 D  6 A  7 B
8 D  9 C  10 D  11 C  12 C  13 B  14 C
15 A  16 D  17 A  18 D  19 C  20 C  21 C

# Chapter 05

# Factor Market and Income Distribution

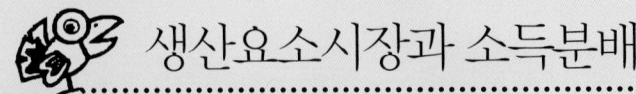

생산요소시장과 소득분배

Chapter5에서는 생산요소시장factor market에 대해 정리하도록 하겠습니다. chapter1에서 배운 상품시장product market과 생산요소시장은 거래 대상이 달라지고 가계와 기업의 역할이 뒤바뀝니다. 최근에 AP 시험에서 더욱 중요해진 부분이기도 합니다. 생산요소시장에서는 수요곡선의 의미와 공급곡선이 어디에서 도출되는지, 수요와 공급의 변화 요인 등이 중요합니다. 또한 완전경쟁 노동시장의 시장과 기업의 Side-by-Side 그래프는 AP FRQ에 단골로 출현하는 문제이기도 합니다.

# Lesson 1: Factor Market
## 생산요소시장

### factor market
### 생산요소시장

The market in which factors of production(land, labor, capital) are bought by firm and sold by household
생산요소(천연자원, 노동, 자본)를 기업이 구매하고 가계는 판매하는 시장

- **Demand for factor is derived from demand for product.**
  생산요소에 대한 수요는 상품에 대한 수요에서 파생된다.
- **In factor market a buyer is a firm and a seller is a household.**
  생산요소시장에서 구매자는 기업이고 판매자는 가계이다.

### determination of wage and employment
### 임금과 고용의 결정

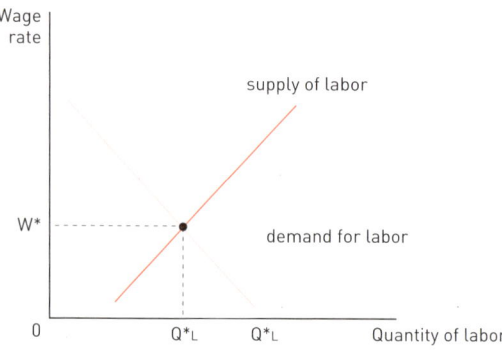

❶ The demand curve in labor market is marginal revenue product curve. By definition the height of the demand curve is willingness to pay. The firm's willingness to pay for one more worker is the marginal benefit the firm can get by hiring the worker, which equals price multiplied by quantity of output, marginal revenue product(MRP). Marginal revenue product curve, which is now egual to the demand curve. demand curve is downward sloping, because of the diminishing marginal product of labor.

노동시장에서 수요곡선은 한계수입 생산곡선이 된다. 정의하면, 수요곡선의 높이는 최대 지불용의금액이다. 기업이 노동자 한 명을 더 고용할 때 지불용의금액은 노동자를 고용함으로써 얻는 한계편익인데, 이 한계편익은 가격 곱하기 생산량, 즉 한계수입생산(MRP)과 같다. 한계수입생산 곡선은 이제 수요곡선이 되고 우하향하는데 이는 노동의 한계수익체감 때문이다.

❷ **The supply curve in labor market is derived from the trade-off between labor and leisure. If the wage rises, the opportunity cost of enjoying leisure increases. People decrease their leisure and increase labor hour. Therefore, the supply curve in the labor market is upward sloping.**

노동시장에서 공급곡선은 노동과 여가의 상충관계에서 도출된다. 임금이 올라가면 여가를 누리는 기회비용이 증가한다. 사람들은 여가를 줄이고 노동시간을 증가시킬 것이다. 따라서 노동의 공급곡선은 우상향한다.

## marginal revenue product(MRP)
### 한계수입생산

The increase in total revenue from an additional unit of input, equals price multiplied marginal product of an input.

요소를 한 단위 추가투입하여 발생하는 총수입의 증가분

## marginal resource cost(MRC) syn marginal factor cost(MFC)
### 한계요소비용

The increase in total cost from an additional unit of an input.

요소를 한 단위 추가투입해서 발생하는 총비용의 증가분

**Tip** 노동시장에서 기업의 이윤극대화 공식: MRP = MRC

## determinants of demand for factors
### 요소수요의 결정요인

- **product price** 상품가격
- **technological advance** 기술진보
- **supply of other factors** 다른 생산요소의 공급

## determinants of supply of factors
요소공급의 결정요인

- **population growth** 인구증가
- **immigration** 이민
- **change in worker preference** 노동자선호의 변화
- **wealth** 부
- **alternative opportunities** 대체 노동기회
- **amenities such as safe and friendly working conditions** 안전하고 친숙한 근무환경

## a firm in perfectly competitive labor market
완전경쟁노동시장에서의 기업

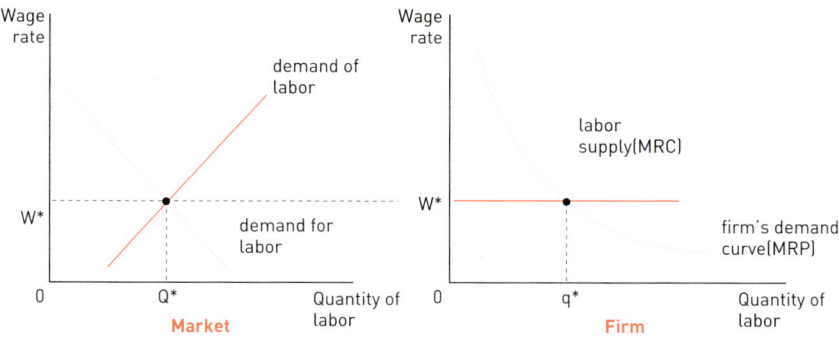

A firm in a perfectly competitive labor market is a wage taker, as a firm in a perfect competition covered in chapter 4 is a price taker. The firm's supply curve is horizontal at wage, W*, determined by the market, which means that the firm can hire as many workers as it wants at the given wage, W*. The firm's demand curve is downward sloping, due to the property of diminishing marginal product of labor. The firm hires workers at q*, because at q* marginal revenue product(MRP) equals marginal resource cost(MRC), maximizing profits. In addition, in a perfectly competitve labor market marginal resource cost equals wage, as the marginal revenue equals price in perfectly competitive product market.

Chapter4에서 다루었던 바와 같이 완전경쟁에서 기업이 가격수용자인 것처럼 완전경쟁 노동시장에서 기업은 임금수용자wage taker이다. 기업의 공급 곡선은 시장에서 결정된 임금인 W*에서 수평인데, 이는 기업이 주어진 임금인 W*에서 원하는 만큼 노동자를 고용할 수 있음을 의미한다. 한계수익이 체감하는 성질 때문에, 기업의 수요곡선은 우하향한다. 기업은 q*에서 노동을 고용한다. q*에서 한계수입생산과 한계요소비용이 같아져서 이윤이 극대화되기 때문이다. 덧붙이자면, 완전경쟁 상품시장에서 한계수입이 가격과 같아졌던 것처럼, 완전경쟁 노동시장에서 한계요소비용은 임금과 같아진다.

## monopsony
수요독점

### A factor market in which one firm is the sole buyer of a resource
한 기업이 요소의 유일한 구매자인 요소시장

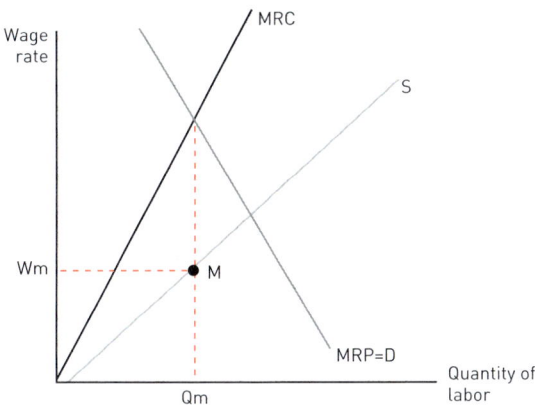

In monopsony, the resource is allocated at point M, where wage is determined at Wm, and the quantity of labor is at Qm. This is because the profit-maximizing quantity of labor employed is determined at MRP = MRC, which is at the point A, and the firm has only to give workers wage Wm because the employees at the employment level of Qm are willing to work at the wage of Wm on the supply curve.

수요독점에서 자원은 M점에서 배분된다. 여기서 임금은 Wm이고 노동고용량은 Qm이다. 이것은 기업의 이윤최대화 노동고용량이 MRP와 MRC가 만나는 A점의 수준에서 결정되기 때문이다. 기업은 노동자에게 Wm의 임금만을 주면 되는데, Qm의 고용수준에서 노동자들은 W의 임금을 받고 일하려고 하기 때문이다.

**Resource allocation in monopsony**
1. Quantity of labor is determined where MRP equals MRC,(Point A)
2. Wage is determined on the supply curve at the quantity of labor where MRP equals MRC

Chapter 5 Factor Market and Income Distribution

## economic rent and transfer
### 경제적 지대와 전용수입

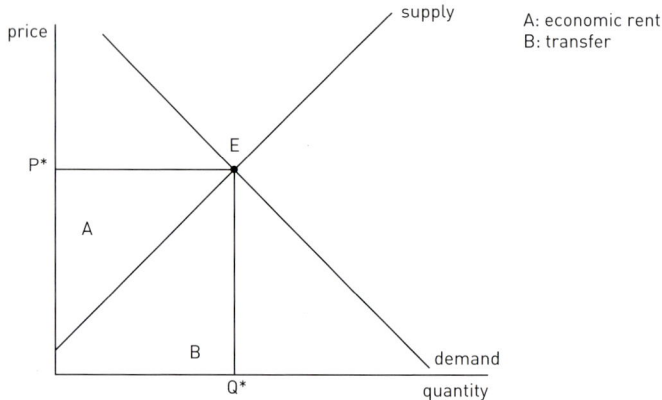

- **Economic rent(A) is the income received by any factor of production above the amount required to induce a given quantity of the factor to be supplied. (the amount of income in excess of the required income.)**
  경제적 지대란 주어진 생산요소를 투입하기 위해 필요한 소득 이상으로 생산요소에게 주어지는 소득을 말한다. (즉, 필요한 소득을 초과하는 소득의 크기를 말한다.)

- **Transfer(B) 전용수입**
  The income required to attract a factor of production from its next-best alternative
  차선의 기회로부터 생산요소를 끌어오기 위해 필요한 수입

> **Tip** 즉, 생산요소에게 주어지는 수입은 경제적 지대와 전용수입으로 나뉘는데, 전용수입을 초과하는 수입이 바로 경제적 지대가 된다.

# Two Special Cases

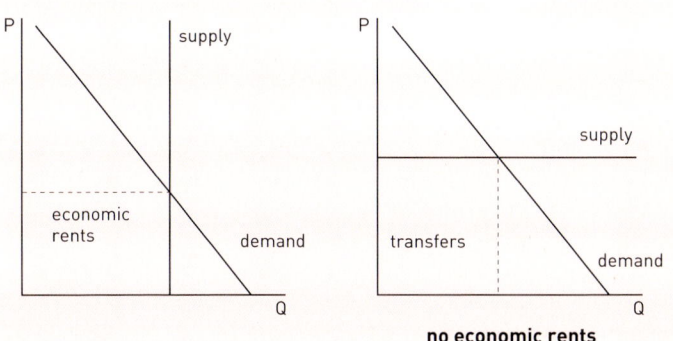

When supply curve is vertical, or perfectly inelastic as in graph A, there is economicrent, but no transfer. On the other hand, when supply curve is horizontal, or perfectly elastic as in graph B there is transfer but no economic rent.

공급곡선이 그래프 A에서 수직, 즉 완전비탄력적이면 전용수입은 하나도 없이 경제적 지대만 존재한다. 반면에 그래프 B에서 공급이 수평이면, 즉 완전탄력적이면 전용수입만 존재하고 경제적 지대는 전혀 존재하지 않는다.

# Lesson 2 | Income Distribution
## 소득분배

## income distribution and inequality
### 소득분배와 불평등

**U.S. Income Distribution in 2006**

| Income group | Income range | Average income | Percent of total income |
|---|---|---|---|
| Bottom quintile | Less than $20,032 | $11,352 | 3.4% |
| Second quintile | $20,032 to $37,771 | 28,777 | 8.6 |
| Third quintile | $37,771 to $60,000 | 48,223 | 14.5 |
| Fourth quintile | $60,000 to $97,030 | 76,329 | 22.9 |
| Top quintile | More than $97,030 | 168,170 | 50.5 |
| Top 5% | More than $174,000 | 297,405 | 22.3 |
| Mean income = 566,570 | | Median income = 548,201 | |

Source: U.S. Census Bureau.

The table above displays the US income distribution in 2006 from the lowest quintile(20%) to the top quintile(20%). The table tells us the top 20% households earn over half of total income.

위의 표는 하위 20%부터 상위 20%까지 2006년 미국의 소득분배를 보여준다. 상위 20% 가구가 전체 소득의 반 이상을 벌어들였다는 것을 알 수 있다.

# Lorenz curve
로렌츠 곡선

**A curve that represents the cumulative distribution of income**
소득의 누적적 분포를 보여주는 곡선

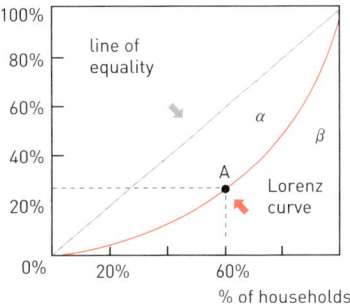

A Lorenz curve illustrates inequality

The percentage of households is cumulatively plotted on the x-axis from the bottom to the top according to the level of income, and the percentage of total income on the y-axis. Point A means that bottom 60% of the households earns over 20% of total income, while top 40% of the households earns almost 80% of total income.

Suppose the area between the Lorenz curve and line of equality is $\alpha$ and, the rightward area of Lorenz curve is $\beta$. The income inequality can be represented by $\frac{\alpha}{\alpha+\beta}$, which is called the Gini coefficient. As the value of the Gini coefficient increases, the income distribution becomes more unequal. As Lorenz curve shifts to the right, Gini coefficient increases, so income inequality gets worse.

가계의 비율은 소득수준에 따라 하위에서 상위까지 X축에 누적적으로 배열되어 있고 소득의 비율은 Y축에 배열되어 있다. 점 A는 하위 60%가 총 소득의 20%를 조금 넘게 벌고 있다는 것을 의미한다. 이는 역으로, 상위 40%가 총 소득의 거의 80%정도를 벌고 있다는 것을 의미한다. 로렌츠 커브와 평등선 사이의 영역을 $\alpha$, 로렌츠 커브의 오른쪽 영역을 $\beta$라고 하면, 소득불평등은 $\frac{\alpha}{\alpha+\beta}$로 나타낼 수 있는데, 이것이 바로 지니계수(Gini coefficient)이다. 지니계수의 값이 커질수록, 소득분배는 더 불평등해진다. 로렌츠 커브가 오른쪽으로 이동하면 지니계수는 증가하고 소득불평등은 더 악화된다.

# Short Answer Question

## Write down a proper word for the definition

**1** the market in which factors of production(land, labor, capital) is bought by firm and sold by household

**2** the increase in total revenue from an additional unit of an input, price multiplied by marginal product

**3** the increase in total cost from an additional unit of an input

**4** a factor market in which one firm is the sole buyer of a resource

**5** the income required to attract a factor of production from its next-best alternative

**6** a curve that represents the cumulative distribution of income

# Define these words

**7** monopsony?

**8** factors of production?

  Answer

1 factor market(market for factors of production, resource market)
2 marginal revenue product(MRP)
3 marginal resource cost(MRC), or marginal factor cost(MFC)
4 monopsony
5 transfer
6 lorenz curve

7 a factor market in which one firm is the sole buyer of a resource
8 land, labor, capital

# Problem Set B: multiple questions

**1.** Which of the following best explain factors of production?

A) Factors of production consist of final and intermediate good
B) Factors of production are some kinds of good and services produced for other use
C) Factors of production are inputs used to produce goods and services such as land, labor, capital
D) Factors of production are things such as wages, interest, rent, and profit

**2.** Which of the following is NOT a factor of production?

A) entrepreneurial efforts
B) money
C) labor
D) natural resources

**3.** The demand for a factor of production is called a derived demand because it is derived from _____.

A) the demand for resources that can be substituted for other uses
B) the demand for good and services the factor of production is used to produce
C) the supply of the factor of production
D) the demand for financial assets

## 4
For a firm in perfect competition, the marginal revenue product is equal to _____.

A) marginal product × marginal cost
B) marginal revenue × quantity sold
C) product price × marginal revenue
D) product price × marginal product

## 5
A firm that aims to maximize profit hires labor _____.

A) until marginal revenue product equals the wage rate
B) up to the point that marginal revenue equals marginal cost
C) until total revenue equals total cost
D) until the difference between marginal revenue product and marginal resource cost is maximized

## 6
Which of the following represents the demand curve for labor?

A) marginal revenue curve
B) marginal cost curve
C) marginal revenue product
D) marginal resource cost

## 7. Which of the following best describes economic rent?

A) the opportunity cost of providing any factor of production
B) income any factor of production earns above its opportunity cost
C) income any factor of production earns below its opportunity cos
D) income that landowner earns by providing the factors of production

## 8. A Lorenz curve?

A) a curve that show only wealth inequality
B) a curve that can be drawn only for the poor
C) a curve that can be drawn only for the rich
D) a curve that cumulative percentage of household is plotted against cumulative percentage of income

## 9-11

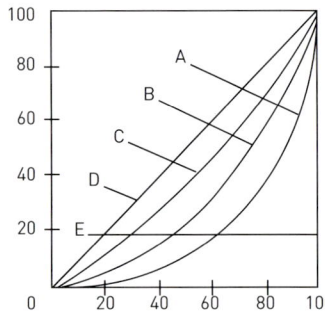

## 9
If each household in a country receives the same amount of income, the Lorenz curve for the country would be _____.

A) curve A
B) curve B
C) curve C
D) curve D

## 10
_____ A country's Lorenz curve would be if only one household earns the entire income in the country.

A) curve A
B) curve B
C) curve D
D) curve E

## 11
Compare the Gini coefficient of the four economies in the graph

A) A 〉 B 〉 C 〉 D 〉 E
B) E 〉 D 〉 C 〉 B 〉 A
C) E 〉 A 〉 B 〉 C 〉 D
D) C 〉 D 〈 E 〉 B 〉 A

1 C  2 B  3 B  4 D  5 A
6 C  7 B  8 D  9 D  10 D  11 C

# Chapter 06

# Market Failure
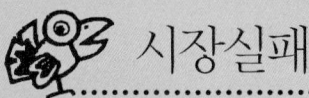
시장실패

Chapter6에서는 시장실패market failure에 대해서 다룹니다. 미시경제학의 많은 분석은 완전경쟁perfect competition을 전제로 하고 이루어지는 경우가 많습니다. 하지만 현실에서는 완전경쟁이 구현되기 힘들며, 시장 실패 현상을 자주 목격할 수가 있습니다. 시장실패는 외부성externalities, 공공재public good, 공유자원common resources, 정보의 비대칭information asymmtry, 불완전경쟁imperfect competition으로 인해 발생합니다. 불완전경쟁은 독과점에서 확인했으니, 여기에서는 외부성, 공공재, 정보비대칭에 대한 개념을 정리하도록 하겠습니다.

# Lesson 1 | Externalities
## 외부성

## market failure
### 시장실패

**The situation in which a market cannot allocate resources efficiently**
시장이 자원을 효율적으로 배분하지 못하는 상황

## externalities
### 외부성(외부효과)

**Costs or benefits caused by producers or consumers to bystanders**
생산자나 소비자에 의해 제삼자에게 발생하는 비용이나 편익

### Market Outcome without Externalities
### 외부성 없는 시장결과

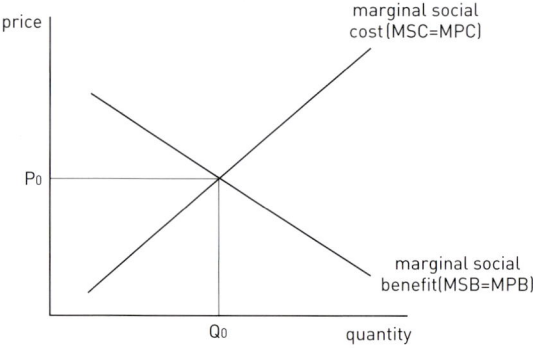

- **Marginal Social Cost** 사회적 한계비용
  Marginal private cost and marginal external cost(spill-over cost)
  사회적 한계비용은 사적 한계비용과 외부 한계비용(파급비용)의 합이다.
- **Marginal Social Benefit** 사회적 한계편익
  Marginal private benefit and marginal external benefit(spill-over benefit)
  사회적 한계편익은 사회적 한계편익과 외부 한계편익(파급편익)의 합이다.

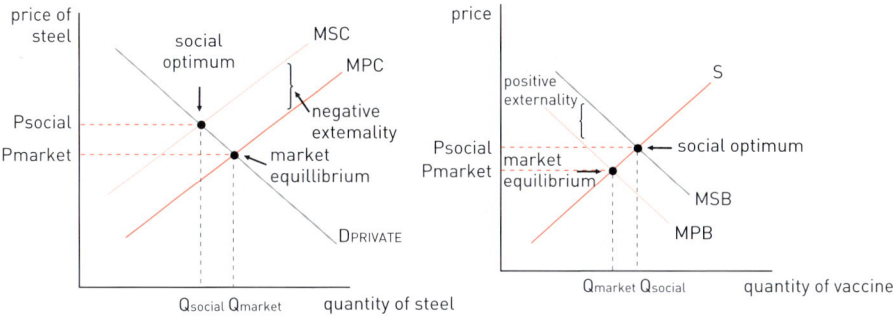

When there is a negative externality, the current market production is larger than social optimal output(overproduced)
외부비경제 발생 시 사회적 최적생산량은 현재 시장생산량보다 작다(과잉생산).

When there is a positive externalites, the current market production is less than social optimal output in positive externalities(underproduced)
외부경제 시 현재 시장생산은 사회적 최적생산보다 적다(과소생산).

## deadweight losses in externalities
### 외부효과의 자중손실

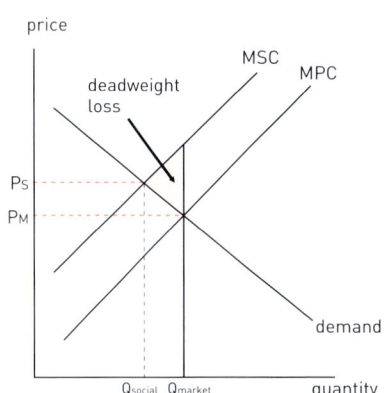

Deadweight loss in negative externalities is the deadweight loss in a negative externality

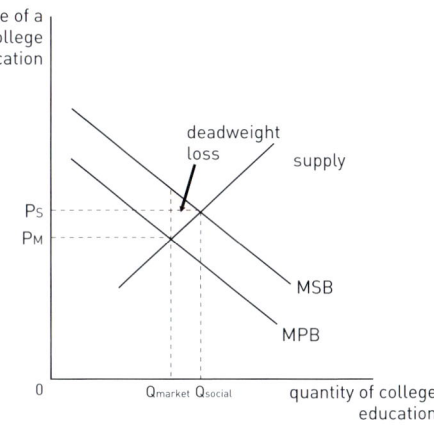

The shaded area is the deadweight loss in a positive externality

Positive externalities and negative externalites alike incur deadweight loss. Social benefits are lost by the difference between social optimal output and current output by externalities. We call the loss deadweigt loss.
긍정적 외부효과와 부정적 외부효과는 모두 자중손실을 발생시킨다. 외부성으로 인해 사회적 최적 생산과 현재 생산의 차이만큼 사회적으로 편익이 감소하게 된다. 그 편익의 감소분을 자중손실이라고 한다.

## internalizing an externality
### 외부효과의 내부화

**Changing incentives so that people consider the external cost or benefit**
사람들이 외부비용과 편익을 고려할 수 있도록 유인을 바꾸는 것

## Coase theorem
### 코즈의 정리

**The argument that private parties can solve the problems of externalities on their own if property rights are well established and there are no free riders, and no transaction costs**
재산권이 잘 확립되고 무임승차자와 거래비용이 없다면, 민간 주체가 스스로 외부성의 문제를 해결할 수 있다는 주장

## Pigovian tax
### 피구세

**A tax enacted to correct the effects of a negative externality**
부정적 외부효과를 교정하기 위한 세금

Tip

| externalities | ways |
|---|---|
| negative externalities (spill-over cost) | private negotiation regulation/ corrective tax pollution permit(pollution license) |
| positive externalities (spill-over benefit) | subsidy |

# Lesson 2
# Common Resources & Public Good
## 공유 자원과 공공재

**four types of good and services according to rivalry and excludability**
경합성과 배재성에 따른 재화와 서비스의 네 가지 유형

|  | exclusive | non-exclusive |
|---|---|---|
| rival | **private good**<br>ex. smart phone, clothing, food | **common resources**<br>ex. clean water and air, natural resources |
| non-rival | **club good(or Artificially scarce good)**<br>ex. satellite television, cinema, tab water | **public good**<br>ex. national defense, free broadcasting |

### 기본 단어 익히기

- **rival good** 경합적인 재화
  A rival good is a good which consumption by one consumer diminishes the possibility of consumption by other consumers
  한 사람의 소비가 다른 사람의 소비가능성을 줄이는 재화

- **excludable good** 배제 가능한 재화
  An excludable good is a good that it is possible to prevent a person from using it.
  사용에서 배제할 수 있는 재화

- **private good** 사적재화
  Rival and excludable good
  경합적이고 배제 가능한 재화

- **club good(or artificially scarce good)** 클럽재화
  Non-rival and excludable good
  비경합적이고 배제 가능한 재화

- **common resources** 공유자원
  Rival and non-excludable good
  경합적이고 비배제적인 재화

Chapter 6 Market Failure

- **tragedy of commons** 공유자원의 비극
  The phenomenon that multiple individuals who behave independently and rationally try to maximize their own self-interest, will ultimately use the common resources excessively.
  독립적이고 합리적으로 행동하는 다수의 개인들이 자기이익을 극대화하기 위해 공유자원을 과도하게 사용하게 되는 현상

- **How we can preserve common resources** 공유자원의 보호 방법
  To establish property rights 재산권의 확립

- **public good** 공공재
  Non-rival and non-excludable good
  비경합적이고 비배제적인 재화

## free-rider
무임 승차자

**A person who consumes a good or service without paying for it**
비용을 내지 않고 상품이나 서비스를 소비하는 사람

## transaction cost
거래비용

**The costs that are involved in the process of bargaining**
거래의 과정에 수반되는 비용

# Lesson 3 | Information Asymmetry
## 정보비대칭

### information asymmetry[3]
정보의 비대칭

**A situation in transaction in which one party has more or better information than the other**
한 쪽이 다른 쪽보다 정보를 더 많이, 또는 더 좋은 정보를 가지고 있는 상황

### adverse selection
역선택

**An exchange process in which bad goods are more likely to be chosen when buyers and sellers have different information**
구매자와 판매자가 다른 정보를 가지고 있을 때 안 좋은 상품이 선택될 가능성이 높은 거래 과정

### lemon market
레몬시장(개살구시장)

**The market in which defective goods are exchanged without buyers' knowledge**
흠있는 물건이 구매자가 알지 못한 채 거래되는 시장

### screening
선별행위

**An action taken by one to reveal the other's hidden information**
한 사람이 다른 사람의 숨겨진 정보를 알기 위해 하는 행동

## signaling
### 신호발송

**An action taken by one to inform his or her private information to the other**
한 사람이 자신의 개별 정보를 다른 사람에게 알려주기 위해 하는 행동


## principal-agent problem
### 주인-대리인문제

**The problem that arises when managers(agents) pursue their own profits, even if that entails lower profits for the owners of the firm(the principals)**
경영자(대리인)가 기업의 소유자(주인)에게 낮은 이익을 가져올 수도 있지만 자기 자신의 이익을 추구할 때 발생하는 문제


## moral hazard
### 도덕적 해이

**The danger, or the tendency that of party of a contract to change his conduct for profits**
계약의 당사자가 이익을 얻으려고 자신의 행동을 바꿀 위험, 혹은 그런 경향

## Problem Set A — Short Answer Question

Write down a proper word for the definition

**1** the situation in transaction in which one party has more or better information than the other

**2** costs or benefits caused by producers or consumers to bystanders

**3** a good whose consumption by one consumer diminishes the possibility of consumption by other consumers

**4** the danger, or the tendency of one party of a contract to change his conduct for profits

**5** a exchange process in which bad goods are more likely to be chosen when buyers and sellers have different information

**6** a good that is possible to prevent a person from using it

**7** the phenomenon that multiple individuals who behave independently and rationally try to maximize their own self-interest, will ultimately use the common resources excessively

**8** rival and non-excludable good

**9** the market in which defective goods are exchanged without buyers' knowledge

**10** an action taken by one to reveal the other's hidden information

**11** an action taken by one to inform his or her private information to the other

**12** the argument that private parties can solve the problems of externalities on their own if property rights are well established and there are no free riders, and no transaction costs

**13** the costs that are involved in the process of bargaining

# Define these words

**14** free-rider problem?

**15** public good?

**16** market Failures?

### Answer

**1** information asymmetry  **2** externalities  **3** rival good  **4** moral hazard  **5** adverse selection
**6** excludable good  **7** tragedy of commons  **8** common resources  **9** lemon market
**10** screening  **11** signaling  **12** Coase theorem  **13** transaction cost

**14** free rider is a person who consumes a good or service without paying for it
**15** non-rival and non-excludable good
**16** the situation that market cannot allocate resources efficiently

## Problem Set B: multiple questions

**1.** A firm discharged chemicals into a river, polluting the river. Choose the right one.

A) The cost of the water pollution is zero for the society, but positive for the pollution-emitting firm
B) The cost of the water pollution is marginal private cost of producing a good
C) The social cost of producing the good increases by the pollution cost
D) The social cost of producing the good remains constant

**2.** A club good(artificially scarce good) is defined as a good or service _____.

A) that is non-rival and excludable
B) that is rival and excludable
C) that is rival and non-excludable
D) that is non-rival and non-excludable

**3.** Problems of externalities will be solved without government intervention if property rights are well established and there are no transaction costs, according to _____.

A) Smith theorem
B) Chaos theorem
C) Coase theorem
D) Ronald theorem

## 4

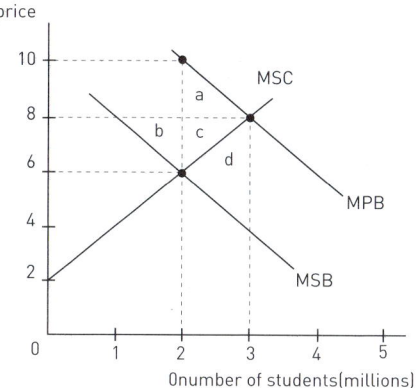

The graph above show the markets for college education. Choose the right combination.

| | deadweight loss | current numbers of student | optimal numbers of student |
|---|---|---|---|
| A) | d | 2 millions | 3 millions |
| B) | a + c | 3 millions | 2 millions |
| C) | b + c | 2 millions | 3 millions |
| D) | a + c | 2 millions | 3 millions |

## 5

Choose the right one.

A) marginal social cost = marginal private cost - marginal external cost

B) marginal social benefit = marginal private benefit + marginal external cost

C) marginal social cost = marginal external benefit + marginal external cost

D) marginal external cost = marginal social benefit - marginal external benefit

Chapter 6 Market Failure 155

## 6. A common resource is defined as a good or service _____.

A) that is non-rival and excludable
B) that is rival and excludable
C) that is rival and non-excludable
D) that is non-rival and non-excludable

## 7. A private good is defined as a good or service_____.

A) that is non-rival and excludable
B) that is rival and excludable
C) that is rival and non-excludable
D) that is non-rival and non-excludable

## 8. A public good is defined as a good or service_____.

A) that is non-rival and excludable
B) that is rival and excludable
C) that is rival and non-excludable
D) that is non-rival and non-excludable

**Answer**

1 C  2 A  3 C  4 D
5 B  6 C  7 B  8 D

# Part 1 Practice Exam Microeconomics
Time : 50 minutes

**1.** Which of the following is the firm's short-run supply curve?

A) the marginal cost itself
B) the average variable cost below average total cost
C) the average fixed cost below average total cost
D) the marginal cost above average total cost
E) the marginal cost above average variable cost

**2.** Which of the following is most likely to increase the demand for college education, which is normal good?

A) a decrease in average income of household
B) a decrease in financial aid provided by the university authority
C) a decrease in college tuition fee
D) an increase in job opportunity to college graduates
E) an increase in unemployment among college graduates

**3.** The equilibrium price of natural gas in the market is $3.00 per liter. When the government imposes a price ceiling of $ 2.00 per liter, which of the following will happen in the natural gas market?

A) Quantity supplied of natural gas will increase
B) The demand for natural gas will increase
C) The supply for the natural gas will decrease
D) Quantity demanded of natural gas will increase
E) No change will occur in the market for natural gas

What will occur to the market price and quantity when firms in a monopolistic competition lose its product differentiation and start to produce the identical goods?

|   | Price | Quantity |
|---|-------|----------|
| A) | Decrease | No change |
| B) | Increase | Decrease |
| C) | Decrease | Increase |
| D) | No change | Decrease |
| E) | No change | Increase |

The employer in an electronic company considers whether the firm hires one more worker. If the change in total revenue by hiring one more worker is less than the change in total cost, which of the following is correct?

A) The firm should hire one more worker.
B) Marginal revenue is greater than marginal cost.
C) The firm should fire one more worker.
D) To maximize profits, the firm shut down the factory.
E) Marginal revenue product is less than marginal resource cost.

Apple, a US electronic manufacture company, raises the price of i-phone by 10 percent, and total revenue earned by i-phone increases 10%. Which of the following is correct?

A) Demand for I-phone is perfectly elastic
B) Demand for I-phone is elastic
C) Demand for I-phone is unit-elastic
D) Demand for I-phone is inelastic
E) Demand for I-phone is perfectly inelastic

**7** When an individual consumes a good, others benefit from the consumption. Which of the following is true?

A) The market is allocatively and productively efficient.
B) The benefit can be called spill-over cost in other words, because it impedes market efficiency.
C) To increase the production, the government should impose tax on the company that produce the good.
D) In perfect competition, the industry will produce the social optimum.
E) Socially optimal output is greater than the current output.

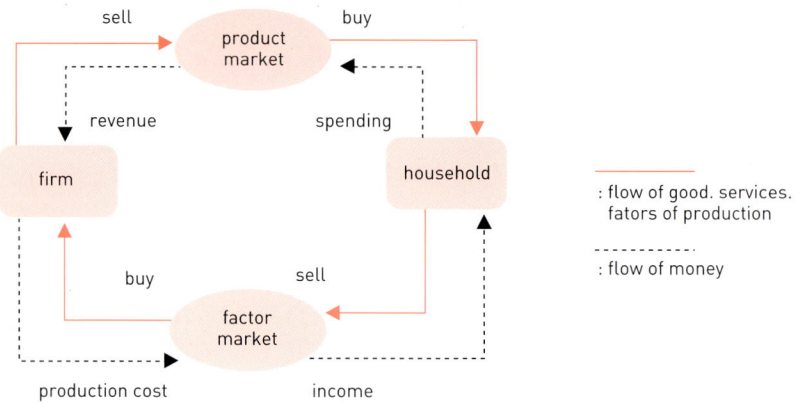

**8** The graph above is circular flow diagram, which shows the circulation among participants through markets in the economy. Which of the following is not true?

A) In the product market, firms supply and households consume.
B) In the factor market, the factors of production, such as land, labor, and capital are traded with each other.
C) The firms receive revenue in the product market, and the households receive income in the factor market.
D) The firms buy land, labor capital in the factor market, and sell good and services in the product market.
E) The household spending should equal the firm's production costs for market equilibrium.

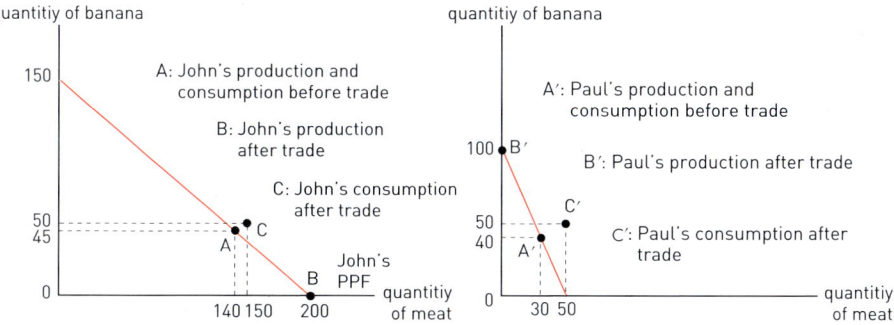

question 9 and 10 refers to the graph above.

**9** Which of the following is true according to the side-by-side production possibilities curve above?

A) John has comparative advantage in the production of both goods.
B) Paul has comparative advantage in the production of bananas.
C) John has no incentives to trade with Paul.
D) John should specialize in coconuts and Paul in fish.
E) Paul will become worse off after trade.

**10** After the specialization according to comparative advantage theory, John could consume 150 meat and 50 bananas, and Paul could consume 50 meat and 50 bananas. Identify the terms of trade in this exchange.

A) 1 meat = 0.5 bananas
B) 1 meat = 1 bananas
C) 1 meat = 1.5 bananas
D) 1 meat = 2 bananas
E) 1 meat = 2.5 bananas

**11** Which of the following is NOT true when it comes to the determinants of price elasticity of demand?

A) the more substitutes the more elastic
B) luxuries are more elastic
C) the smaller proportion of expenditure on the good, the more elastic
D) the more broadly defined the market is, the less elastic
E) the longer the time horizon, the more elastic

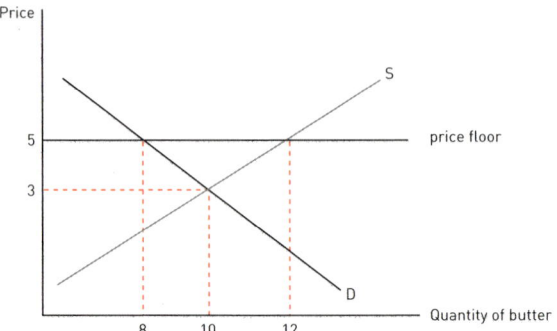

## 12

Suppose that government suppose price floor on the market for butter. Choose the right combinations of quantity sold(millions of pounds) before and after price floor.

|    | Before | After |
|----|--------|-------|
| A) | 9      | 12    |
| B) | 10     | 12    |
| C) | 12     | 10    |
| D) | 10     | 9     |
| E) | 12     | 9     |

## 13

Which of the following is not correct?

A) The magnitude of deadweight loss is 150,000.
B) After price floor the consumers become worse off, and the suppliers become better off.
C) The price floor leads to surplus, excess supply, which will lower the price of the good.
D) This kind of price floor is often found in the agriculture sector.
E) The magnitude of excess supply is 3 millions of pounds.

question 14 refers to the graph below.

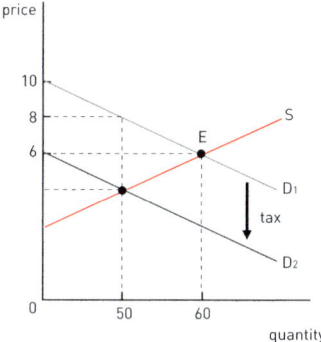

**14** In the market for books point E is a initial equilibrium point. with equilibrium price at $8, equilibrium quantity at 60. Suppose that the government imposes tax on consumers in the market for a good. Which of the following is NOT true about the graph above?

A) The magnitude of tax imposed on the good is $4.
B) The magnitude of deadweight loss is 20.
C) When tax is imposed on the consumers, the demand curve of the good shifts down.
D) When tax is levied on the market, the market shrinks.
E) The government tax revenue is 100.

question 15, 16 refers to the graph below.

| Pizza($2) | | Hamburger($1) | |
|---|---|---|---|
| Quantity | Total utility | Quantity | Total utility |
| 0 | 0 | 0 | 0 |
| 1 | 30 | 1 | 20 |
| 2 | 55 | 2 | 30 |
| 3 | 75 | 3 | 35 |
| 4 | 90 | 4 | 38 |
| 5 | 100 | 5 | 40 |

## 15

Paul want to maximize his total utility by consuming pizza and hamburger. His income is $8. Which of the following is the best combination of utility maximizing consumption?

|    | Pizza | Hamburger | Total Utility |
|----|-------|-----------|---------------|
| A) | 1     | 2         | 60            |
| B) | 2     | 2         | 85            |
| C) | 3     | 1         | 95            |
| D) | 3     | 2         | 105           |
| E) | 3     | 3         | 110           |

## 16

Price of hamburger rises to $2, and his income has increased to $14. Which of the following is the best combination of utility maximizing consumption?

|    | Pizza | Hamburger | Total Utility |
|----|-------|-----------|---------------|
| A) | 3     | 4         | 113           |
| B) | 4     | 2         | 120           |
| C) | 4     | 3         | 125           |
| D) | 5     | 2         | 130           |
| E) | 5     | 3         | 135           |

question 17 refers to the graph below.

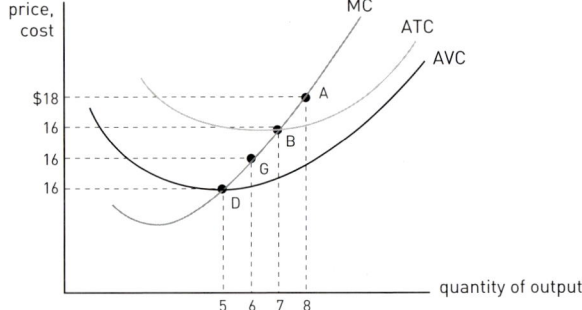

164  Part 1 Microeconomics 미시경제학

## 17

The graph above shows cost curves of a firm operation in the market for peanuts. Which of the following is NOT true?

A) If the price lowers below $10, the firm should shut down.
B) If the price is $14, the firm is making normal profits.
C) If the price is $18, the firm must be making economic profits.
D) If the firm is operating at point B, the firm is making a loss, but should keep producing in the long run.
E) The marginal cost curve above the average variable cost curve is the firm's short-run supply curve.

## 18

When the price of a good changes, income effect and substitution effect occur simultaneously. Which of the following is NOT true about income and substitution effect?

A) When price falls, income effect is positive in case of normal good because the real income increases.
B) When price falls, substitution effect is positive regardless of types of good.
C) When price rises, income effect is positive in case of inferior good.
D) When price rises, substitution effect dominates income effect in case of giffen good.
E) Income effect and substitution effect have opposite directions in case of giffen good.

question 19 and 20 refers to the graph below.

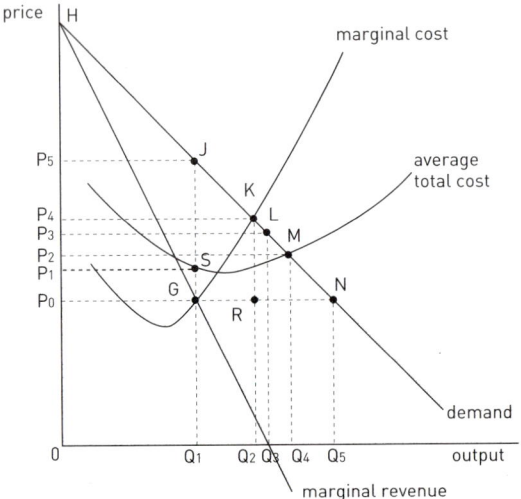

## 19
The graph above shows the monopoly market. Which of the following are the correct points on the demand curve?

|   | Profit maximizing point | Revenue maximizing point | Allocative Efficiency point |
|---|---|---|---|
| A) | J | K | L |
| B) | J | L | K |
| C) | K | K | M |
| D) | J | M | K |
| E) | J | M | L |

## 20
If the monopoly firm is operating without any government intervention, which of the following is most likely to be the economic profit area of monopoly firm?

A) P5JGP0
B) P5JSP1
C) P4KRP0
D) P3KRP0
E) P5JSP0

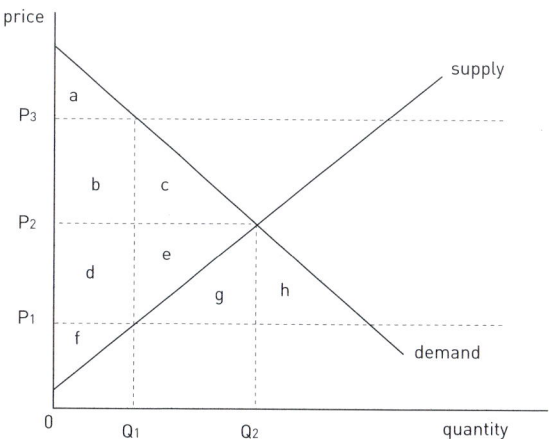

**21** Suppose that the government impose price floor at P3, Choose the correct combinations on consumer surplus, producer surplus, and efficiency loss(deadweight loss) after price floor.

|   | consumer surplus | producer surplus | efficiency loss |
|---|---|---|---|
| A) | a + b + c | d + e + f | g + h |
| B) | a + c | b + d + f | g + h |
| C) | a | b + d + f | c + e |
| D) | a + b + c | d + e + f | g + h |
| E) | a + b + d | f | c + e |

**22** Under which of the following conditions of price elasticity of supply will a factor of production NOT earn transfer, which means the income required to attract a factor of production from its next-best alternative?

A) perfectly inelastic
B) inelastic
C) unit elastic
D) elastic
E) perfectly elastic

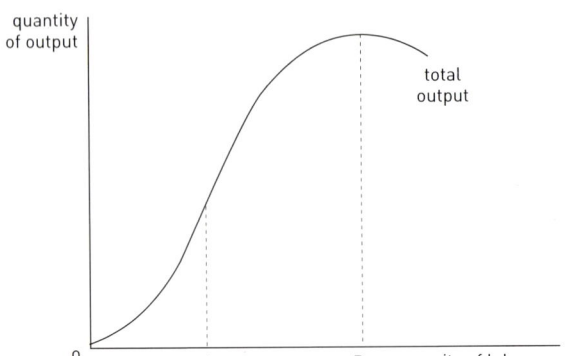

## 23

**According to the law of diminishing returns(diminishing marginal product), which of the following is NOT true?**

A) The law of diminishing returns states that the additional change in total product from hiring one more worker decreases.
B) When marginal product is decreasing, total product is increasing as long as the marginal product is positive.
C) When the firm hires more workers between A and B, the average product increases and then decreases.
D) When total product is decreasing, marginal product is still positive.
E) When total product is decreasing, average product is still positive.

## 24

**A farmer grows two plants, wheat and corn in his land. If the price of corn rises, which of the following is NOT likely to happen in the markets of wheat and corn?**

A) The quantity demanded of wheat will decrease.
B) The quantity supplied of corn will increase.
C) The supply of wheat will increase.
D) The supply of corn will not change.
E) The price of wheat will rise.

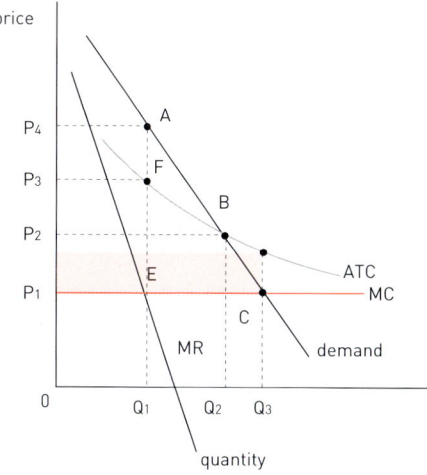

 The graph above shows natural monopoly. D is demand curve, MR is marginal revenue curve, ATC is average total cost curve, MC is marginal cost curve. . Point A, B, and C and area E is displayed on the graph. Which of the following is NOT true?

A) Without any government intervention the monopolist will produce Q1 at P4.
B) Without government intervention the monopolist will enjoy economic profits by the amount of P4AFP3.
C) By raising its price to sell more products at point A, the monopolist can increase total revenue because marginal revenue is still positive.
D) Total Revenue is maximized at the production between Q1 and Q2.
E) The monopolist is enjoying economies of scale.

## 26

The government plans to regulate monopoly to cure market failures incurred by monopoly and enhance market efficiency. Which of the following is NOT true?

A) The government will set price ceiling at P1 if the government is to achieve social optimum.
B) At P1, the monopolist will make a economic loss by the amount of area E.
C) The government will set price ceiling at P2 if the government is to guarantee fair returns to the monopolist.
D) The government should levy tax the monopolist to achieve social equity and allocatively efficient output.
E) If the monopolist emit pollution, the marginal cost in the social perspective, marginal social cost will shift up and social optimal output will decrease.

## 27

A firm in perfect competition is producing computers. The average variable cost of producing 9 unit of a good is $ 7, and average fixed cost of 9 units is $10. The total cost of producing 10 units is $163. Which of the following is the marginal cost of 10th unit?

A) $5
B) $10
C) $15
D) $20
E) $25

## 28

Which of the following is the best example of the good or services that incur tragedy of commons?

A) national defense
B) police service
C) light houses
D) clean air and water
E) pollution emitting

**29** Paul started sell computers in the market, instead of working at the manufacture firm receiving annual salary of $50,000. After one year, his total revenue is $100,000. He used small building he owns as a trading place. He could rent the building for $15,000 per year. He hired one clerk at the salary of $15,000 per year. The cost of materials and other expenses is $40,000, Which of the following is his economic profit?

A) -$20,000
B) -$5,000
C) $0
D) $10,000
E) $45,000

**30** A clerk in convenience store knows that if the store charge $5 a hamburger, 200 people buy hamburgers. and if store charge $8 a hamburger, 100 people buy hamburgers. Which of the following can be inferred from this knowledge?

A) The convenience store is the price taker of the market for hamburger.
B) The convenience store is the price maker of the market for hamburger.
C) The price elasticity of demand of hamburger is elastic.
D) The income elasticity of demand of hamburger is inelastic.
E) There is no substitutes for hamburgers.

**31** The table below shows the numbers of time consumed by John and Paul when washing dishes and cleaning the house. Which of the following is true according to the table?

|  | cleaning the house | washing the dishes |
|---|---|---|
| John | 30 minutes | 30 minutes |
| Mary | 50 minutes | 45 minutes |

**question 32** refers to the graph below.

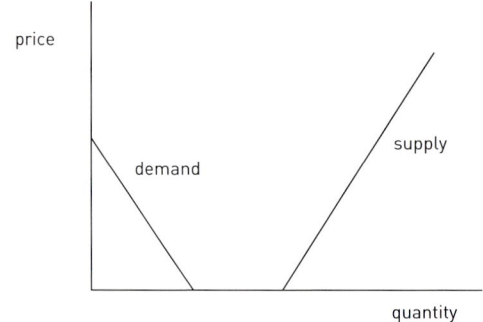

 The graph above shows a special case of supply-demand relationship in the market for a good. Which of the following is NOT true?

A) At price of $0, there is a surplus of the good.
B) The good must be a free good.
C) Because the quantity supplied is greater than quantity demanded at every price level, there is no scarcity of the good.
D) The good is not currently traded in the market
E) If demand decreases or supply increases, the good will be traded in the market.

**question 33 refers to the graph below.**

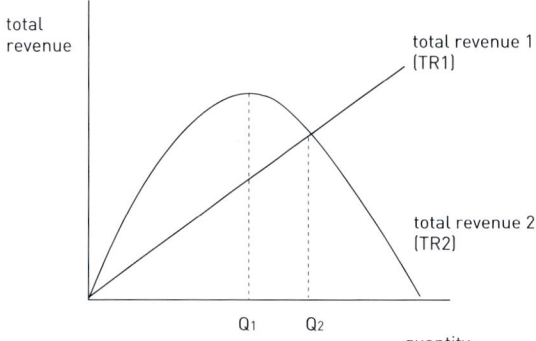

 There are two total revenue curves of each firm. TR1 is the total revenue curve of firm 1, and TR2 is the total revenue curve of firm 2. Which of the following is true concerning the graph above?

A) The firm of TR1 is a price maker in monopoly, the case of firm pursuing the maximization of total revenue.
B) The firm of TR2 is a price taker in perfect competition, with the maximum total revenue capped.
C) At Q1, the marginal cost and marginal revenue of firm 2 must be equalized.
D) At Q2, the average revenue of firm 1 is greater than that of firm 2.
E) At Q1, the marginal revenue of firm 1 is price, and the marginal revenue of firm 2 is zero.

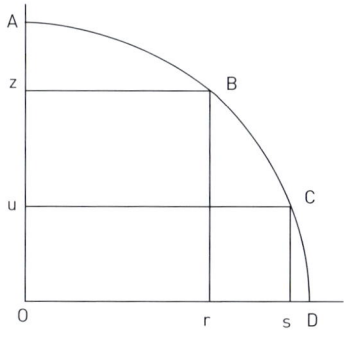

**34** The graph above shows production possibilities curve of an economy producing two goods. Which of the following is the opportunity cost of moving from point C to point B?

A) sr quantity of good X
B) or quantity of good X
C) ou quantity of good Y
D) zu quantity of good Y
E) oz quantity of good Y

**35** Which of the following situations best illustrates the law of supply?

A) As more producers enter the market for the smart phones, the supply of smart phones increases.
B) The new introduction of tariff on wheat has led to increase in domestic price of corn.
C) The price increase of tomato raises total revenue for producers.
D) The increase in the price of corn has led to an increase in the production of corn.
E) If suppliers expect price of a good to rise in the near future, the quantity supplied will decrease.

**36** Which of the following is NOT true about market structures?

A) In perfect competition, all firms are price takers.
B) If one industry consists of one firm, the market must be monopoly.
C) In monopolistic competition, brand names play important roles in sales.
D) In oligopoly, under mutual interdependence, many firms act strategically.
E) If the barriers to entry would be lifted in monopoly, the market could be more competitive.

question 37-38 refers to the graph below.

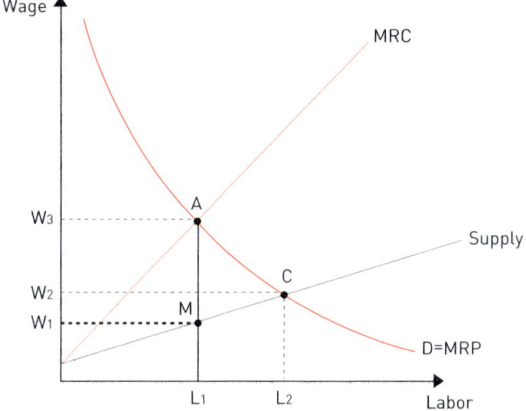

The graph shows the market for factors of production, labor market. S is the supply curve of labor. MRP is marginal revenue product curve, MRC is marginal resource cost curve, or marginal factor cost curve.

## 37  Which of the following is NOT true?

A) MRP is the demand curve for the firm operating in this market.
B) The supply curve represents the trade-off between leisure and income.
C) If the price of the good rises, MRP will shift to the right.
D) If there is a technological advance, the supply curve will shift to the right.
E) In factor market households are suppliers and firms are sellers.

# 38

**Which of the following is NOT true about the equilibrium of the graph?**

A) In perfect competition labor market, the equilibrium will be the point C.
B) The firm will maximize profits at the output that marginal revenue product equals marginal resource cost.
C) In the market equilibrium wage will be W1 and quantity of labor will be L1
D) If the market becomes more competitive, wage will rise and quantity of labor will fall.
E) The segment AM shows the difference between the marginal contribution of an additional worker to firm's total revenue and the amount of wage she receives.

**question 39 and 40 refers to the table below.**

|  | Paul deny | Paul confess |
|---|---|---|
| John deny | Paul gets 5-year sentence. / John gets 5-year sentence. | Paul gets 2-year sentencel. / John gets 20-year sentence. |
| John confess | Paul gets 20-year sentence. / John gets 2-year sentence. | Paul gets 10-year sentence. / John gets 10-year sentence. |

The two players, John and Paul are in the strategic situation. They have two strategy, 'confess' or 'deny', and they receive pay-offs according to their choice. The game is played just one time. The two players cannot communicate each other.

# 39

**Which of the following is true?**

A) This kind of situation is different form the strategic situation in oligopoly.
B) Paul has dominant strategy but John has not.
C) Paul's dominant strategy is 'deny'.
D) They will be sentenced to 10 years in prison.
E) John has no incentive to change his strategy in any situations.

## 40 Which of the following is NOT true?

A) There is dominant strategy equilibrium for the two players.
B) The dominant strategy is 'confess' for both players.
C) The equilibrium is also Nash equilibrium, the situation that no single player can be better off by unilaterally changing her strategy
D) If the game is repeated and there are some incentives to cooperate, the result will be different.
E) It would be better for two players not to cooperate, if possible.

# Answer Practice Microeconomics

**1 | E**  The marginal cost above the average variable cost is the firm's short-run supply curve and the marginal cost above the average total cost is the firm's long-run marginal cost

**2 | D**  Normal good is the good for which the demand increases when income increases. When income increases, the demand for college education will increases. There are many non-price determinants that shift the demand or supply curve. In this question, (D) is the correct answer because the more job opportunities for college graduates is an incentive to enter college.

**3 | D**  Change in quantity demanded and change in demand, or change in quantity supplied and change in supply is different. Change in quantity demand and quantity supplied is caused by the change in price. On the other hand, change in demand and supply results from the change in non-price determinants. Price control by government alters the market price, which changes the quantity demanded and quantity supplied. In case of price ceiling, the quantity demanded increases and the quantity supplied decreases.

**4 | C**  When firms in imperfect competition become more competitive, the price will decrease and quantity increase.

**5 | E**  If the change in total revenue by hiring one more worker is less than the change in total cost, the marginal revenue product of the good is less than marginal resource cost or marginal factor cost. The firm should not hire one more worker.

**6 | E**  When Apple raises the price of I-phone by 10 percent and total revenue earned by iphone increases 10%, it means that there is no change in quantity sold. If there was no change in quantity demanded to a change in price, the price elasticity of demand is zero, perfectly inelastic.

**7 | E**  The situation in the question is positive externalities. The market is not efficient and does not produce socially optimal output. The current output in the industry is less than social optimum. To increase production, the government should give subsidy to producers or consumers.

**8 | E**  The household spending has no direct relationship to the production cost in the   diagram.

**9 | B**  John has absolute advantage in the production of both goods, because he can produce more good with the same amount of resources. In the production of fish, John has comparative advantage, because John's opportunity cost of producing one unit of fish, 3/4 coconut is less than Paul's, 2 coconuts. In the production of coconuts, Paul has comparative advantage, because, Paul's opportunity cost, 1/2 fish, is less than John's, 4/3 fish. Therefore John specializes in fish, and Paul specializes in coconut.

**10 | B**  Terms of trade depends on the domestic rate of exchange before trade. Before trade, 1 fish can be traded for 3/4 coconut for John. For Paul, 1 fish can be traded for 2 coconuts. The terms of trade is determined between the two domestic rates of exchange. In the case of the question, according to comparative advantage theory, John specialize in the production of fish, producing 40 fish, Paul in the production of coconut, producing 20 coconuts. On the PPC above, the consumption after trade is that John consumes 30 fish, 10 coconuts, and Paul consumes 10 fish, 10 coconuts. John and Paul trade 10 fish with 10 coconut. The terms of trade is 1 fish: 1 coconut

**11 | C**  The smaller the proportion of expenditure on a good, the less elastic, because the small proportion of expenditure on the good is not likely to be influenced by price change.

**12 | D**  At the initial equilibrium point, price is $1, quantity is 10 million. After imposing price floor, the good is allocated at the point where, price at $1.2, quantity at 9 million.

**13 | C**  In case of price floor, the price will not lowered by downward pressure on price, because the government supports the price.

**14 | E**  The government tax revenue is 2000, 50(quantity sold) × 4(tax size).

## 15-16

**D | D**  Refer to the table below. Find the each combination that equalize marginal utility per dollar given price and budget constraint.

| Pizza($2) | | | | Hamburger | | | | |
|---|---|---|---|---|---|---|---|---|
| Quantity | Total utility | Marginal Utility | $\frac{MU_x}{P_x}$ | Quantity | Total utility | Marginal Utility | $\frac{MU_y}{P_y}$ price=$1 | $\frac{MU_y}{P_y}$ price=$2 |
| 0 | 0 | | | 0 | 0 | | | |
| 1 | 30 | 30 | 15 | 1 | 20 | 20 | 20 | 10 |
| 2 | 55 | 25 | 12.5 | 2 | 30 | 10 | 10 | 5 |
| 3 | 75 | 20 | 10 | 3 | 35 | 5 | 5 | 2.5 |
| 4 | 90 | 15 | 2.5 | 4 | 38 | 3 | 3 | 1.5 |
| 5 | 100 | 10 | 5 | 5 | 40 | 2 | 2 | 1 |

**17 | D**  If the firm is operating at point B in the long run, the firm is making a loss and should exit the market.

**18 | D**  When price changes, quantity demanded changes. The change in quantity demanded can be explained by income effect and substitution effect. If price falls, quantity demanded rises. This rise in quantity demanded is composed of income effect and substitution effect. Income effect occurs due to change in purchasing power, and substitution effect occurs because of change in relative price. If price falls, income effect of normal good is positive. If price rises, income effect of inferior good is negative. Substitution effect has always the opposite direction with the change in price irregardless of the types of goods. If price falls, substitution effect is positive, and if price rises, substitution effect is negative. Giffen good is a special case. In case of giffen good the income effect as a inferior good dominates the substitution effect. When price rises, the positive
income effect of giffen good is greater than negative substitution effect. So, the quantity demanded increases when price rises. This phenomenon violates of the law of demand. This kind of good that quantity demanded increases when price rises is called giffen good.

**19 | E**  Profit is maximized at MR = MC, revenue is maximized at MR=0, and allocative efficiency is achieved at P = MC.

**20 | B**  Economic profit is the area of total revenue minus total cost. The monopolist is producing at the profit-maximizing output at which marginal revenue equals marginal cost. In the graph, Total revenue is P5JQ10 and total cost is P1SQ10. The difference between total revenue and total cost is economic profit, P5JSP1

**21 | C**  The consumer surplus is the area below demand curve and above price. The producer surplus is the area below price and above supply curve. Deadweight loss is the forgone area due to price floor that used to be a part of total surplus. The allocation point after price floor is P3, Q1.

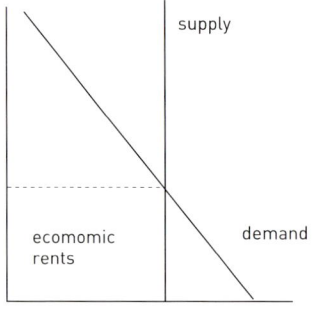

If supply of the good is vertical, or the price elasticity of supply is perfectly

**22** | **A**    inelastic, there is no transfer.

**23** | **D**    When total product is decreasing, marginal product is negative.

**24** | **C**    The supply of wheat will decrease, because the farmer will grow more corn.

**25** | **C**    At point A the monopolist should lower its price to sell one more unit of output, increasing total revenue.

**26** | **D**    If government imposes tax on the monopolist, the price will rise and output will decrease due to rise in marginal cost, which will deteriorate current market allocation.

**27** | **B**    Total cost of producing 9 units is $153(Total cost($153) = Total fixed cost($90) + Total variable cost($63)). Total cost of producing 10 units is $163. So the marginal cost of producing 10th unit is $10

**28** | **D**    Tragedy of commons refers to the phenomenon that multiple individuals who behave independently and rationally try to maximize their own self-interest, will ultimately use the common resources excessively. Tragedy of commons have to do with common resources. Good examples of common resources are clean water and air, natural resources.

**29** | **A**    Economic profit is the difference between total revenue and total cost. In the question total revenue is $100,000, Total cost is composed of explicit cost and implicit cost. His explicit cost is the cost of materials and other expenses, $40,000, and the salary given to the clerk, $15,000. His implicit cost is his forgone salary, 50,000, and the forgone rent, $15,000. His total opportunity cost is $120,000. His economic profit is -$20,000($100,000 - $120,000= -$20,000)

**30** | **C**    When price rises, total revenue falls. The price elasticity of demand for hamburger is elastic.

**31** | **C**    John has absolute advantage in both works and has comparative advantage in cleaning the house due to the lower opportunity cost in cleaning the house.

**32** | **E**    If demand increases or supply decreases, the good will be traded in the market.

**33** | **E**    TR1 is the total revenue of firm 1 in perfect competition, and TR2 is the total revenue of firm 2 in monopoly(with maket power). At Q1, marginal revenue is zero and marginal cost is not zero for firm 2. At Q2, the average revenue is the same.

**34| A** The opportunity cost of a choice is foregone benefits, income, production and etc. that one could enjoy if one would choose different way. In this case, the foregone benefit or production the producer could enjoy is sr units of good X.

**35| D** The law of supply represents the positive relationship between price and quantity supplied. It states that when price rises, all other things being constant, quantity supplied increases.

**36| D** In oligopoly, few firms act strategically under mutual interdependence.

**37| D** If there is a technological advance, the demand curve will shift to the right, because the MRP, MP×P, which is the demand curve for the firm, will increase due to the technological advance.

**38| D** If the market becomes more competitive, wage will rise and quantity of labor will also increase.

## 39-40|

This game matrix shows typical prisoners' dilemma. Let's think about the solution of this game in terms of strategic situation. For John, if Paul chooses not to confess, confess is a better choice for John and if Paul chooses to confess, confess is a better choice for John, too. Regardless of Paul's choice, confessing is a better choice for John. This kind of choice is called dominant strategy. The same logic is with Paul. So both choose to confess and both get a 15-year sentence. This is worse result than both players' not to confess strategy.

**39| D** The dominant strategy for both players is 'confess', which would lead to 15-year sentence for both.

**40| E** It would be better for two players to cooperate, because they will be sentenced to be in prison for fewer years.

# Part 02

## Macroeconomics
# 거시경제학

"how the economy as a whole works?"

거시경제학 macroeconomics은 국가경제 전체가 어떻게 움직이는가를 연구하는 학문입니다. 국가의 경제활동을 보여주는 가장 중요한 지표는 물가 price level와 국내총생산 GDP Gross Domestic Product입니다. 물가는 인플레이션과 직결되어 있고, 국내총생산은 실업문제와 밀접하지요. 한 국가의 물가와 국내총생산은 총수요-총공급 AD-AS model으로 설명됩니다. 정부는 재정정책 fiscal policy과 통화정책 monetary policy이라는 두 가지 방법을 사용하여 경제안정화정책을 실시합니다. 거시경제운용의 장기적인 목표는 경제성장 economic growth 입니다. 국내경제는 무역시장 trade market과 환율시장 foreign exchange market을 통해 해외경제와 연결되어 영향을 주고받습니다.

## Chapter 01
**Measuring Economic Performance**
경제 성과 측정하기

## Chapter 02
**Income-Expenditure and AD-AS Model**
총지출과 AD-AS 모델

## Chapter 03
**Money, Banking and Financial Market**
화폐, 은행 그리고 금융시장

## Chapter 04
**Economic Stabilization Policy and Economic Growth**
경제안정화정책과 경제성장

## Chapter 05
**Open Economy**
개방경제

# Microeconomics Map for AP Macroeconomics

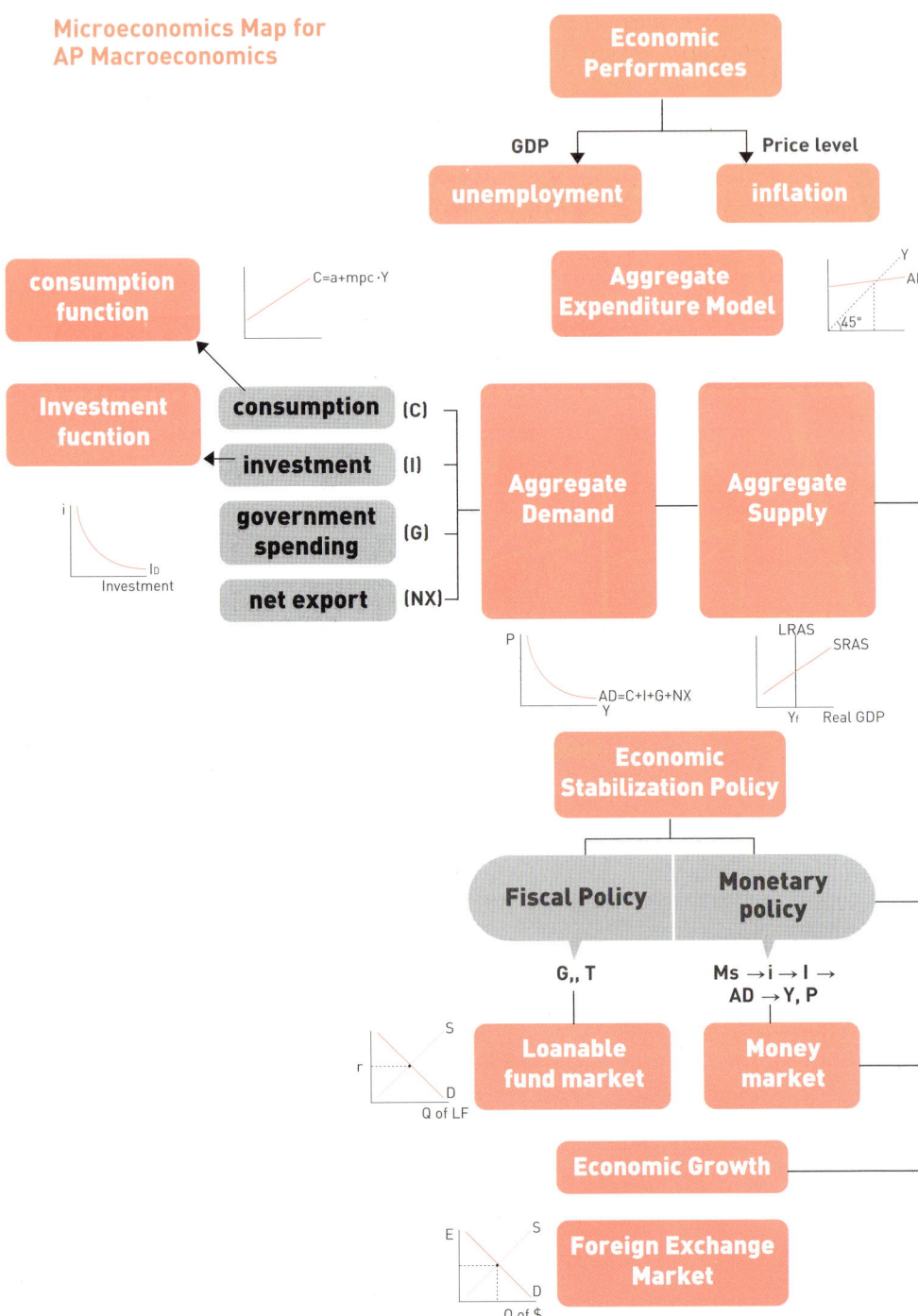

# Two big schools of economic thoughts

**Classical Tradition** vs. **Keynsian Tradition**

- Supply creates its own demand
- Prices and wages are flexible.
- Market is self-correcting mechanism.

- Demand creates its own supply
- Price and wage are sticky(rigid)
- Goverment should inteveneth in the market in the period of economic downturn.

**Classical (1776-)**

$LARS = A \cdot F(L, K, H, N)$
Labor(L)
Capital(C)
Human Capital(H)
Natural Recource(N)
Technology(A)

$SRAS = P^e \cdot A \cdot F(L, K, H, N)$
$P^e$: price expectation

**Monetarist** — (1960s) MV=PQ Monetary Neutrality

**Rational Expectation** — (1970s) Policy Ineffectiveness

**Supply Siders** — [1980s] Tax cut

· Open Market Operations
· discount rate
· reserve requirements

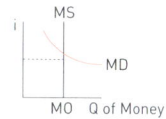

**Keynesian (1929-)**

**New classical (1990s)**

**New Keynesian (1990s)**

## 학파에 대한 설명 - Must Read! (거시경제학파 이해에 필수)

애덤 스미스 이후의 영국을 중심으로 한 고전학파classical school는 자유방임주의를 주장하면서 시장에 대해 정부의 간섭은 최소화하고 정부가 치안과 국방 등의 일에만 집중하고 경제운용에는 간섭하지 말아야 한다는 야경국가론을 주장했다. 고전학파는 세이J. Say의 법칙에 따라 공급이 스스로 그 수요를 창출하며, 요소가격은 단기에도 신축적으로 움직이므로 시장은 자신의 문제를 스스로 해결할 수 있다고 믿었다. 하지만 1929년 10월에 미국 뉴욕의 주식시장의 붕괴를 시작으로 전 세계를 휩쓴 대공황Great Depression이 오래 지속되며 경제상황이 갈수록 악화되었고 기존의 고전학파의 경제이론은 혁명적으로 수정되었다.

거시경제학의 창시자라고 할 수 있는 존 메이나드 케인즈John Maynard Keynes가 1936년 『고용, 화폐, 이자에 대한 일반이론』General Theory on Employment, Interest, and Money이라는 기념비적인 저작을 통해 유효수요 effective demand 창출을 위해 정부가 개입할 것을 주장했다. 이후 탄생한 케인즈학파는 불황에 빠진 경제가 완전고용생산을 회복하기 위해서는 정부가 총수요를 증가시켜 경기를 살리고 또 과열된 경제는 냉각시키는 경제 안정화 정책을 펼쳐야한다는 이론적 기반을 제공하였다. 케인즈 학파의 핵심적인 아이디어는 물가와 임금은 단기에 경직적이며 수요가 공급을 창출하기 때문에 정부 지출을 통해 경제를 회복해야 한다는 것이다.

케인즈의 유명한 말대로 고전학파의 주장을 따르게 되면 '장기에는 모두 죽고 만다In the long run, we are all dead'. 시장의 자기규제능력 self-regulation을 기약없이 믿고 있을 수만 없고 민간경제주체에게 무언가를 기대할 수 없기 상황에서 정부가 나서서 할 수 있는 걸 해야 한다는 것이다. 1940년대와 50년대에 미국의 하버드대학과 MIT대학을 중심으로 정계와 학계에 크게 영향력을 발휘하던 케인스학파는 1960년대부터 시카고 대학의 밀턴 프리드먼을 중심으로 하는 통화주의학파 monetarist, 같은 시카고 대학의 로버트 루카스Robert Lucas를 중심으로 하는 1970년대 합리적 기대론자 rational expectationist들의 등장으로 위축되기 시작하였다.

무엇보다 1973년에 전 세계 경제를 강타한 오일 파동으로 인플레이션과 실업이 동시에 증가하는 스태그플레이션 stagflation이 발생하자 인플레이션과 실업이 상충관계에 있는 전통적인 필립스 커브에 집착하였던 케인스 학파는 문제의 해법을 제시하지 못하여 그 기세가 크게 꺾였다. 고전학파의 전통에 서 있는 통화주의자들과 합리적 기대론자들은 스테그플레이션의 원인이 정부의 과도한 개입과 규제에 있다고 단언하며 고전학파의 명제로 다시 돌아가서 정부의 경제 개입을 최소화할 것을 주장하였다. 통화주의자들은 재량discretion에 의한 통화정책을 배격하며 준칙에 의한 통화정책을 강조하였고 합리적 기대론자들은 예상된 정부정책은 단기에 조차 무용하다는 정책무력성명제government policy ineffectiveness hypothesis를 들고 나왔다.

1980년대는 무엇보다 경제적 보수주의자들의 시대였다. 정치권에서 영국의 대처, 미국의 레이건의 등장과 더불어 래퍼(A. Laffer)와 같은 공급주의학파supply-sider들이 등장하여 세금 인하가 경제활동을 증가시키고 세금기반을 넓혀서 재정적자를 해결해 줄 것이라고 주장하였지만 정책의 실시 결과 미국의 재정적자는 더 심화되었다. 특히 영국과 미국을 중심으로 한 이들의 정책은 신자유주의 세계화neoliberal globalization로 나타나게 되었다.

하지만 신자유주의가 주장하는 지나친 탈규제deregulation, 민영화privatization는 2008년 미국발 서브프라임모기지 사태에 일정한 원인을 제공하였으며 경제양극화economic polarization를 더욱 심화시켰다는 평가를 받는다. 지난 30년간 세계를 휩쓴 신자유주의적 세계화는 현재는 한풀 꺾인 상태로, 지나친 단기자본의 이동에 대한 규제 등이 제시되며 고삐 풀린 시장에 대한 정부의 재(再)규제reregulation에 대한 논의가 진행 중이다.

# Chapter 01

# Measuring Economic Performance

 경제 성과 측정하기

"Measuring a nation's income and price level"

Part2의 Chapter1에서는 거시경제의 가장 핵심적인 변수인 국민소득과 물가수준에 대한 정의와 그 측정방법에 대해 알아보고 그와 직결된 실업과 인플레이션 문제에 대해 다루겠습니다. 국민소득의 대표적인 지수는 국내총생산 Gross Domestic Product 이고 대표적인 물가지수는 GDP디플레이터와 소비자물가지수 Consumer Price Index 입니다. 각각의 정의와 그 측정방식, 그 한계에 대해서 정확하게 알아두어야 합니다. 또한 인플레이션에서는 원인과 비용, 예상치 않은 인플레이션 Unanticipated Inflation 의 효과가 중요하며, 실업에서는 실업의 유형 Types of Unemployment, 실업률의 측정방식, 통계실업률 측정의 문제 등에 대해서 확실하게 익혀두어야 합니다.

# Lesson 1 | Macroeconomics
## 거시경제학

### macroeconomics
### 거시경제학

**The study of how an economy operates as a whole**
경제가 전체적으로 어떻게 작동하는가를 연구하는 학문

### business cycle or economic fluctuation
### 경기순환과 경제변동

**The ups and downs of economic performance**
경제 성과의 기복

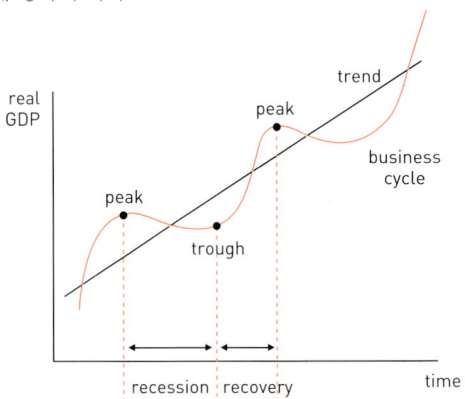

- **recession: the period of falling real GDP**
  경기침체: 실질GDP가 떨어지는 시기
- **expansion: the period of rising real GDP**
  경기확장: 실질GDP가 증가하는 시기
- **peak: the top of a business cycle**
  정점: 경기변동의 최고점
- **trough: the bottom of a business cycle**
  저점: 경기변동의 바닥점

## two ways to measure a nation's income
### 국민소득의 두 가지 측정방법

**❶ expenditure approach** 지출접근법
Calculation of a nation's income by adding the expenditures of market participants (GDP = C + I + G + NX)
시장참여자들의 지출을 합함으로써 국민소득을 계산하는 방법
(국내총생산= 소비+투자+정부지출+순수출)

**❷ income approach** 소득접근법
Calculation of nation's income by summing incomes earned by providing factors of production
생산요소를 제공함으로써 얻은 소득을 합해서 국민소득을 계산하는 방법

**Tip** expenditure approach = income approach

- Why is total expenditure equal to total income?
  → Because someone's expenditure becomes someone's income.
  누군가의 지출은 누군가의 소득이 되기 때문이다.

## GDP
### 국내총생산

**Total market value of all final goods and services produced in an economy during a period of time.**
일정한 기간 동안 한 경제 내에서 생산된 최종재화와 서비스의 총시장가치

- **Included in GDP** GDP에 포함되는 것
  Domestically produced final goods and services (including capital goods), new construction of structures, changes to inventories
  국내생산된 최종재화와 서비스(자본재 포함), 새로운 구조물 건설, 재고의 변동

- **Not Included in GDP** GDP에 포함되지 않는 것
  Intermediate goods and services, inputs, used goods, financial assets like stocks and bonds, foreign-produced goods and services
  중간재화와 서비스, 투입요소, 중고품, 주식과 채권 등의 금융상품, 해외에서 생산된 재화와 서비스

**The limitation of GDP as an index of well-being[5]**

GDP excludes non-market activities such as a housewife's work, underground economy, volunteer work and so forth. GDP does not consider the value of leisure, quality of environment. GDP cannot tell us about income distribution.

GDP는 가정주부일, 지하경제, 자원봉사 등의 비시장활동을 제외한다. GDP는 여가의 가치, 환경의 질을 고려하지 않는다. GDP를 통해 소득분배에 대해서 알 수 없다.

## GNP
### 국민총생산

- **NNP(Net National Product) = GNP-depreciation**
  순국민생산 = 국민총생산-감가상각
- **NI(National Income) = NNP-sales tax + business subsidies**
  국민소득 = 순국민생산-판매세 + 기업보조금
- **PI(Personal Income) = NI-corporate income taxes-retained earnings-social security taxes + government transfer payments**
  개인소득 = 국민소득-법인세-회사보유금-사회보장세 + 정부 이전지출
- **DPI(Disposable Personal Income) = P-personal taxes**
  개인가처분소득 = 개인소득-개인세금

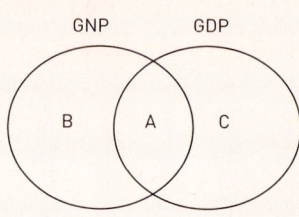

A: citizens' domestic income(product)
　시민의 국내소득(생산)
B: citizens' foreign income
　시민의 해외소득
C: Foreigners' domestic income
　외국인의 국내소득

GNP(A+B)=GDP(A+C) + NFI(Net factor Income from the rest of the world; B-C)

# Lesson 2

## Real GDP and Nominal GDP
### 실질 GDP와 명목 GDP

### real GDP
### 실질 GDP

The total market value of all final goods and services produced in an economy during a period of time, calculated using the price of a base year.

기준년도 가격을 사용하여 계산한, 일정 기간 동안 한 경제 내에서 생산한 모든 최종재의 총시장가치

### nominal GDP
### 명목 GDP

The total market value of all final goods and services produced in an economy during a period of time, calculated using the price of current year

해당년도 가격을 사용하여 계산한, 일정기간 동안 한 경제 내에서 생산한 모든 최종재의 총시장가치

### base year
### 기준년도

The year in which data are identified as 100 (sometimes 1) when constructing an index number such as GDP and price level.

GDP나 물가수준 등을 지수로 구성할 때 100이나 1의 값으로 동일시되는 연도

**Tip** real GDP와 nominal GDP가 달라지는 이유는 물가상승 때문이다.

|  | 2010(base year) |  | 2011 |  |
| --- | --- | --- | --- | --- |
|  | P($) | Q | P($) | Q |
| apple | 5 | 10 | 8 | 12 |
| cookies | 2 | 15 | 3 | 17 |
| Nominal GDP | 5×10 + 2×15 = 85 | | 8×12 + 3×17 = 147 | |
| Real | 5×10 + 2×15 = 85 | | 5×12 + 2×17 = 94 | |

real GDP를 구하는 이유는 nominal GDP의 증가분에서 물가상승분을 제거함으로써 실질적인 의미에서 GDP의 증가를 측정하기 위해서이다. 진정한 생활수준은 물가상승이 아니라 실제 생산의 증가에 달려 있기 때문이다.

# Lesson 3

## Price Level
## 물가

### price level
### 물가

**A measure of overall prices for goods and services**
재화와 서비스의 전반적인 가격을 재는 척도

### GDP deflator
### GDP 디플레이터

**The ratio of nominal GDP to real GDP; a measure of the overall price level. Gives the average prices of the final goods and services produced in an economy**
실질 GDP에 대한 명목 GDP의 비율, 전반적인 가격수준을 재는 척도 중 하나, 한 경제에서 생산되는 최종재화와 서비스의 평균가격을 제시한다.

- GDP Deflator = $\dfrac{Nominal\ GDP}{Real\ GDP} \times 100$

### CPI(Consumer Price Index)
### 소비자 물가지수

**The cost of a basket of goods and services bought by a typical consumer**
평균적인 소비자가 구매하는 재화와 서비스의 상품 바구니 비용

|         | 2010(base year) | 2011  |
|---------|-----------------|-------|
|         | Price($)        | Price |
| apple   | 5               | 8     |
| cookies | 2               | 3     |

❶ Fix the basket(Base Year = 2010, basket = apple 3 units, cookies 5 units)
❷ Compute the costs of baskets in each year
   The cost of the basket in 2010 = 3×5 + 5×2 = $25
   The cost of the basket in 2011 = 3×8 + 5×3 = $39

❸ Compute the CPI of the compared year(the CPI of the Base Year =100)

$= \dfrac{39}{25} \times 100 = 156$

❹ Compute the inflation rate

Inflation rate of the year 2011 $= \dfrac{CPI_{2011} - CPI_{2010}}{CPI_{2010}} = \dfrac{156-100}{100} \times 100 = 56\%$

## PPI(Producer Price Index)
생산자 가격지수

**A price index of the basket of goods and services purchased by firms**
기업이 구매하는 상품과 서비스에 대한 가격지수

# Lesson 4: Inflation and Unemployment
## 인플레이션과 실업

## inflation
### 인플레이션

**A continuous increase in the overall price level**
전반적인 물가의 지속적 상승

## causes of inflation
### 인플레이션의 원인

❶ **demand-pull inflation 수요견인 인플레이션**
Inflation that is caused when aggregate demand increases.
총수요의 증가로 인해 발생하는 인플레이션

❷ **cost-push inflation 비용상승 인플레이션**
Inflation that is caused when aggregate supply decreases.
총공급의 감소로 인해 발생하는 인플레이션

❸ **long-term cause of inflation 인플레이션의 장기적인 원인**
money growth
통화증가

## equation of exchange
### 교환방정식

**MV=PQ (M:money supply, V:velocity of money, P: Price level, Q: real GDP)**
통화량 × 화폐유통속도 = 명목GDP

- **This equation argues monetary neutrality.**
  이 방정식은 화폐의 중립성을 주장한다.

## monetary neutrality
### 화폐의 중립성

**The proposition that an increase in money supply has no effect on real output but is reflected entirely by a proportional increase in the price level**

통화량의 증가는 실질생산에는 아무런 영향을 미치지 못하지만, 물가를 통화량 증가비율만큼 상승시키는 것으로 나타난다.

## Fisher hypothesis
### 피셔 가설

**The proposition that an increase in money growth is reflected in an identical increase in both the inflation rate and the nominal interest rate in the long run**

통화량의 증가는 장기적으로 인플레이션과 명목이자율이 같은 크기로 상승하는 것으로 나타난다는 주장

- **nominal interest rate(i) = real interest rate(r) + expected inflation rate($\pi^e$)**
  
  명목이자율 = 실질이자율 + 기대 인플레이션율

> **Tip** The nominal interest rate is the interest rate expressed in dollar terms.
> 명목이자율은 달러 기준으로 표현된 이자율이다.
> 
> The real interest rate is the nominal interest rate minus the rate of inflation.
> 실질이자율은 명목이자율에서 인플레이션율을 뺀 이자율이다.

## cost of inflation
### 인플레이션의 비용

- **Shoe-leather cost is the increased cost of transaction caused by inflation.**
  구두창 비용은 인플레이션으로 인해 증가되는 거래비용이다.
- **Menu cost is the cost of changing prices.**
  메뉴 비용은 가격을 바꿀 때 발생하는 비용이다.
- **Unit-of-account costs arise because inflation makes money a less reliable unit of measurement.**
  회계단위 비용은 인플레이션이 화폐의 가치의 측정 단위로서 신뢰성을 떨어뜨리므로 발생하는 비용이다.

> **Tip** Unanticipated Inflation brings arbitrary redistribution of wealth. Unanticipated inflation makes the debtor better off, but the creditor worse off because the money

becomes cheaper than before the unexpected inflations.
예기치 않은 인플레이션은 부의 자의적인 재분배를 가져온다. 예기치 않은 인플레이션은 채무자에게 이득을 주고 채권자에게는 손해를 끼친다. 왜냐하면 인플레이션 이전보다 돈의 가치가 떨어졌기 때문이다.

Disinflation is the process of lowering the inflation rate.
디스인플레이션은 인플레이션율을 줄이는 과정을 말한다.

## unemployment
## 실업

- **Adult Population(working-age population)** 성인 인구(노동 가능 인구)
  Those who are able to work over age 16 and older
  16세 이상의 일할 수 있는 인구

- **Labor force** 경제활동인구
  The sum of the employed and the unemployed
  취업자와 실업자의 합계

- **Employed** 취업자
  Usually paid employes, but includes those who work in their own business, or worked as unpaid workers in a family member's business.
  대개 유급 피고용자이며 자영업자와 가족 사업에서 일하는 무급 노동자를 포함한다.

- **Unemployed** 실업자
  Those who do not have a job, but are available for work, and have actively looked for work during the previous 4 weeks. .
  직장이 없으나 일이 주어지면 할 수 있고 지난 4주 동안 적극적으로 일을 구한 사람들

- **Not in the labor force** 비경제활동인구
  Those who are not in the labor force among the adult population
  성인 인구 중에서 경제활동인구에 속해 있지 않은 인구

- **Labor force participation rate** 경제활동 참가율
  Labor force divided by adult population
  경제활동인구를 성인 인구로 나눈 값

- **Unemployment rate** 실업률
  Unemployed divided by labor force
  실업자를 경제활동인구로 나눈 값.

## the limits of unemployment statistics
### 실업통계의 한계

**Discouraged workers are excluded from the labor force, and part-time workers, who are actually underemployed are regarded as employed. These fallacies make the genuine unemployment rate underestimated.**

실망 노동자는 경제활동인구에 없는 것으로 여겨지고, 사실상 저고용 되어 있는 시간제 근무 노동자는 취업자로 간주된다. 이 두 가지 오류는 진정한 실업률을 과소평가하게 만든다.

### 기 본 단 어 익 히 기

**discourage worker** 실망노동자
**underemployment** 저고용
**part-time worker** 시간제 근무 노동자

## types of unemployment
### 실업의 유형

**❶ frictional unemployment  마찰적 실업**

Unemployment that results from the time workers spend in job search.
구직활동에 사용하는 시간 때문에 발생하는 실업

**❷ structural unemployment  구조적 실업**

Unemployment that results when there are more people seeking jobs in a labor market than there are jobs available at the current wage.(minimum wage, union, efficiency wages)

현재 임금에서 얻을 수 있는 직장보다 구직자의 수가 더 많을 때 발생하는 실업(최저임금제, 노동조합, 효율임금)

**❸ cyclical unemployment  경기적 실업**

Unemployment that results from the economic downturns such as recession or depression.
경기 침체나 불황처럼 경제 하강으로 인해 생기는 실업

# natural rate of unemployment
## 자연실업률

**The unemployment rate at which full employment is achieved**
완전고용이 달성되었을 때의 실업률

- **Natural unemployment 자연실업**

  = Frictional unemployment + Structural unemployment
  마찰적실업 + 구조적 실업

- **Actual unemployment 실제실업**

  = Natural unemployment + Cyclical unemployment
  자연실업 + 경기적 실업

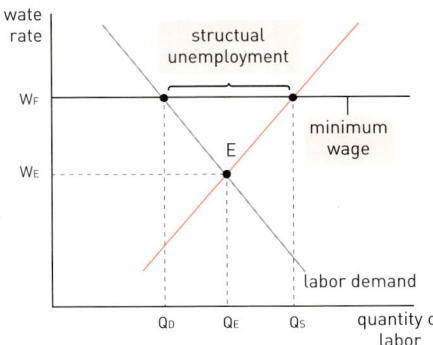

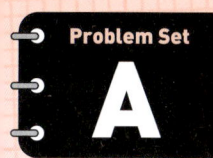

# Short Answer Question

Write down a proper word for the definition

**1** the study of how an economy operates as a whole

**2** total market value of all final goods and services produced in an economy during a period of time

**3** the cost of a basket of goods and services bought by a typical consumer

**4** the ups and downs of economic performance

**5** the ratio of nominal GDP to real GDP; a measure of the overall price level

**6** the period of rising real GDP

**7** the total market value of all final goods and services produced in an economy during a period of time, calculated using the price of current year

**8** the top of the business cycle

**9** the bottom of business cycle

**10** the total market value of all final goods and services produced in an economy during a period of time, calculated using the price of a base year

**11** the period of falling real GDP

**12** the increased costs of transactions caused by inflation

**13** a continuous increase in the overall price level

**14** unemployment that results from the time workers spend in job search

**15** the cost of changing prices due

**16** unemployment that results when there are more people seeking jobs in a labor market than there are jobs available at the current wage

**17** Inflation that is caused when aggregate demand increases

**18** the unemployment rate at which full employment is achieved

**19** Inflation that is caused when aggregate supply decreases

**20** the proposition that an increase in money growth is reflected in an identical increase in both the inflation rate and the nominal interest rate in the long run

**21** those who do not have a job, were available for work, and have actively looked for work during the previous 4 weeks.

**22** unemployment that results from the economic downturns such as recession, depression

# Define these words

**23** expenditure approach ?

**24** income approach ?

### Answer

**1** macroeconomics  **2** GDP  **3** CPI  **4** business cycle or economic fluctuation
**5** GDP deflator  **6** expansion  **7** nominal GDP  **8** peak  **9** trough  **10** real GDP
**11** recession  **12** shoe-leather costs  **13** inflation  **14** frictional unemployment
**15** menu cost  **16** structural unemployment  **17** demand-pull inflation
**18** natural rate of unemployment  **19** cost-push inflation  **20** Fisher hypothesis
**21** unemployed  **22** cyclical unemployment

**23** calculation of nation's income by adding the expenditures by market participants
**24** calculation of nation's income by summing of incomes earned by providing factors of production

# Problem Set B: multiple questions

**1.** Gross Domestic Product is measured by _____.

A) adding quantity of all goods and services
B) adding the market value of all final goods and services
C) adding the difference between the whole sale prices and retail prices for all final goods
D) adding the difference between the market price of final good and the market price of the intermediate goods

**2.** According to expenditure approach, Gross Domestic Product equals _____.

A) Consumption + Investment + Government Spending + Export
B) Consumption + Investment + Government Spending + Import
C) Consumption + Investment + Government Spending + Export +Import
D) Consumption + Investment + Government Spending + Export − Import

**3.** All other things being equal, if the purchase of new houses increases by $100 billion and imports of French wine increases by $100 billion in the United States, then GDP of the United States _____.

A) increases by $200 billion
B) increases by $100 billion
C) decreases by $100 billion
D) does not change

## 4

The table below shows the total expenditures of a country.

| Components | Millions of dollars |
|---|---|
| Consumption | 6,800 |
| Investment | 1,700 |
| Government spending on goods and services | 1,800 |
| Net exports of goods and services | -400 |

Based on the data on the table above, what much is the GDP of the country?

A) 10,700
B) 10,300
C) 9,900
D) 8,900

## 5

The income approach measures GDP by summing _____.

A) the market value of all final goods and services produced within a country in a given period of time
B) Consumption + Investment + Government Spending + Net Exports
C) the national wealth possessed by households, businesses, and government
D) the incomes households receive in return for providing factors of production

## 6-7

|  | 2010 | | 2011 | |
| --- | --- | --- | --- | --- |
|  | Quantity | Price | Quantity | Price |
| Hamburger | 20 | $7 | 25 | $8 |
| Coke | 35 | $2 | 40 | $3 |

**6** The table above gives the production and prices for a small nation that produces only bread and soda. The base year is 2010. What is nominal GDP, real GDP, and approximate price index of 2011?

A) $210, $255, 82.4
B) $255, $340, 75
C) $340, $255, 133
D) $340, $233, 146

**7** Compute the Consumer Price Index of 2011. Then find the approximate inflation rate between 2010 and 2011. The basket for CPI covers only 5 hamburgers and 5 Cokes. Year 2010 is the base year.

A) 111, 11%
B) 122, 22%
C) 133, 33%
D) 144, 44%

**8** Investment is defined as the purchase of _____.

A) financial assets such as stocks and bonds
B) new capital good such as equipment, machinery, and building and additions to inventories
C) both capital good and financial assets
D) foreign capital goods and stocks

**9** Each of the following is omitted when measuring GDP. Which of the following underestimates GDP as a standard of economic well-being?

I. Underground economy
II. Leisure time
III. Home production
IV. Cost of Cleaning environmental pollution

A) I, II.
B) I, II and III
C) I, II, and IV
D) I, II, III, and IV

**10** The Consumer Price Index (CPI) measures _____.

A) the cost of a fixed basket of goods and services bought by a typical consumer
B) the quantities of a fixed basket of goods produced by firm
C) the lowest cost of a fixed basket of good and services bought by a typical consumers
D) the cost of a fixed basket of production resources paid by a typical firm

**11** Which of the following is a source of distortion in the CPI as price index?

I. unmeasured quality change
II. introduction of new goods
III. substitution bias

A) I, II, only
B) II, III only
C) III only
D) I, II and III

**12** The difference between nominal and real value is that _____.

A) nominal is measured in current-year dollars and real is measured in base-year dollars
B) real is measured in current-year dollars and nominal is measured in base-year dollars
C) nominal is stated in physical unit and real is stated in monetary unit
D) real is a number stated in dollars and nominal is stated with an index number

**13** The real interest rate equals _____.

A) nominal interest rate − expected inflation rate
B) nominal interest rate + expected inflation rate
C) nominal interest rate ÷ inflation rate
D) expected inflation rate − nominal interest rate

## 14. A person is considered unemployed if s/he _____.

A) is working without pay
B) is without a job
C) has a job and is looking for another one
D) does not have a job and is looking for one

## 15. The unemployment rate is defined as _____.

A) (labor force) ÷ (working-age population) times 100
B) (number of the employed) ÷ (labor force) times 100
C) (number of the unemployed) ÷ (labor force) times 100
D) (number of the unemployed) ÷ (working-age population) times 100

## 16. If Sheldon, age 24, had no job but had tried to find one during the week, Sheldon is classified as _____.

A) underemployed
B) unemployed
C) a discouraged worker
D) not in the labor force

**17** When calculating the unemployment rate, part-time workers over the age of 16 are counted as _____.

A) underemployed
B) unemployed
C) not in the labor force
D) employed

**18** The adult or working-age population in a country is 300 million people; 200 million people are employed, 50 million people are unemployed, and the unemployment rate is _____.

A) 25 %
B) 20 %
C) 16.6 %
D) 15 %

**19** During the 2008 sub-prime mortgage crisis the unemployment rate was exceptionally high since the Great Depression in 1930s. What kind of unemployment was caused by this financial crisis?

A) Cyclical
B) Seasonal
C) Structural
D) Frictional

**20** As the unemployment rate increases, _____.

A) potential GDP decreases
B) real GDP decreases
C) potential GDP increases
D) full employment GDP decreases

**21** Potential GDP is reached when _____.

A) unemployment is zero
B) there is no cyclical unemployment
C) unemployment is above full employment
D) unemployment is below full employment

Answer

1 B  2 D  3 D  4 C  5 D
6 C  7 B  8 B  9 B  10 A  11 D
12 A  13 A  14 D  15 C  16 B  17 D
18 B  19 A  20 B  21 B

# Chapter 02

# Income-Expenditure and AD-AS Model

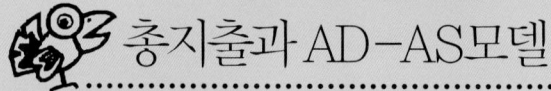
총지출과 AD-AS모델

거시경제학 Chapter2에서는 국민소득과 물가가 어떻게 결정되는가에 대해서 배워봅니다. 소득-지출모형(총지출모형)에서는 국민소득이 생산과 지출의 차이인 재고의 변동을 통해 이루어지는 과정을 배우게 됩니다. 총수요-총공급 모형에서는 소득-지출모형에서 총수요곡선이 도출되는 것을 보게 되고, 경제 내의 생산요소와 기술에 따라 총공급곡선이 도출되는 것을 배우게 될 것입니다. 무엇보다 총수요곡선이 우하향하게 되는 이유와 단기 총공급곡선은 우상향하지만 장기 총공급곡선은 수직인 이유를 명확하게 이해하기 바랍니다. 거시경제의 균형은 총수요곡선과 총공급곡선이 만나는 점에서 이루어지며 거시경제의 모든 현상은 바로 이 총수요-총공급 모형에서 설명되므로, 이 모형의 중요성을 깨닫고 자기 것으로 꼭 만들어봅시다.

# Lesson 1 | Consumption
## 소비

## consumption function
### 소비함수

**The relationship between income and consumption**
소득과 소비의 관계

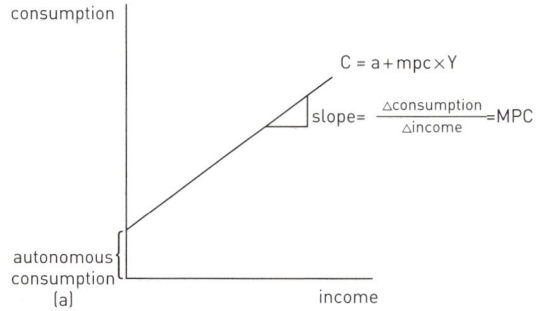

- Consumption 소비 = autonomous consumption 기초소비 + marginal propensity to consume 한계소비성향 × income 소득

## marginal propensity to consume
### 한계소비성향

**The effect of an additional dollar of disposable income on consumption**
가처분소득 1달러의 증가가 소비를 증가시키는 정도

- Income = Consumption + Saving 소득 = 소비 + 저축
  △Y(Change in Income)소득변화 = △C(Change in Consumption)소비변화 + △S(Change in Saving)저축변화

## average propensity to consume
### 평균소비성향

**Consumption spending divided by disposable income**
소비지출을 가처분소득으로 나눈 값

## autonomous consumption
### 기초소비

**The amount of consumption that does not depend on the level of disposable income. The minimum consumption when a man has no income**
가처분소득과 관계없는 소비액, 소득이 없을 때 최소한의 소비액

## paradox of thrift[6)]
### 절약의 역설

**When families and businesses are worried about the possibility of economic hard times, they prepare by cutting their spending. This reduction in spending depresses the economy as consumers spend less and businesses react by laying off workers. As a result, families and businesses may end up worse off than if they hadn't tried to act responsibly by cutting their spending.**
경제가 어려워질 것이라고 예상할 때 가계와 기업은 지출을 줄여서 대비한다. 가계가 소비를 줄이고 기업이 노동자들을 해고하면서 지출을 줄이면 경제가 침체된다. 결과적으로 가계와 기업은 지출을 줄여서 대응하지 않았을 경우보다 더 경제상황이 악화된다.

## investment function
### 소비함수

**The inverse relationship between interest rate and investment**
이자율과 투자의 역관계

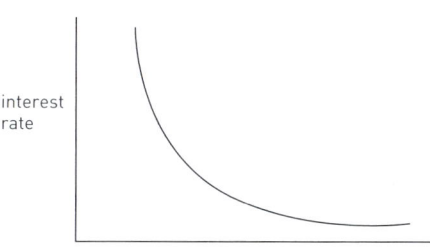

> **Tip** Interest is the opportunity cost of investment.
> 이자는 투자의 기회비용이다.

## government spending
### 정부 지출

**Spending on goods and services by local, state, and federal governments. Government spending does not include transfer payments because transfer payments are made without any exchange of goods or services.**

재화와 서비스에 대한 지방·주·연방정부의 지출
정부 지출은 이전 지출을 포함하지 않는다. 재화와 서비스의 교환 없이 이루어지기 때문이다.

- **Transfer payments** 이전 지출

    **redistribution of income such as unemployment benefits, and business subsidy**

    실업 급여, 기업 보조금 같은 소득의 재분배

## net export
### 순수출

**The difference between export and import. Price level and income is the main determinants of net export. When price level rises in a country, net export of the country falls, because export decreases and import increases. When income rises in a country, net export of the country falls, because import increases.**

수출과 수입의 차이, 물가수준과 소득이 순수출의 주요 결정요인이다. 어느 국가의 물가가 상승하면 수출이 감소하고, 수입이 증가하기 때문에 순수출은 떨어진다. 어느 국가의 소득이 상승하면 수입이 증가하기 때문에 그 국가의 순수출은 떨어진다.

# Lesson 2 | Aggregate Expenditure (AE) Model
## 총지출곡선

### aggregate expenditure
### 총지출

The sum of consumption, investment, government spending, and net export.
소비, 투자, 정부 지출, 그리고 순수출의 합

- **Aggregate expenditure curve the vertical summation of consumption(C), investment(I), government spending(G) and net export(NX)**
  총지출곡선은 소비, 투자, 정부 지출, 순수출의 수직 합이다.

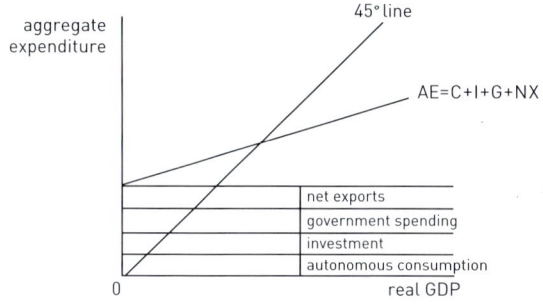

### the determination of national income
### 국민소득의 결정

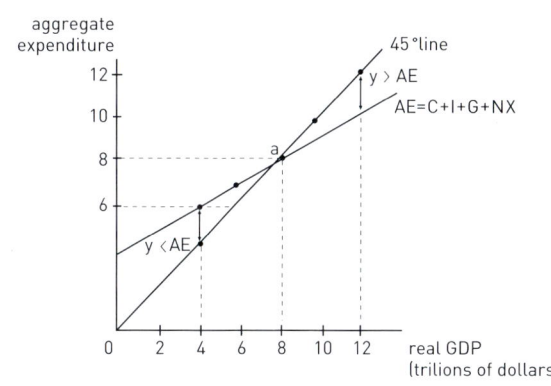

Chapter 2 Income-Expenditure and AD-AS model

National income is determined at $8 trillions. At $12 trillion, production is greater than expenditure, which will increases inventories. Then firms will decrease production. At $ 4 trillion, expenditure is greater than production, so inventories will decrease. Then firms will increase production. At $8 trillion, production equals expenditure.

국민소득은 8조 달러에서 결정된다. 12조 달러에서 생산이 지출보다 커서 재고가 증가한다. 그러면 기업은 생산을 줄일 것이다. 4조 달러에서는 지출이 생산보다 커서 재고가 감소한다. 그러면 기업은 생산을 증가시킬 것이다. 8조 달러에서 생산과 지출이 같아지고 국민소득이 결정된다.

## three kinds of economic situations in AE model
### 세 가지 경제정세를 나타낸 총지출 곡선

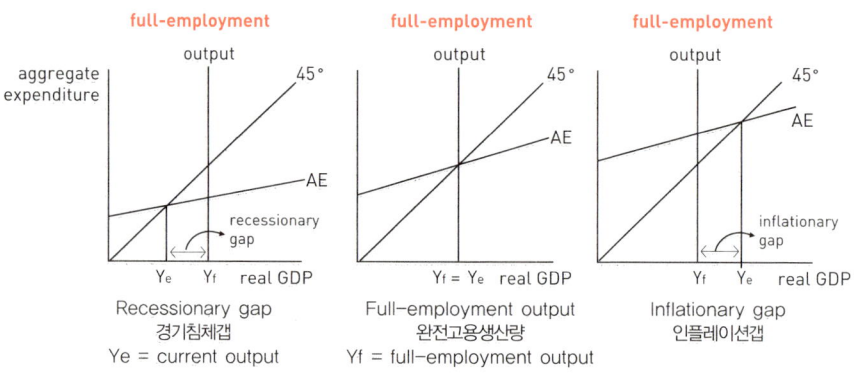

Recessionary gap
경기침체갭
Ye = current output

Full-employment output
완전고용생산량
Yf = full-employment output

Inflationary gap
인플레이션갭

## connecting aggregate expenditure to aggregate demand
### 총지출모형을 총수요곡선과 연결하기

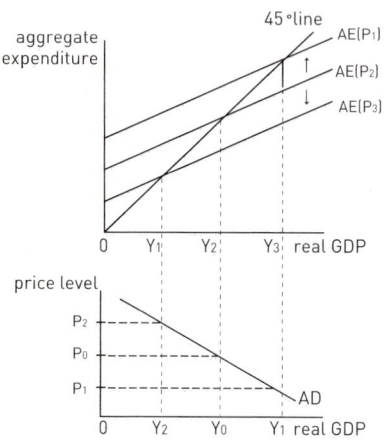

Aggregate expenditure model assumes that the price level is given. But in a real economy, price level changes. We need a new model that shows price level. We can derive the new diagram, AD(aggregate demand) from aggregate expenditure model.
총지출모형은 물가가 주어진 것으로 가정한다. 하지만 현실 경제에서 물가는 변한다. 물가 수준을 보여주는 새로운 모형이 필요하고 총지출모형에서 총수요곡선을 도출할 수 있다.

**When price level falls, what happens to AE?**
물가가 떨어지면 총지출에 어떤 일이 생기는가?

**❶ Wealth effect(or real balance effect) 부의 효과(실질잔고 효과)**
When price level falls. consumption increases because real income rises.
물가수준이 떨어지면 실질소득이 증가하기 때문에 소비가 증가한다.

**❷ Interest rate effect 이자율효과**
When price level falls, investment increases because people demand less money, which lowers interest rate. When interest rate falls, investment rises.
물가수준이 떨어질 때, 투자는 증가한다. 사람들의 화폐수요가 줄어들어 이자율이 떨어지기 때문이다.

**❸ Net-export effect 순수출효과**
When price level falls, net-export increases because domestic goods are cheaper than foreign ones.
물가가 떨어지면 순수출은 증가한다. 국내재화가 외국재화보다 더 싸기 때문이다.

Therefore, we can conclude that real GDP increases when price level falls. The price level and real GDP is inversely related. Aggregate demand curve, which represents the relationship between price level and real GDP, is downward sloping.
따라서 우리는 물가가 떨어지면 실질 GDP가 증가한다고 결론을 내릴 수 있다. 물가와 실질 GDP는 역관계이다. 물가와 실질 GDP의 관계를 보여주는 총수요는 우하향한다.

## aggregate supply
총공급

### The relationship between price level and quantity of output
물가와 총생산량과의 관계

## aggregate supply
## 총공급

**The relationship between price level and quantity of output**
물가와 총생산량의 관계

### the determinants shifting aggregate supply
### 총공급곡선의 이동요인

1 **labor** 노동(L)
2 **capital** 자본(K)
3 **natural resources** 천연자원(N)
4 **entrepreneurship** 기업가 정신
5 **technology** 기술(A)
6 **price expectation** 물가예상($p^e$)

- Increase in labor, capital, natural resources, and expected price level and technological advances shift the aggregate supply curve to the right. Notice that price expectation does not affect the long-run aggregate supply curve, but only short-run aggegate supply curve. When people expect price level to rise, wage will increase. Then, short-run aggegate supply shift to the left. When people expect price level to fall, wage will decrease. Then short-run aggregate supply will shift to the right.

노동, 자본, 천연자원, 예상물가 증가, 기술의 발전은 총공급곡선을 오른쪽으로 이동시킨다. 물가예상은 장기 공급곡선에는 영향을 주지 못하고 단지 단기 총공급곡선만을 움직인다. 사람들이 물가가 상승할 것이라고 예상하면 임금이 오르게 될 것이다. 그러면 단기 총공급곡선은 왼쪽으로 이동한다. 사람들이 물가가 하락할 것이라고 예상하면 임금이 떨어지게 될 것이다. 그러면 단기 총공급곡선은 오른쪽으로 이동할 것이다.

- SRAS = $P^e \cdot A \cdot F(L, K, H, N)$

- LRAS = $A \cdot F(L, K, H, N)$

## Why would producers be willing to increase output when the price level increases? 물가가 상승할 때 생산자들은 왜 생산을 늘리려고 하는가?

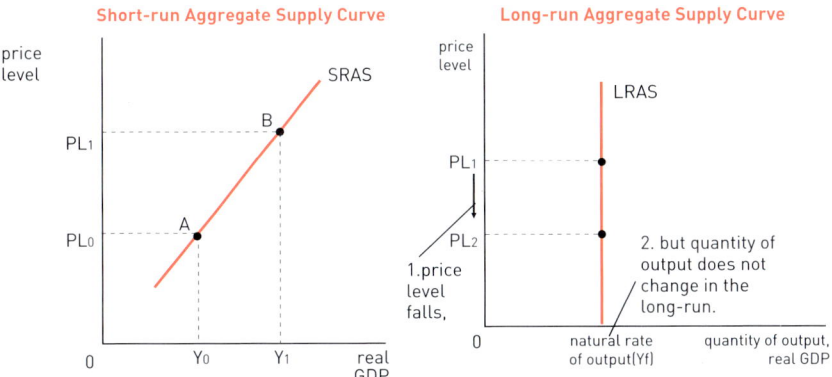

In the short run, firms are willing to supply more output at a higher price level, because the firms would make more profits due to rigid wages and other input prices in the short run. On the other hand, in the long run, firms will always produce at the maximum sustainable level allowed by their capital, labor, and technological inputs, regardless of the price level. Therefore, the short-run aggregate supply curve(SRAS) is upward-sloping, and the long-run aggregate supply(LRAS) curve is vertical at full-employment output.

단기에 기업은 가격이 높아지면 공급량을 증가시키려고 한다. 왜냐하면 임금이나 다른 투입요소가격이 경직적이기 때문에 이윤이 더 커지기 때문이다. 다른 한편으로 장기에 기업은 가격수준에 관계없이 자본, 노동, 기술에 의해 지속가능한 최대량을 생산할 것이다. 따라서 단기 총공급곡선은 우상향하고 장기 총공급곡선은 완전고용 생산량에서 수직이다.

Any change in the quantity of factors of production such as capital, entrepreneurship, land, or labor can cause a shift in both the long-run and short-run aggregate supply curves. An increase in any of these factors can shift both the LRAS and SRAS curves to the right. A decrease in any of these factors can shift both the LRAS and SRAS curves to the left.

자본, 경영능력, 자원, 노동 같은 생산요소량의 변화는 장기 총공급곡선과 단기 총공급곡선 모두를 이동시킬 수 있다. 생산요소의 증가는 장기 총공급곡선과 단기 총공급곡선을 모두 오른쪽으로 이동시킬 수 있다. 생산요소의 감소는 장기 총공급곡선과 단기 총공급곡선을 왼쪽으로 이동시킨다.

## macroeconomic equilibrium in AD-AS model
### AD-AS모델에서 거시경제 균형

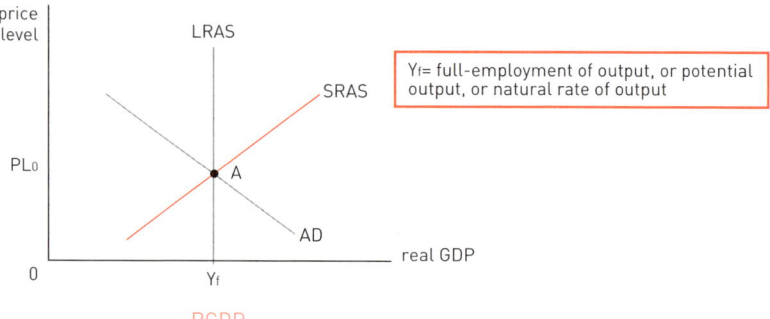

The long-run macroeconomic equilibrium occurs where short-run aggregate supply and aggregate demand meets at a point on the long-run aggregate supply curve(Point A). At the long-run equilibrium real GDP equals potential GDP at the full employment, the expected price level equals the actual price level.

장기 거시경제균형은 단기총공급과 총수요가 장기 총공급곡선에서 만나는 점 A에서 이루어진다. 이 장기균형점에서 실질 GDP는 완전고용에서 잠재 GDP와 같아지고 예상물가는 실제물가와 같아진다.

## recessionary gap and inflationary gap
### 경기침체 갭과 인플레이션 갭

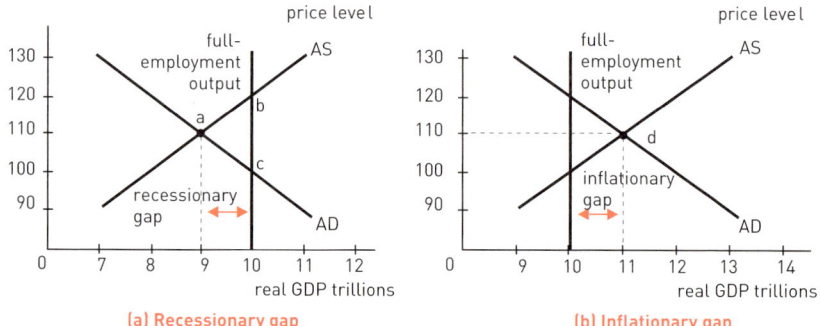

In graph A, the current equilibrium is at point a, making recessionary gap between potential GDP, $10 trillion and current real GDP, $9 trillion.

그래프 A에서 현재 균형은 점 a이고 경기침체 갭이 잠재 GDP와 실질 GDP사이에 발생한다.

In graph, B, the current equilibrium is at point d, making inflationary gap between current real GDP, $11 trillion and potential GDP, $10 trillion.

그래프 B에서는 현재 균형은 d이고 현재 실질 GDP와 잠재 GDP사이에 인플레이션 갭이 발생한다.

## long-run adjustment process
## 장기조정과정

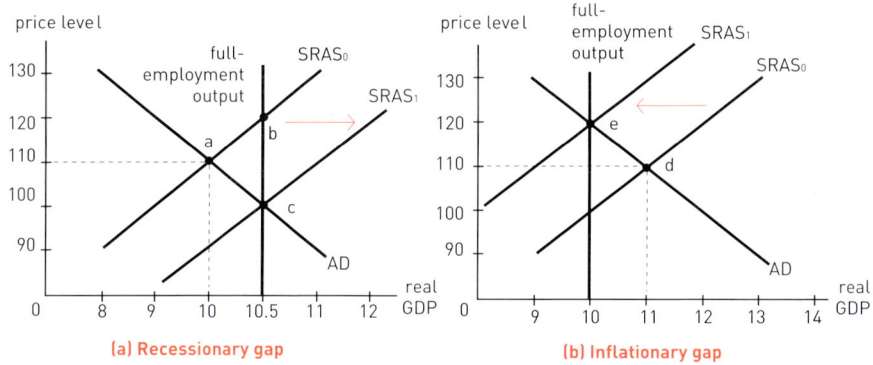

(a) Recessionary gap

(b) Inflationary gap

In graph A, the economy does not stay at point a, because in recession people expect price level to fall due to underemployment of resources. Over time SRAS shifts to the right due to fall in production cost.

그래프 A에서 경제는 a점에 머물러 있지 않는다.
경기침체 시에 경제주체들은 자원의 저고용으로 인해 물가가 떨어질 것을 예상하기 때문이다. 시간이 흐르면서 생산비용의 하락으로 단기 총공급곡선은 오른쪽으로 이동한다.

In graph B, the economy can not sustain point d, because the output at d is beyond the normal production capacity of the economy, and resources are overemployed at the output. So there are rising inflation expectation at the point d. In the long run, the SRAS shifts to the left due to rise in production cost.

그래프 B에서 경제는 d점을 지탱할 수가 없다. d점에서의 생산은 경제의 정상적인 생산능력을 초과해 있고 자원이 과도하게 사용되고 있기 때문이다. 그래서 d점에서는 인플레이션 기대가 상승한다. 장기적으로는 단기 총공급곡선이 생산비용의 상승으로 인해 왼쪽으로 이동한다.

# Problem Set A: Short Answer Question

## Write down a proper word for the definition

**1** the effect on consumption of an additional dollar of disposable income

**2** the opportunity cost of investment

**3** spending on goods and services by local, state, and federal governments

**4** redistribution of income such as unemployment benefits, business subsidy

**5** the difference between export and import

**6** when price level falls, consumption increases because real income rises

**7** when price level falls, investment increases because people demand less money, which lowers interest rate. when interest rate falls, investment rises

**8** when price level falls, net-export increases because domestic goods are cheaper than foreign ones

**9** consumption spending divided by disposable income

**10** the situation that if everyone try to save more money in recession, total spending will fall, so will total income, which in turn will decrease total savings

**1** marginal propensity to consume  **2** interest  **3** government spending  **4** transfer payments
**5** net export  **6** wealth effect (or real balance effect)  **7** Interest rate effect  **8** net-export effect
**9** average propensity to consume  **10** paradox of thrift

# Problem Set B: multiple questions

**1.** Aggregate demand in the United States _____.

A) increases if the international value of the currency rises
B) increases if government spending decrease
C) decreases if business expects profits to rises
D) increases if the consumer confidence rises

**2.** The short-run aggregate supply curve illustrates that _____.

A) the quantity of output increases as the price level rises
B) the quantity of output decreases as the price level rises
C) the price level determines aggregate demand curve
D) the quantity of output does not change as the price level changes

**3.** Recession is defined as _____.

A) a period of economic downturn in main sectors of the economy
B) a decrease in nominal GDP for at least two consecutive quarters
C) a decrease in real GDP for at least two consecutive quarters
D) an increase in unemployment from one quarter to the next

**4** The real wage definitely _____ if the nominal wage stays the same and the price level _____.

A) falls, rises
B) falls, falls
C) rises, rises
D) remains constant, rises

**5** Which of the following increases aggregate demand and shifts the AD curve to the right?

A) a tax increase
B) an decrease in government expenditures
C) an decrease in the price of exported goods and services
D) an increase in potential GDP

**6** If the United States enters a recession, _____.

A) the EU aggregate demand increases because EU imports decreases
B) the EU aggregate demand decreases because EU exports decreases
C) the quantity of output in the United States increases
D) the quantity of output in the EU increases

## 7. Which of the following is true according to the AD-AS model?

A) Equilibrium quantity of output and quantity of money available in an economy are determined at the intersection of aggregate supply curve and aggregate demand curve
B) The aggregate quantity supplied is equal to aggregate quantity demanded at equilibrium, and the equilibrium is not always at full employment output(potential GDP)
C) The aggregate quantity demanded is usually greater than the aggregate quantity supplied, thereby leading to depression
D) The long-run aggregate supply is horizontal at the natural rate of output

## 8. According to the AD-AS model, if the AD curve shifts to the left, then _____.

A) both the price level and real GDP will decrease
B) the price level will decrease but real GDP will remain constant
C) the price level will not change but real GDP will increase
D) both the price level and real GDP will increase

## 9. Stagflation is defined as a period when real GDP _____ and the price level _____.

A) increases; increases
B) increases; decreases
C) decreases; increases
D) decreases; decreases

## 10-11

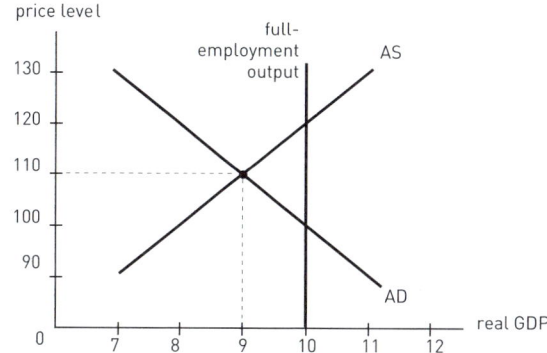

**10** The economy in the figure above is in _____.

A) inflation
B) hyperinflation
C) full-employment equilibrium.
D) recession

**11** The economy in the figure above is at an equilibrium with real GDP of $9 trillion and a price level of 110. Without any government intervention, the _____ curve shifts _____ in the long run

A) aggregate demand; to the left
B) aggregate supply; to the right
C) aggregate demand; to the right
D) aggregate supply; to the left

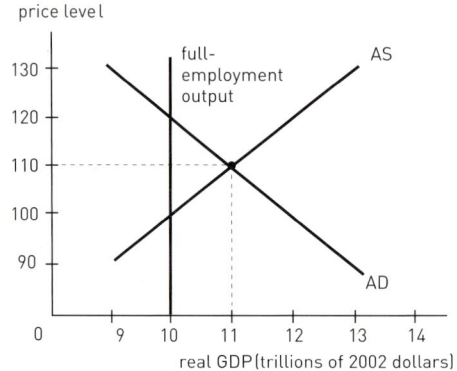

## 12
The economy in the figure above is in(at) _____.

A) inflationary gap of $1 trillion
B) deflationary gap of $1 trillion
C) a full-employment equilibrium
D) potential output

## 13
The economy in the figure above is at an equilibrium with real GDP of $11 trillion and a price level of 110. Without any government intervention, the _____ curve shifts _____ in the long run.

A) aggregate demand; to the left
B) aggregate supply; to the right
C) aggregate demand; to the right
D) aggregate supply; to the left

 Answer

1 D  2 A  3 C  4 A  5 C  6 B  7 B  8 A  9 C  10 D  11 B  12 A  13 D

# Chapter 03

# Money, Banking and Financial Market

 화폐, 은행 그리고 금융시장

경제에서 화폐의 흐름은 신체의 혈액 순환에 비유됩니다. 혈액이 잘 순환하지 않으면 동맥경화에 걸릴 수 있는 것처럼 화폐가 잘 돌지 않으면 '돈맥경화'에 걸릴 수 있습니다. 경제학 용어로는 '신용경색', '유동성 부족'으로 표현되는 이 현상은 자본주의 경제에 심각한 피해를 끼칩니다.

Chapter3에서는 자본시장financial market의 주요 개념을 간단히 살피고, 대부자금시장, 화폐시장money market에서 수요와 공급을 통해 이자율이 결정되고 통화창조의 핵심적 기관인 은행의 대차대조표, 그리고 중앙은행의 통화정책의 도구에 대해서 살펴보도록 하겠습니다.

# Lesson 1: Saving, Investment and Loanable Fund Market
## 저축, 투자와 대부자금시장

### financial market
### 금융시장

**Markets where financial assets are traded**
금융자산이 거래되는 시장

### bond
### 채권

**A certificate of debt**
채무증서

### stock
### 주식

**A financial asset that its owner has a claim to partial ownership in a firm**
소유자가 기업의 부분소유권을 주장할 수 있는 금융자산

### mutual fund
### 뮤추얼 펀드

**A financial institution that pools money from the public to purchase financial assets**
사람들에게서 돈을 모아서 금융자산을 구매하는 금융기관

Saving equals investment in market equilibrium.
시장균형에서 저축은 투자와 같아진다.

Y총소득 = C소비 + I투자 + G정부 지출(assume closed economy)
Y총소득 − C소비 − G정부지출 = I투자
(Y−C−T) 민간 저축 + (T−G) 정부 저축 = I투자
Total Saving 총저축 = Investment 투자

## loanable funds market
### 대부자금시장

**The market where the interaction of demand for loanable fund and supply of loanable determine real interest rate.**
대부자금에 대한 수요와 공급이 실질이자율을 결정하는 시장

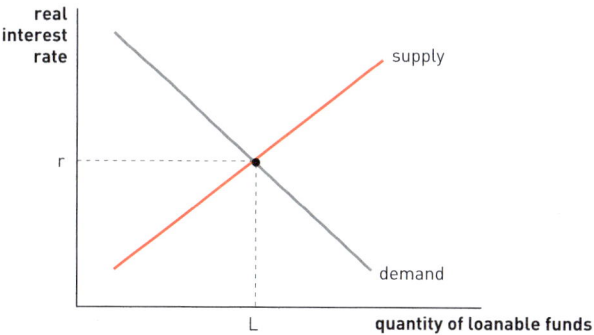

### 기본 단어 익히기

**demand for loanable fund** 대부자금의 수요
investment, consumption, government spending 투자, 소비, 정부지출
**supply of loanable fund** 대부자금의 공급
saving 저축

# Lesson 2 | Money Market
## 화폐 시장

### three functions of money
화폐의 세 가지 기능

**❶ A medium of exchange** 거래수단
An asset that people acquire for the purpose of trading rather than for their own consumption.
사람들이 소비보다는 거래의 목적으로 획득하는 자산

**❷ A store of value** 가치저장
Means of holding purchasing power over time.
시간이 지나도 구매력을 유지해주는 수단

**❷ A unit of account** 회계단위
A measure used to set prices and make economic calculations
가격을 정하고 경제적 계산을 하는데 사용되는 척도 역할

### kinds of money
화폐의 종류

**❶ Commodity money** 상품화폐
commodity which is used as money and has intrinsic value.
화폐로 사용되며 내재적 가치를 가진 상품

**❷ Fiat money, legal tender** 법정화폐
Paper and coin without intrinsic value that is used as money because the government mandates it by law
내재적 가치는 없지만 정부가 법에 위임하였기 때문에 화폐로 사용되는 지폐나 동전

**❸ A unit of account** 회계단위
A measure used to set prices and make economic calculations
가격을 정하고 경제적 계산을 하는데 사용되는 척도 역할

## central bank
### 중앙은행

**An institution that oversees and regulates the banking system and controls the monetary base**
은행시스템을 감독하고 규제하며 통화 기반을 통제하는 기관

- **federal reserve notes 연방 준비 은행권**
  Federal currency issued by the Federal Reserve in the United States that is legal tender
  법정화폐로 연방 준비 위원회(미국의 중앙은행)이 발행한 현금통화

**Tip** credit card is not money!! 신용카드는 화폐가 아니다!!

## index of money supply
### 통화량지표

- **M1:** the index of money supply that is made up of currency, demand deposit(checking account), and traveler's checks
  현금통화, 요구불예금, 여행자수표 등으로 이루어진 통화량지표

- **M2:** M1 plus saving deposits, money market mutual funds, time deposit, and etc.
  M1에 정기적립금, 뮤추얼펀드, 정기예금이 더해진 통화량지표

- **Money Supply = currency + demand deposit(M1 base)**
  통화량(M1) = 현금통화 + 요구불예금

- **Money supply is determined by the central bank.**
  통화공급은 중앙은행이 결정한다.

## money market
### 화폐시장

**The market where interest rate is determined by money demand and money supply**
화폐수요와 화폐공급에 의해 이자율이 결정되는 시장

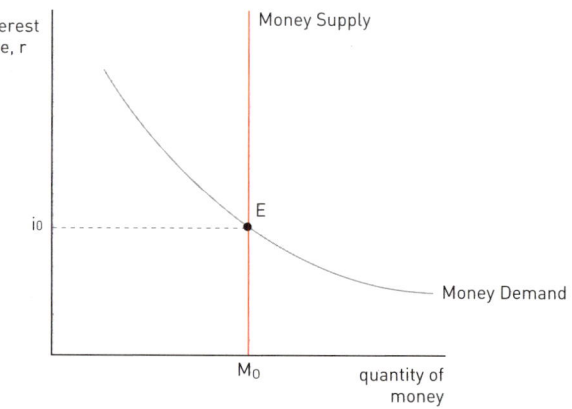

The money market assumes that people can choose between money and bond(financial assets). People choose to hold money instead of bond which offers higher returns because money is easily traded, or highly liquid.
화폐시장은 사람들이 화폐와 채권(금융상품) 사이에서 선택을 한다고 가정한다. 사람들이 더 높은 수익률을 제공하는 채권 대신 화폐를 보유하는 이유는 화폐는 쉽게 거래에 사용될 수 있기 때문이다. 즉 유동성이 높아서이다.

## theory of liquidity preference
### 유동성선호이론

**Keynes's theory that interest rate adjusts to bring the money supply and demand into equilibrium**
이자율이 화폐공급과 화폐수요를 균형으로 가져다준다는 케인스의 이론

### 기본 단어 익히기

**liquidity** 유동성
The property that the asset can be easily traded.
자산이 쉽게 거래될 수 있는 성질

## three motives to hold money
### 화폐보유의 세 가지 동기

**❶ transaction motive** 거래적 동기
needed for liquidity for daily transaction
일일거래를 위한 유동성에 대한 필요 때문

**❷ precautionary motive** 예비적 동기
To prepare for unexpected situations
예상치 못한 상황에 대비

**❸ speculative motive** 투기적 동기
To make a profit by holding money when the rate of return of holding bonds falls
채권보유의 수익률이 떨어질 때, 화폐를 소유함으로써 이익을 얻기 위해

# Lesson 3 | Tools of Monetary Policy
## 통화정책의 수단

### three tools to control money supply by the central bank
### 중앙은행의 통화량 조절 세 가지

- **reserve requirements** 법정지급 준비제도
  the control on the minimum amount of reserves that a commercial bank must hold
  일반은행이 보유해야할 최소지급준비금에 대한 통제

- **open market operation** 공개시장 조작정책
  the purchase or sale of government bonds by the central bank
  중앙은행이 정부채권을 구매하고 판매하는 행위

- **discount rate** 재할인율정책
  the interest rate at which commercial banks borrows from the Federal Reserves(central bank)
  상업은행이 중앙은행으로부터 자금을 빌릴 때 적용되는 이자율

### bank balance sheet
### 은행의 대차대조표

**Transaction 1: T-account**

| assets | | liabilities | |
|---|---|---|---|
| loans | 900,000 | deposits | $1,000,000 |
| reserves | $100,000 | | |

- **T- account**: a simplified financial record that shows the balance between a bank's assets and liabilities. On the left side of T- account above are the bank's assets of $1,000,000, and on the right side are the banks liabilities of $100. Notice that the assets and liabilities of the bank are the same. In the example, suppose that the central bank mandates 10% of reserve requirements.
  은행의 자산과 부채의 균형을 보여주는 단순화된 재정기록. 위에 있는 T-account의 왼

쪽에는 은행의 자산이 100만 달러 있고, 오른쪽에는 은행의 부채가 100만 달러 있다. 부채와 자산은 균형을 이룬다. 보기에서는 중앙은행이 10%의 법정지급준비금을 명령했다고 가정하자.

- **reserves** 지급준비금
  Deposits that banks received but have not loaned out. Reserves consists of required reserves and excess reserves
  은행이 예금으로 받았지만 대출하지 않은 액수. 지급준비금은 법정지급준비금과 초과지급준비금으로 구성

- **required reserves** 법정지급준비금
  The minimum amount of deposits that bank should hold as reserves by the mandates of the central bank
  중앙은행의 명령으로 지급준비금으로 보유해야 할 최소한의 예금

- **reserve requirements(required reserve ratio)** 법정지급준비율
  The minimum ratio of reserves that banks must hold in proportion to checkable deposits
  요구불예금에 비례하여 은행이 보유하고 있어야 하는 최소한의 지급준비율

- **excess reserves** 초과지급준비금
  Reserves held by bank more than the amout(required by the central bank)
  중앙은행이 요구한 이상으로 보유하고 있는 지급준비금

- **fractional reserve banking system** 부분지급준비금제도
  A banking system that requires banks to hold a fraction of deposits as reserves
  은행이 예금의 일정 부분을 준비금으로 보유하도록 요구하는 은행 시스템

**Transaction 2: change in bank account due to deposit**

| assets | | liabilities | |
|---|---|---|---|
| loans | | deposits | + $1,000 |
| reserves | + $1,000 | | |

- **When deposit increased by $1000, reserves increased by the same amount.**
  예금이 1000달러가 증가하자 부채항목의 예금과 자산항목의 지급준비금이 1000달러만큼 똑같이 증가했다.

## Transaction 3: change in bank account due to new loans

| assets | | liabilities |
|---|---|---|
| loans | + $900 | No change |
| reserves | - $900 | |

- **Bank loaned $900 to the public.**
  
  대출이 900달러만큼 이루어졌다.

## Transaction 4: Money Creation 통화창조

| Bank | (1) Acquired Reserves and Deposits | (2) Required Reserves(Reserve Ratio=0.1) | (3) Excess Reserves (1)−(2) | (4) Amount bank can lend(new money created) |
|---|---|---|---|---|
| Bank A | $100.00 | $10.00 | $90.00 | $90.00 |
| Bank B | 90.00 | 9.00 | 81.00 | 81.00 |
| Bank C | 81.00 | 8.00 | 72.90 | 72.90 |
| Bank D | 72.90 | 7.29 | 65.61 | 65.61 |
| ⋮ | ⋮ | ⋮ | ⋮ | ⋮ |
| Total | | | | 900 |

- Suppose that people do not hold money, and banks do not hold excess reserves. Reserve required ratio is 10%. Bank A receives $100 deposit. Bank A reserves the exact amount of required reserves, $10 and loans out excess reserves, $90. People who borrow $90 spend the borrowed money, and people who earn all the money loaned deposited $90 at Bank B. In this way, the money is created through the banking system. The amount of money created by this process is $\frac{1}{R}$ multiplied by initial excess reserves.

사람들이 화폐를 보유하지 않으며 은행은 초과지급준비금을 갖지 않는다고 가정하자. 법정지급준비금은 10%이다. 은행 A에 100달러가 예금되었다. 은행 A는 정확하게 법정지급준비금 액수인 10달러만을 준비하고, 나머지 초과지급준비금인 90달러는 대출한다. 90달러를 빌린 사람들은 그 돈을 다 쓰고 그 돈을 번 사람들은 은행 B에 90달러를 예금한다. 이런 식으로 은행시스템을 통해 통화가 창조된다. 이 과정에서 창조되는 통화의 크기는 '$\frac{1}{R}$×최초 초과지급준비금' 이다.

## open market operation
공개시장조작

**The purchase and sale of government securities by central banks.**
중앙은행이 정부 채권을 사고파는 것

### Transaction 5: Open Market Purchase of $ 100 million securities
공개시장조작으로 1억달러 채권(treasury bill: 미국 재무부채권) 구매

| Federal Reserve | assets | | liabilities | |
|---|---|---|---|---|
| | Treasury bills | + $100 million | Monetary base | + $100 million |

| commercial banks | assets | | liabilities |
|---|---|---|---|
| | Treasury bills | - $100 million | |
| | Reserves | + $100 million | |

- When the central bank purchases $100 million government securities, the central bank's assets and liabilities increases by $100 million. Commercial banks government securities decreases by $100 million, and reserves increases $100 million, so there is no change in assets of commercial banks.

  중앙은행이 재무부채권을 1억 달러를 사자 중앙은행의 자산과 부채가 1억 달러만큼 증가하고 시중은행은 자산항목에서 채권이 1억 달러 감소되고, 지급준비금이 1억 달러만큼 증가하여 결국 시중은행의 자산항목에 변화는 없다.

- **federal funds rate**

  The interest rate on short-term loans between commercial banks
  시중은행 사이에 단기 자금에 대한 이자율

## Transaction 6: Open Market Sale of $100 million Securities

| | assets | | liabilities | |
|---|---|---|---|---|
| Federal Reserve | Treasury bills | - $100 million | Monetary base | - $100 million |

| | assets | | liabilities |
|---|---|---|---|
| Commercial banks | Treasury bills | + $100 million | |
| | Reserves | - $100 million | |

- 중앙은행이 재무부채권을 1억 달러를 팔자 중앙은행의 자산과 부채가 1억 달러만큼 감소하고 시중은행은 자산항목에서 채권이 1억 달러가 증가되고, 지급준비금이 1억 달러만큼 감소한다.

## discount rate policy
### 재할인율정책

**Controlling the interest that the central banks charges to commercial banks for the loans it lends to them**

중앙은행이 시중은행에 빌려준 자금에 부과되는 이자율

**Bank balance sheet that shows the recent changes in released exam**
은행대차대조표 관련 최근 출제 경향 변화

| assets | | liabilities | |
|---|---|---|---|
| Required reserves | $2,000 | Demand deposits | $10,000 |
| Excess reserves | $0 | Qwner's equity | $10,000 |
| Customer loans | $8,000 | | |
| Government securities(bonds) | $7,000 | | |
| Building and fixtures | $3,000 | | |

It seems complicated, but notice that the recent exams often ask questions about change in assets brought by buying and selling government purchases.
최근 시험은 자산항목에서 정부채권을 사고팔아서 발생하는 변화에 대해 종종 질문하고 있다.

| assets | | liabilities | |
|---|---|---|---|
| Cash(reserves) | $2,000,000 | Transaction deposits (Checking deposits) | $5,000,000 |
| Loans | 6,100,000 | | |
| Bonds(U.S. govt. and municipal) | 1,500,000 | Savings and time deposits | 4,000,000 |
| Bank building, Equipment, fixtures | 400,000 | Total Liabilities | 9,000,000 |
| | | Capital | 1,000,000 |
| Total Assets | $10,000,000 | Total Liabilities and Capital | $10,000,000 |

# Problem Set A: Short Answer Question

Write down a proper word for the definition

**1** the markets where financial assets are traded

**2** a certificate of debt

**3** the market where the interaction of demand for loanable fund and supply of loanable determine real interest rate

**4** commodity which is used as money and has intrinsic value

**5** paper and coin without intrinsic value that is used as money because the government mandates it by law

**6** an institution that oversees and regulates the banking system and controls the monetary base

**7** the market where interest rate is determined by money demand and money supply

**8** Keynes's theory that interest rate adjusts to bring the money supply and demand into equilibrium

**9** the minimum amount of deposits that bank should hold as reserves by the mandates of the central bank

**10** reserves held by bank above that required by the central bank

**11** the purchase and sale of the government securities by the central banks

## Define these words

**12** federal funds rate

**13** discount rate

**14** three functions of money

**15** one motive to hold money

1 financial market
2 bond
3 loanable funds market
4 commodity money
5 fiat money, legal tender
6 central bank
7 money market
8 theory of liquidity preference
9 required reserves
10 excess reserves
11 open market operation

12 the interest rate on short-term loans between commercial banks, overnight interest rate
13 the interest that the central banks charges commercial banks for the loans it lends to them
14 medium of exchange, store of value, unit of account
15 transaction motive, precautionary motive, speculative motive(asset motive)

## Problem Set B: multiple questions

**1.** Choose the functions of money.

I. medium of exchange
II. unit of account
III. medium of barter system
IV. store of value

A) I only
B) I, II, only
C) I, II, III, only
D) I, II, IV, only

**2.** An institution that oversees and regulates the banking system and controls the monetary base is called _____.

A) government
B) commercial bank
C) mutual fund
D) central bank

**3.** The monetary policy tools the central bank uses are controlling _____.

A) open market operations, taxation, and government spending
B) subprime rate and discount rate and federal fund rate
C) discount rate, open market operations, and the reserve requirements
D) federal find rate, prime rate, and tax rates

**4** The reserve requirement is 10 percent and Mischell withdrew $100 from her checking account. What happened to the balance sheet of bank?

A) required reserves increases by $10
B) excess reserves increases by $90
C) required reserves decreases by $10
D) There was no change in balance sheet of bank

**5** When the central bank decreases the required reserve ration, the quantity of money will generally _____.

A) decrease
B) increase
C) not be changed
D) be uncertain

**6** The interest rate on the short-term loans the central bank lend to commercial banks _____.

A) federal fund rate
B) reserve ratio
C) discount rate
D) prime rate

**7** When the central bank decreases the discount rate, the quantity of money in the economy will _____.

A) increase
B) decrease
C) no be changed
D) be uncertain

**8** The purchase and sale of government bond(securities) is _____.

A) fractional banking
B) discount rate policy
C) prime rate policy
D) open market operation

**9** When the central bank increases the required reserve ratio, the money supply will generally _____.

A) not be changed
B) be uncertain
C) decrease
D) increase

**10** Currency issued by the Federal Reserve in the United States that is legal tender are _____.

A) federal reserve checks
B) bond
C) federal reserve notes
D) treasury bills

**11** The financial statement that summarized bank's assets and liablities is _____ _____.

A) bank report
B) financial report
C) bank balance sheet
D) equilibrium report

**12** Paul deposits $100 into his checking account at JP Bank, a commercial bank. The immediate effect of his deposit is _____.

A) an increase in bank liabilities by $100 and no change in bank assets
B) an increase in bank assets and liabilities by $100
C) a decrease in bank liabilities by $100 and no change in bank assets
D) an increase in bank assets by $100 and a decrease in bank liabilities by $100

**13** JC Bank, a commercial bank sells $1,000,000 worth of government securities. This sale of government securities _____.

A) increases the assets and liabilities by $1,000,000
B) decreases the assets and liabilities by $1,000,000
C) decreases the liabilities by $1,000,000 and increases the assets by $1,000,000
D) does not change the total value of the assets

**14** When Harold deposits $100 in currency in his checkable account at JC Bank, the immediate effect on the money supply is that _____.

A) money supply increases by $100
B) money supply decreases by $100
C) money supply depends on the amount of excess reserves JC Bank holds
D) money supply does not change because money supply is the sum of currency and demand deposit

**15** Lucy deposits $500 cash in her checkable account at the City Bank. If the required reserve ratio is 10 percent, City Bank's _____.

A) assets increase but its liabilities decrease
B) assets do not change but its liabilities increase
C) required reserves increase by $50 and its excess reserves increase by $450
D) required reserves increase by $500

**16** Penny Bank's required reserves increase by $6,000 when Robert deposits $30,000 cash in his checkable account at the Penny Bank and the required reserve ratio is _____.

A) 5 percent
B) 10 percent
C) 15 percent
D) 20 percent

**17** Mary deposits $500 in her bank. The required reserve ratio is 20 percent. What is the maximum change in money supply that the entire banking system can create _____.

A) $1,200
B) $1,500
C) $1,800
D) $2,000

**18** The opportunity cost of holding money _____.

A) increases as the nominal interest rate decreases
B) decreases as the nominal interest rate increases
C) increases as the nominal interest rate increases
D) has nothing to do with interest rates

**19** When the price level decreases, the demand for money _____.

A) shifts to the right
B) shifts to the left
C) does not change
D) has nothing to do with price level

**20** When real GDP(income) deceases, the demand for money _____.

A) shifts to the right
B) shifts to the left
C) does not change
D) has nothing to do with real GDP

**21** When the quantity of money demanded exceeds the quantity of money supplied in the money market, the interest rate will _____ and the prices of assets will _____.

A) rise; increase
B) rise; decrease
C) fall; increase
D) fall; decrease

## 22

The central bank purchases $1,000,000 government securities in open market operations. The required reserve ratio is 20 percent. What is the maximum increase in money supply that the entire banking system can create _____.

A) $2,000,000
B) $3,000,000
C) $4,000,000
D) $5,000,000

1 D  2 D  3 C  4 C  5 B  6 C  7 A  8 D  9 C  10 C
11 C  12 B  13 D  14 D  15 C  16 D  17 D  18 C  19 B  20 B  21 B  22 D

# Chapter 04

# Economic Stabilization Policy and Economic Growth

 경제안정화정책과 경제성장

Chapter4에서는 거시경제의 꽃이라고 할 수 있는 경제안정화 정책, 필립스곡선, 경제성장에 대해 공부하도록 합시다. 경제정책에 관심이 많은 거시경제학도들은 경제를 어떻게 안정적으로 운용할 수 있을까에 대해서 고민을 많이 합니다. 경제정책은 크게 통화정책 monetary policy와 재정정책 fiscal policy로 이루어져 있으며, 각각의 정책은 장단점을 가지고 있지요. 또한 함께 학습할 필립스 곡선은 실업률과 인플레이션율의 장단기 관계를 보여주는 곡선으로 경제정책의 효과를 나타나며 총수요-총공급 모형의 다른 면이라고 생각하면 됩니다. 끝으로 거시경제정책의 장기적인 목표인 경제성장에 대해서 그 정의와 요인에 대해 알아보도록 합시다.

# Lesson 1 | Economic Stabilization Policy
## 경제안정화정책

## economic stabilization policy
### 경제안정화정책

**Government policy to promote full employment and price stabilization by implementing countercyclical measures.**
경기완전고용과 물가안정을 촉진하는 정부정책

## monetary policy
### 통화정책

**The control on money supply by the central bank to influence the economy**
경제에 영향을 주기 위해 중앙은행이 통화량을 조절하는 정책

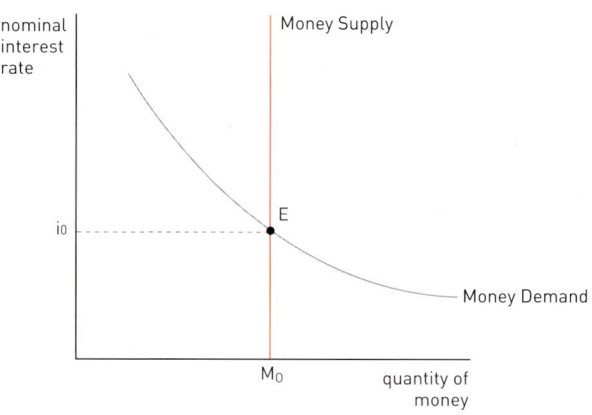

- **liquidity preference** 유동성 선호
- **liquidity** 유동성
  The property that the asset can be easily traded
  자산이 거래되기에 쉬운 정도

- **liquidity trap** 유동성 함정

A situation in which monetary policy cannot stimulate an economy because people are extremely reluctant to trade liquid assets

사람들이 극단적으로 유동성 있는 자산을 거래하지 않으려고 해서 통화정책으로 경제를 부양시키지 못하는 상황

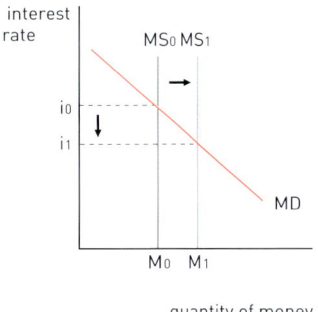

Expansionary(easy) monetary policy

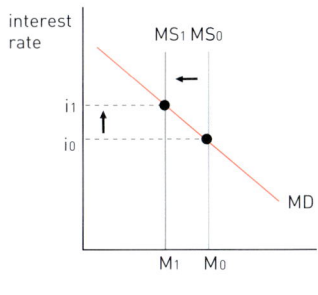

Contractionary(tight) monetary policy

## expansionary monetary policy
### 확장적 통화정책(이자율인하정책)

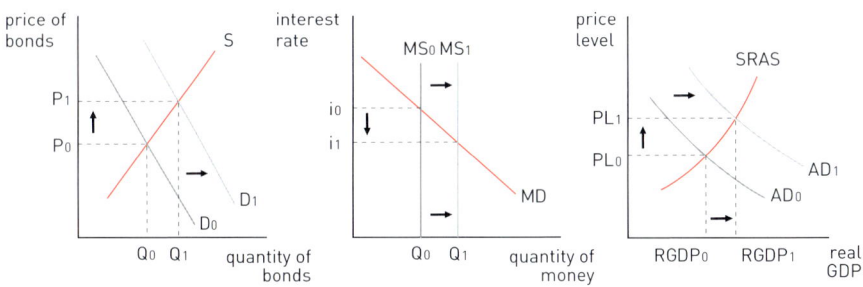

Suppose that the central bank increases money supply by purchasing government securities. When the central bank buys government securities, demand for the government securities increases. Therefore, the price of bond(securities) increases, and the interest rate that is return rate of bond falls, because bond price and interest rate are inversely related. When interest rate falls, investment increases because the opportunity cost of investment that is interest rate, falls. When investment increases, aggregate demand increases because investment is a component of aggregate demand. When aggregate demand increases, the real GDP and the price level rises.

중앙은행이 정부채권을 구매해서 통화량을 증가시킨다고 가정하자. 중앙은행이 정부채권을 살 때 정부채권에 대한 수요가 증가한다. 따라서 채권의 가격이 증가하고 채권가격과 채권의 수익률이라고 할 수 있는 이자율은 역관계이기 때문에 이자율은 떨어진다. 이자율이 떨어지면 투자는 증가하는데, 투자의 기회비용이 떨어지기 때문이다. 투자가 증가하면 투자는 총수요의 구성요소이므로 인해 총수요가 증가한다. 총수요가 증가하면 실질 GDP와 물가가 상승한다.

## contractionary monetary policy
긴축통화정책(이자율인상정책)

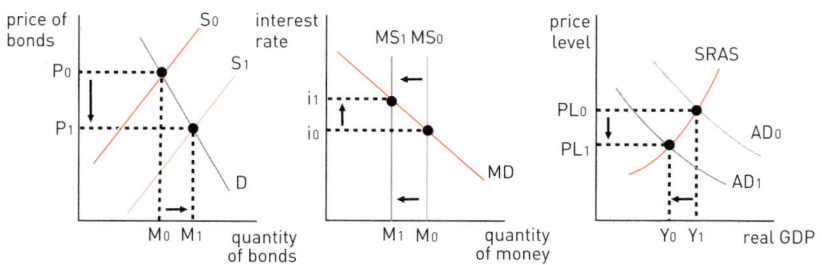

Suppose that the central bank decreases money supply by selling government securities. When the central bank sells government securities, the supply of the government securities increase. Therefore, the price of bond(securities) decreases, and the interest rate that is return rate of bond, rises, because bond price and interest rate are inversely related. When interest rate rises, investment falls because the opportunity cost of investment that is interest rate, falls. When investment decreases, aggregate demand decreases because investment is a component of aggregate demand. When aggregate demand decreases, the real GDP and the price level falls.

중앙은행이 정부채권을 판매하여 통화량을 감소시킨다고 가정하자. 중앙은행이 정부채권을 팔 때 정부채권의 공급이 증가한다. 따라서 채권의 가격이 하락하고 채권가격과 채권의 수익률이라고 할 수 있는 이자율은 역관계이기 때문에 이자율은 상승한다. 이자율이 상승하면 투자는 감소하는데, 투자의 기회비용이 증가하기 때문이다. 투자가 감소하면 투자는 총수요의 구성요소이므로 인해 총수요가 감소한다. 총수요가 감소하면 실질 GDP와 물가가 하락한다.

## three conditions for monetary policy to be most effective
통화정책이 가장 효과적이기 위한 세 가지 조건

### Money demand is not sensitive to a change in interest rate
통화수요가 이자율에 민감하지 않아야하고

**Investment demand is sensitive to a change in interest rate**
투자가 이자율에 민감해야 하고
**Marginal propensity to consume is great.**
한계소비성향이 커야 한다.

통화 정책이 효과적일 조건은 'MLS IS BIG'으로 기억할 것

MLS: **M**oney demand is **L**ess **Se**nsitive to a change in interest rate
화폐수요는 이자율변화에 덜 민감하고

IS: **In**vestment is **S**ensitive to a change in interest rate
투자는 이자율에 민감하고

BIG: MPC is **Big**
한계소비성향은 크다.

## rational expectation hypothesis
합리적기대가설

**The theory according to which people forecast the future using all the optimal information available to them.**
사람들이 결정을 내릴 때 입수가능한 최선의 정보로 미래를 예측한다는 이론

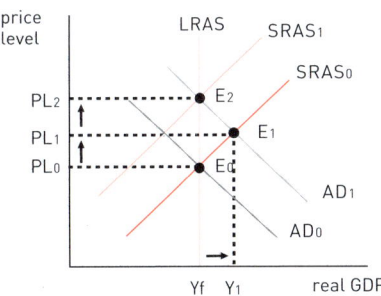

Let's think about the effects of government policy using AD-AS model. Suppose that the economy is in long-run equilibrium at E0. Keynesians argue that expansionary policy moves the economy from E0 to E1, increasing output from RGDf to RGDP1. But over time the economy can not sustain RGDP1, because the output at E1 is beyond the normal production capacity of the economy, and resources are overemployed at the output. So there are inflation expectation at the point E1. In the long run, the SRAS shifts to the left due to rise in production cost. This means that the government policy is effective in the short run, not long run. However, the rational expectation theorists. argue that government policy has no effect even in the short-run, because people behave based on the optimal information available to them. Rational expectationists argue that when the government announces the expansive policy, people thinks that the price level will increase eventually. So, people negotiates wage increase at E0, not E1. When the government implements the policy, aggregate demand curve shifts to the right, and the short-run aggregate supply curve shift to the left. So the economy moves from E0 to E2, not from E0 to E1. They argue that government policy is ineffective even in the short run.

AD-AS모형을 사용하여 정부정책의 효과에 대해서 생각해보자. 경제가 E0에 장기균형 상태에 있다고 가정을 하자. 케인즈학파는 확장 정책이 경제를 E0에서 E1으로 이동시며 생산은 RGDPf에서 RGDP1으로 이동한다고 주장한다. 하지만 시간이 지나면서 경제는 RGDP1을 지탱할 수가 없게 된다. 왜냐하면 E1에서의 생산은 그 경제의 정상적인 생산능력을 초과해서 자원이 과도하게 사용되고 있기 때문이다. E1에서는 인플레이션 상승기대가 존재하게 된다. 장기적으로 생산비용의 상승으로 단기총공급곡선이 왼쪽으로 이동한다. 이것은 정부 정책이 장기에는 효과가 없고 단기에 효과가 있다는 것을 의미한다. 하지만 합리적기대이론가들은 정부정책은 단기에서조차 효과가 없다고 주장한다. 왜냐하면 사람들은 그들에게 이용 가능한 최적의 정보에 기초해서 행동하기 때문이라는 것이다. 합리적기대론자들은 정부가 확장정책을 발표할 때, 사람들은 물가가 결국은 상승하게 될 것이라고 생각한다고 주장한다. 그래서 사람들은 E1에서가 아니라 E0에서 임금인상 협상을 한다. 정부가 정책을 시행하면 총수요곡선은 오른쪽으로 이동하고, 단기 총공급곡선도 왼쪽으로 이동을 한다. 그래서 경제는 E0에서 E1이 아니라 E0에서 E2로 이동한다는 것이다. 정부정책은 단기에서도 효과가 없다고 그들은 주장한다.

## fiscal policy
### 재정정책

**Government's action on its spending and tax collection**
지출과 세금징수에 대한 정부 활동

## multiplier effect
### 승수효과

**An increase in a component of aggregate demand creates a larger increase in nation's income. For instance, an increase in government spending by $1million can create $5 million increase in national income.**
총수요의 어느 구성요소 증가가 국민소득에 더 큰 변화를 만드는 것. 예를 들면, 정부지출이 백만 달러 증가할 때 국민소득이 오백만 달러 증가할 수도 있다.

## three multipliers
### 세 가지 승수

❶ **Spending multiplier** 지출승수
1/1-mpc, the amount by which real GDP change when spending changes by $1
지출이 1달러 변할 때 실질 GDP가 변하는 정도

❷ **Tax multiplier** 조세승수
mpc/1-mpc, the amount by which real GDP change when tax changes by $1
세금이 1달러 증가할 때 실질 GDP의 증가크기

❸ **Balanced budget multiplier** 균형재정승수
1, the amount by which real GDP change when government spending and tax increases by $1
정부지출과 세금이 똑같은 1달러 변할 때 실질 GDP가 변화하는 정도

 **crowding-out effect 구축효과**

The phenomenon that when government increases its spending, private investment decreases due to a rise in interest rate incurred by the government borrowing
정부가 지출을 증가시킬 때 정부차입으로 인한 이자율 상승으로 민간투자가 감소하는 현상

## AD-AS and crowding-out effect
### AD-AS와 구축효과

- **Horizontal segment: Keynes area: no crowding out**
  수평 부분: 케인즈 영역: 구축효과 없음
- **Upward-sloping segment: intermediate area: partially crowding out**
  우상향 부분: 중간 부분: 부분적으로 구축효과
- **Vertical segment: Classical area-completely crowded-out**
  수직부분: 고전학파영역, 완전구축효과

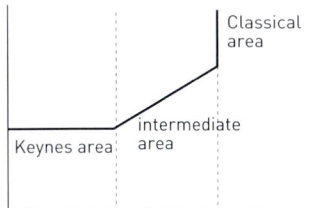

## automatic stabilizer
자동안정화장치

**Built-in mechanism that stabilizes the economy countercyclically without policy makers' extra deliberate action, such as unemployment benefits in recession, progressive tax system in overheated economy.**

정책결정자가 추가적으로 의도적인 행동을 취하지 않고서도 경제를 안절화시키는 내장 커니즘. 과열 경제 시에 실업급여나 경제 과열시의 누진세 제도

### Fiscal Policy and Monetary Policy

|  | Expansionary (easy) policy | Contractionary (tight, restrictive) policy | Tools |
|---|---|---|---|
| Fiscal policy | G increase tax decreae | G decrease tax decrease | government spending, transfer payments(unempolyment benefits  tax |
| Monetary policy | increase money supply | decrease money supply | open market operation, discount rate, reserve requirement |
| Time to implement | recesson, economic downturn, contraction in business cycle | overheated economy |  |

## Basic argument, preferred policy, opinion on time lag according to economic schools

|  | Basic argument | Peferred government policy | Opinion about time lag in government policy (Keynesian vs. Monetarist) |
|---|---|---|---|
| Classical | supply creates it own demand | no | |
| Monetarist | money growth leads only to inflation(monetary neutrality) | k%-rule monetary policy, no fiscal policy | monetary policy has short implementation lag |
| Rational Expectation | government policy ineffectiveness | no | |
| Supply Siders | tax cut | tax cut | |
| Keynesian | demand creates its own supply | discretionary fiscal and monetary policy, fiscal policy preferred | fiscal policy is more powerful. |

# Lesson 2
# Philips Curve
## 필립스 곡선

## Philips curve
### 필립스 곡선

**The curve that shows the relationship between inflation rate and unemployment**
인플레이션율과 실업률의 관계를 보여주는 곡선

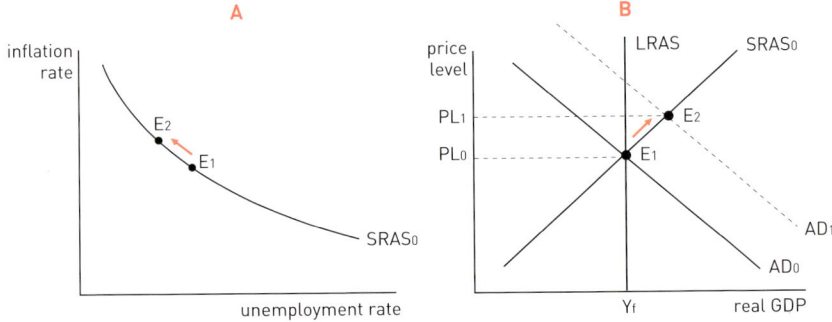

- The Philips curve can be derived from the shift in the aggregate demand. Suppose that the economy is at E1 in graph A. When government implements expansionary fiscal policy, aggregate demand shifts to the right, moving economy from E1 to E2. If this change in economy is observed in terms of unemployment rate and inflation rate, the inflation increases because of the excess demand and unemployment decreases because output rises. The economy moves from E1 to E2 in the graph B. The line connecting E1 to E2 in the graph B is the short-run philips curve. The short-run philips curve(SRPC) is downward sloping, which means the trade-off between inflation and unemployment in the short run.

필립스 곡선은 총수요곡선이 이동할 때 도출된다. 그래프 A에서 경제가 E1에 있다고 가정하자. 정부가 확장적 재정정책을 실행할 때 총수요곡선은 단기 총공급곡선을 따라 오른쪽으로 이동하며 경제는 E1에서 E2로 변화한다. 이 경제적 변화를 실업률과 인플레이션율을 기준으로 관찰한다면 초과수요로 인해 인플레이션은 증가하고, 생산증가로 실업률은 감소한다. 그래프 B에서 경제는 E1에서 E2로 이동한다. 이 E1과 E2를 잇는 선이 바로 단기 필립스 곡선이다. 단기 필립스 곡선은 우하향한다. 이는 인플레이션율과 실업률이 단기에는 상충관계에 있다는 것을 의미한다.

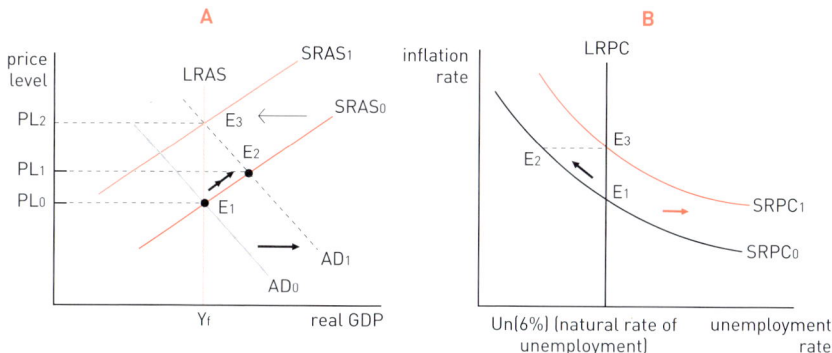

- Over time the economy moves from E2 to E3 in graph A because SRAS shifts to the left due to increase in production cost. When short-run aggregate supply curve shifts to the left, both inflation and unemployment rise. Therefore short-run philips curve shifts upward due to increase in inflation expectation in the graph B. In the long-run, there is no change in unemployment, but inflations rate rises. The line connecting E1 to E3 in the graph B is the long-run philips curve. The long-run philips curve is vertical at natural rate of unemployment(6% in the graph B), which means that there is no trade-off between inflation and unemployment in the long run. As we see above, the philips curve and the AD-AS model is the both side of a coin of AD-AS model. LRPC is the other expression of LRAS. Shifts in AD means movement along the SRPC, and shifts in SRAS means shifts in the SRPC.

시간이 지나면 경제는 그래프 A에서 E2에서 E3으로 이동한다. 단기 총공급곡선이 생산비용증가로 인해 왼쪽으로 이동하기 때문이다. 단기 총공급곡선이 왼쪽으로 이동할 때 인플레이션과 실업 모두 증가한다. 그래프 B에서 단기 필립스 곡선은 인플레이션 기대의 증가로 인해 오른쪽으로 이동한다. 장기에 실업률의 변화는 없고 인플레이션율만 증가했다. 그래프 B에서 E1과 E3를 잇는 선이 바로 장기 필립스 곡선이다. 장기 필립스 곡선은 자연실업률(그래프 B의 경우는 6%)에서 수직이다. 이는 장기에는 인플레이션과 실업 사이에 상충관계가 없다는 의미이다. 위에서 보듯이 필립스 곡선과 총수요-총공급 모형은 동전의 양면과 같다. 장기 필립스 곡선은 장기 총공급곡선의 다른 표현이다. 총수요곡선의 이동은 단기 필립스 곡선 상의 운동movements이고 총공급곡선의 이동은 단기 필립스 곡선의 이동이다.

## natural rate hypothesis
### 자연실업률가설

**The hypothesis argued by Milton Friedman that there is no trade-off between inflation and unemployment in the long run and the long-run philips curve is vertical at the natural rate of unemployment**

밀턴 프리드먼의 주장으로 인플레이션과 실업 사이에는 장기에 아무런 상충관계가 없으며, 필립스 곡선은 장기에 자연실업률에서 수직이라는 가설

# Okun's law
## 오쿤의 법칙

**The proposition that the difference between the unemployment rate and the natural unemployment rate determines the gap between potential GDP and real GDP. Put simply, as unemployment rises, output falls.**

현재실업률과 자연실업률의 차이가 잠재 GDP와 현재 실질 GDP를 결정한다는 주장. 간단하게 말하면 실업률이 상승하면 생산이 줄어든다는 법칙이다.

### AD-AS vs. Philips curve

❶ AD shift = movement along the SRPC

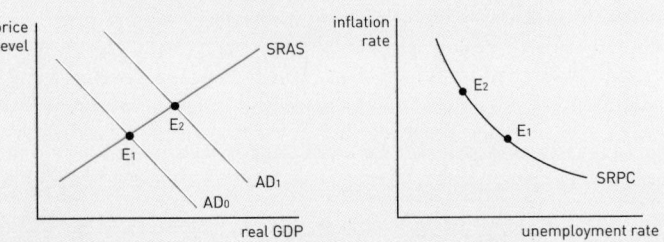

When AD shift right, the economy in the SRPC moves along from E1 to E2.
AD가 오른쪽으로 이동할 때, 경제는 E1에서 E2로 단기 필립스 곡선을 따라 운동한다.

❷ AS shift = shift in the SRPC

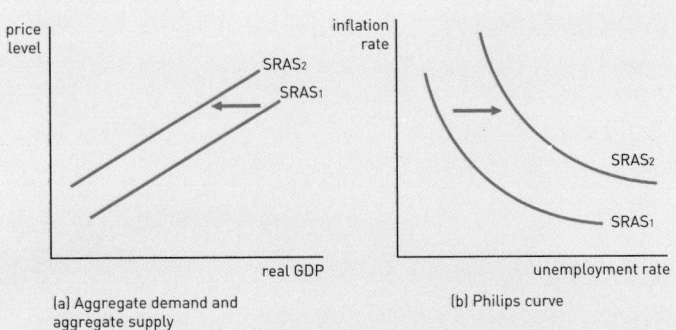

(a) Aggregate demand and aggregate supply  (b) Philips curve

When SRAS shifts to the left, SRPC shifts to the right due to increase in inflationary expectation.

단기 총공급곡선이 왼쪽으로 이동할 때, 단기 필립스 곡선은 예상 인플레이션의 증가로 인해 오른쪽으로 이동한다.

❸ LRAS ≡ LRPC

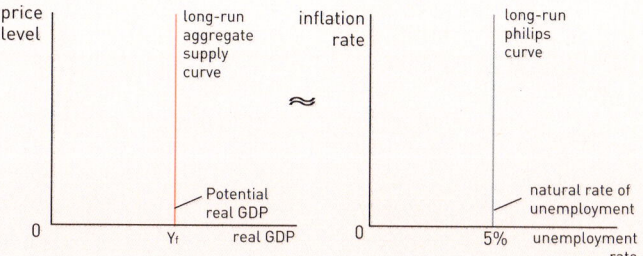

LRAS is vertical at the full employment output or potential output, and LRPC is vertical at the natural rate of output.
장기 총공급곡선은 완전고용생산 또는 잠재생산량에서 수직이다. 장기 필립스 곡선은 자연실업률에서 수직이다.

# Lesson 3 | Economic Growth
## 경제성장

### economic growth
### 경제성장

**The rise in real GDP, or the rise in real GDP per person. Standard of living or the level of well-being is measured by real GDP per person, not by real GDP.**

실질 GDP의 증가, 또는 1인당 실질 GDP의 증가. 생활수준이나 복지수준은 실질 GDP가 아니라 1인당 실질 GDP로 측정한다.

### Show the economic growth using Production Possibilities Curve(PPC) or Long-Run Aggregate Supply Curve(LRAS)

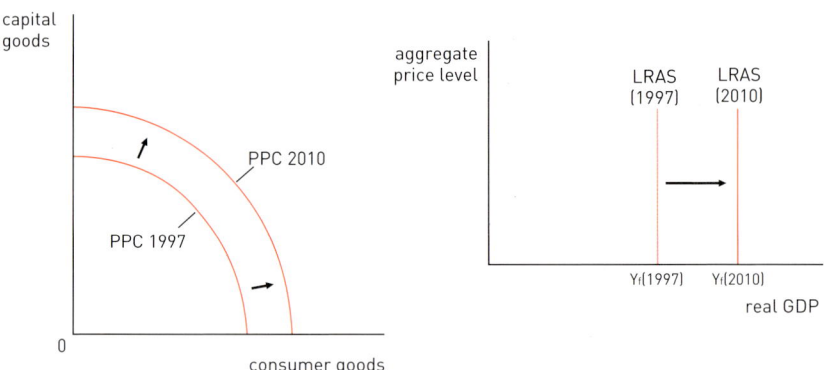

**Outward shift of the PPC**

**Rightward shift of LRAS**

Economic growth can be displayed on the production possibilities curve(PPC) and by the long-run aggregate supply curve(LRAS). The outward shift of PPC and the rightward shift of LRAS represent rise in real GDP, which means economic growth.

경제 성장은 생산가능곡선과 장기 총공급곡선에 의해 표현될 수 있다. 생산가능곡선의 외부이동, 장기 총공급곡선의 오른쪽 이동은 실질 GDP의 증가를 표현하며 이는 경제성장을 뜻하게 된다.

- **Rule of 70**

    the rule that let us know the time it takes for a variable to double is roughly 70 divided by the variable's changing rate. For instance, if a country's economic annual growth rate is 7%, the country's real GDP will double in ten years.

70의 법칙
어떤 변수가 그 값이 2배가 되는데 걸리는 시간을 알려주는 공식으로 70을 변수의 변화율로 나눈 값이다. 예를 들어 어느 나라의 연평균 경제성장률이 7%라고 하면 이 나라의 실질 GDP는 10년이 지나면 2배가 된다.

$$\text{Number of years for variable to double} = \frac{70}{\text{Annual growth rate of variable}}$$

- t년도의 경제성장률 = $\frac{RGDP_{t-1} - RGDP_{t-1}}{RGDP_{t-1}} \times 100$

## factors of economic growth
### 경제성장의 요인

❶ **Quantity of labor** 노동의 양(L)
❷ **Quantity of physical capital** 실물자본의 양(K)
❸ **Quantity of human capital** 인적자본의 양(H)
❹ **Quantity of natural resources** 천연자원의 양(N)
❺ **Technological advance** 기술의 발전(A)

## government policies that encourage economic growth
### 경제성장을 촉진하는 정부정책

❶ **Saving, investment, capital stock, and economic growth**
저축, 투자, 자본스톡, 경제성장
❷ **Education and human capital and economic growth**
교육, 인적자본, 경제성장
❸ **Research and development and economic growth**
연구개발과 경제성장
❹ **Protection of property rights and economic growth**
재산권보호와 경제성장
❺ **Free trade and economic growth**
자유무역과 경제성장

# Problem Set A: Short Answer Question

Write down a proper word for the definition

**1** the phenomenon that when government increases its spending, private investment decreases due to a rise in interest rate incurred by the government borrowing

**2** government policy to promote full employment and price stabilization by implementing countercyclical measures

**3** the rule that let us know the time it takes a variable to double is roughly 70 divided by the variable's average growth rate

**4** the amount by which real GDP change when government spending and tax increases by $1

**5** built-in mechanism that stabilize economy countercyclically without policy makers' extra deliberate action, such as unemployment benefits in recession, progressive tax system in overheated economy

**6** the curve that shows the relationship between inflation rate and unemployment

**7** the control on money supply to influence the economy by the central bank

**8** the property that the asset can be easily traded

**9** 1/1-mpc, the amount by which real GDP change when spending changes by $1

**10** a situation where monetary policy cannot stimulate an economy because people are extremely reluctant to trade liquid assets

**11** the theory according to which people forecast the future using all the optimal information available to them

**12** government's action on its spending and tax collection

**13** a increase in a component of aggregate demand creates a larger increase in nation's income

**14** -mpc/1-mpc, the amount by which real GDP change when tax changes by $1

**15** the hypothesis argued by Milton Friedman that there is no trade-off between inflation and unemployment in the long run and the long-run philips curve is vertical at the natural rate of unemployment

**16** the proposition that the difference between the unemployment rate and the natural unemployment rate determines the gap between potential GDP and real GDP

## Define these words

**17** Economic growth?

**18** productivity?

### Answer

**1** crowding-out effect **2** economic stabilization policy **3** rule of 70
**4** balanced budget multiplier **5** automatic stabilizer **6** the philips curve
**7** monetary policy **8** liquidity **9** spending multiplier **10** liquidity trap
**11** rational expectation theory **12** fiscal policy **13** multiplier effect
**14** tax multiplier **15** natural rate hypothesis **16** Okun's law

**17** the rise in real GDP, or the rise in real GDP per person
**18** a worker's output per hour

# Problem Set B: multiple questions

**1** The situation that government spending is greater than tax revenues is called a _____.

A) budget surplus
B) budget excess
C) budget shortage
D) budget deficit

**2** The situation tax collection equal government spending is referred to as _____.

A) budget surplus
B) budget deficit
C) budget equilibrium
D) balanced budget

**3** The situation that government spending is less than tax revenues is called a _____.

A) budget surplus
B) budget excess
C) budget shortage
D) budget deficit

## 4

When the government spending in a country has continued to be greater than tax revenue, the national debt is the accumulation _____.

A) of past tax revenues
B) of past budget deficits
C) of past government spending
D) of government borrowings

## 5

The government spending multiplier is _____.

A) greater than the tax multiplier
B) equal to the tax multiplier
C) less than the tax multiplier
D) varying depending on the type of government

## 6

Why is the government spending multiplier greater than tax multiplier?

A) Because the government spending is usually greater than tax revenue
B) Because the government spending has indirect impact on economy
C) Because people save some portion of tax cut
D) Because government spending is more effective

**7** The balanced budget multiplier is _____.

A) negative
B) zero
C) one
D) dependent on the magnitude of governmen spending and tax change

**8** Of $100 million increase in government spending and a $100 million decrease in tax revenue, which is the greater impact on national income?

A) $100 million decrease in tax revenue
B) $100 million increase in government spending
C) Both are equal
D) It depends on marginal propensity to consume.

**9** If current GDP of a country at equilibrium is less than full employment output, there is _____ and a fiscal policy such as _____ is appropriate.

A) an inflationary gap; increase in government spending
B) an inflationary gap; decrease in government spending
C) a recessionary gap; increases in tax collection
D) a recessionary gap; decreases in tax collection

**10** If current real GDP of a country at equilibrium is greater than full employment output, there is _____ and a fiscal policy such as_____ is appropriate.

A) an inflationary gap; increase in government spending
B) an inflationary gap; decrease in government spending
C) a recessionary gap; increases in tax collection
D) a recessionary gap; decreases in tax collection

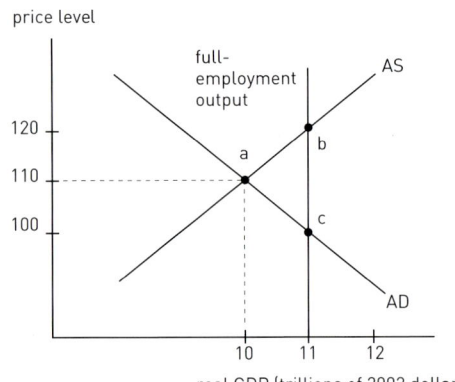

**11** An economy is in equilibrium at point a. An proper fiscal and monetary policy for the economy to reach full employment output is to _____.

| fiscal policy | monetary policy |
|---|---|
| A) increase tax collection | buy government securities |
| B) increase budget surplus | sell government securities |
| C) decrease government debt | raise reserve requirements |
| D) decrease tax rate | lower discount rate |

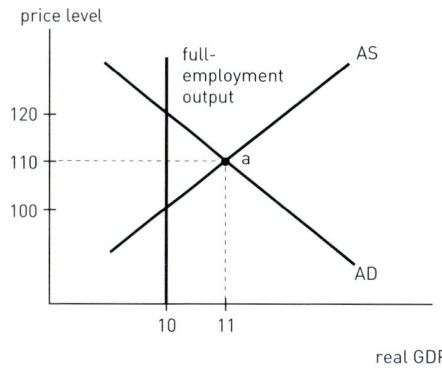

**12** An economy is in equilibrium at point a. An proper fiscal and monetary policy for economy to reach full employment output is to _____.

        fiscal policy            monetary policy
A) increase tax collection     buy government securities
B) increase budget surplus    sell government securities
C) decrease government spending   raise reserve requirements
D) decrease tax rate          lower discount rate

**13** Economic growth is defined as _____.

A) an increase in budget surplus
B) an increase in productivity
C) an increase in real GDP
D) an increase in labor force available

## 14

If real GDP was $20 billion in 2011 and is $22 billion in 2012 in a country, what is the economic growth rate of this country?

A) 10%
B) -10%
C) 20%
D) -20%

## 15

The short-run Phillips curve shows the relationship between the _____.

A) expected inflation rate and the natural rate unemployment
B) actual inflation rate and the actual inflation rate
C) actual unemployment and the expected inflation rate
D) natural rate of unemployment and the balanced inflation rate

## 16

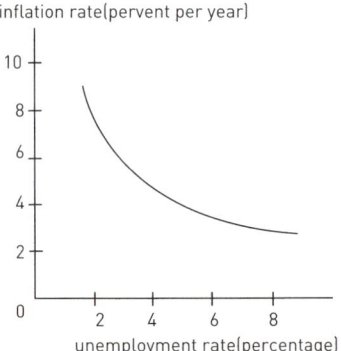

Which one displays the graph above correctly?

A) aggregate demand curve
B) demand for money curve
C) Okun curve
D) Philips curve

## 17
**Why is short-run aggregate supply curve upward sloping and the short-run Phillips curve is downward sloping?**

A) Because each represent other side of economy
B) Because supply creates its own demand
C) Because in the long run we are all dead
D) Because input prices are rigid in the short run

## 18
**According to Okun's Law say, _____ is determined by the difference between the unemployment rate and the natural unemployment rate.**

A) full employment output
B) current real GDP
C) the gap between full employment output and real GDP
D) the gap between the inflation rate and the natural rate of unemployment

## 19-20  Refer to the graph below.

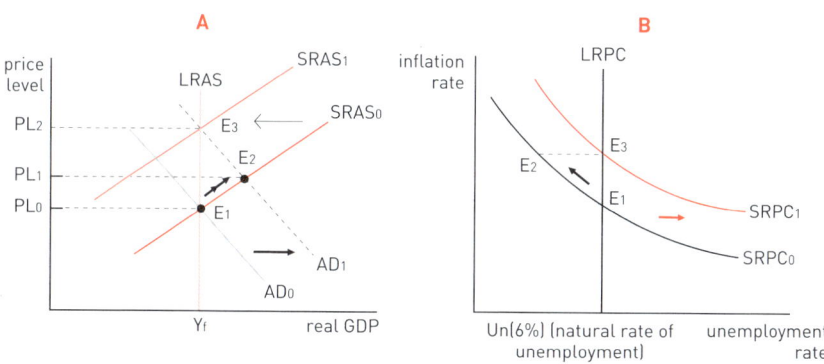

Chapter 4 Economic Stabilization Policy and Economic Growth

**19** If the economy is at 4% unemployment rate on its short-run Phillips curve(SRPC), real GDP in AD-AS model is definitely _____.

A) less than full-employment output
B) greater than potential GDP
C) equal to potential GDP
D) less than potential output

**20** If the aggregate demand shifts to the right in the AD-AS diagram, this shift is shown by a _____ in the short-run Phillips curve(SRPC)

A) movement along the SRPC
B) movement downward along SRPC
C) rightward shift of SRPC
D) leftward shift of SRPC

**21** The long-run Phillips curve suggests that _____.

A) There is a short-run tradeoff between the inflation rate and the unemployment rate i
B) There is a long-run tradeoff between the inflation rate and the unemployment rate
C) Unemployment rate and inflation rate have a upward-sloping relationship
D) Any inflation rate can be realized at the natural rate of unemployment

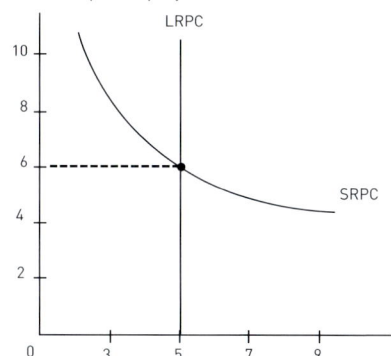

**22** The natural rate of unemployment in the figure above is _____.

A) 3 percent
B) 5 percent
C) 7 percent
D) 9 percent

**23** The expected inflation in the figure above is _____.

A) 2 percent
B) 4 percent
C) 6 percent
D) 8 percent

## 24. If the expected inflation rate falls, the long-run Phillips curve _____ and the short-run Phillips curve _____.

A) does not shift; shifts downward
B) does not shift; shifts upward
C) shifts rightward; shifts upward
D) shifts rightward; shifts downward

## 25. If the natural rate of unemployment rises, long-run Philips curve _____.

A) shifts to the left
B) shifts to the right
C) does not shift
D) has no relation to the change in the natural rate of unemployment

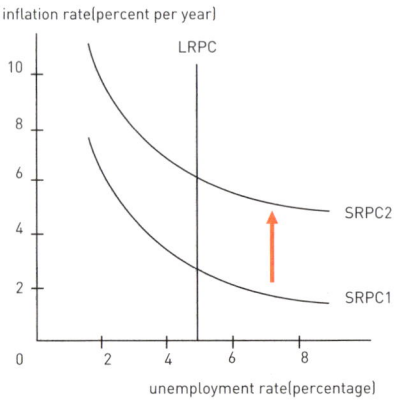

**26** The shift of the short-run Phillips curve in the figure above is the result of _____.

A) an increase in the inflation rate
B) a decrease in the inflation rate
C) an increase in the expected inflation rate
D) a decrease in the expected inflation rate

**27** When people use all the optimal information available in order to make a choice, they are making _____.

A) adaptive expectation
B) static expectation
C) rational expectation
D) perfect expectation

Answer

1 D  2 D  3 A  4 B  5 A  6 C  7 C  8 B  9 D  10 B
11 D  12 C  13 C  14 A  15 B  16 D  17 D  18 C  19 B
20 A  21 D  22 B  23 C  24 A  25 B  26 C  27 C

Chapter 4 Economic Stabilization Policy and Economic Growth

# Chapter 05

# Open Economy
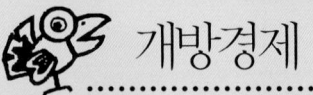
개방경제

이번 Chapter5는 마지막 부분으로, 개방경제 open economy 에서 국제무역 international trade 과 국제수지 balance of payment, 외환시장 foreign exchange market 에 대해 알아보도록 합니다. 또 국제무역의 두 가지 형태인 수출 export 과 수입 import 이 시장의 균형과 시장참여자들의 편익을 전체적으로 어떻게 변화시키는지를 배워 봅니다. 또 국가 간 상품과 자본의 이동을 기록하는 국제수지표 balance of payment 에 대해서 익히며 각 국가의 통화가 거래되는 외환시장에서 환율이 어떻게 결정되는가를 공부하게 될 것입니다.

# Lesson 1 | Free Trade
## 자유무역

### free trade and imports
### 자유무역과 수입

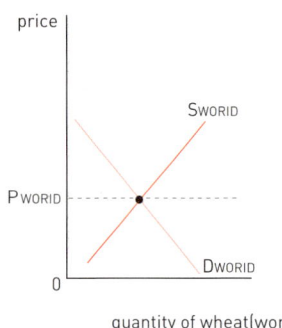

World market

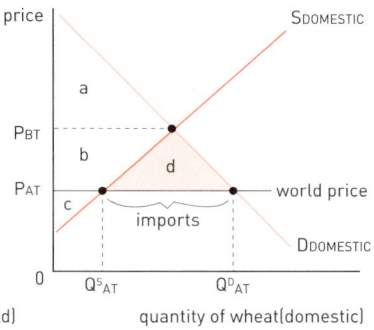

Domestic market

$P_{BT}$: price before trade
$P_{AT}$: price after trade
$Q^D_{AT}$: quantity demanded after trade
$Q^S_{AT}$: Quantity supplied by domestic producers after trade

Whether a country is to import a good or to export it is determined by price. If the country's domestic price of a good is higher than world price, the country would be an importer. If domestic price is lower than world price, the country would be an exporter. In the graph above, because the country's domestic price without trade is higher than world price, the country becomes a importer. The market size of the country is so small that the country takes world price as given, which makes world price horizontal at $P_{AT}$. The volume of import is ($Q^D_{AT} - Q^S_{AT}$). Notice that there is a large change in consumer surplus and producer surplus. The detailed changes in market participants' net benefit is summarized on the table below. In conclusion, the consumers are better off, but the producers are worse off. The net benefit of the country is area d.

한 나라가 상품을 수입하느냐 수출하느냐의 여부는 가격이 결정한다. 그 나라의 국내가격이 세계가격보다 높으면 수입국이 되고, 낮으면 수출국이 된다. 위의 그래프에서 무역이 없을 때 그 나라의 국내가격이 세계가격보다 높으므로, 그 나라는 수입국이 된다. 이 나라의 시장규모는 매우 작아서 세계가격을 주어진 것으로 받아들여 이로 인해 세계가격은 $P_{AT}$에서 수평으로 나타난다. 수입량은 ($Q^D_{AT} - Q^S_{AT}$)이다. 소비자잉여와 생산자 잉여에 큰 변화가 나타나는 것에 주목해야 한다. 시장참가자들의 순편익의 변화에 대한 자세한 사항은 아래 표에 요약되어 있다. 결론적으로 소비자들은 더 좋아졌고, 생산자들은 악화되었다. 국가 전체의 순편익 변화는 d 영역이다.

Domestic gains and losses from free trade(imports)

| Area | Before Trade | After Trade |
|---|---|---|
| consumer surplus(CS) | a | a + b + d |
| producer surplus(PS) | b + c | c |
| total surplus(=CS+PS) | a + b + c | a + b + c + d |

## free-trade and exports
자유무역과 수출

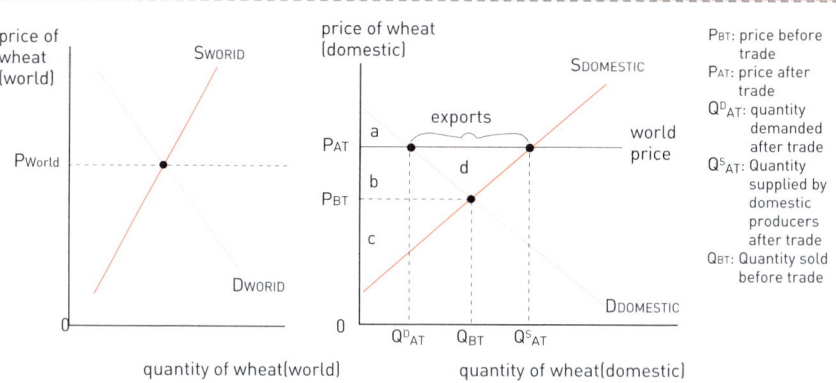

$P_{BT}$: price before trade
$P_{AT}$: price after trade
$Q^D_{AT}$: quantity demanded after trade
$Q^S_{AT}$: Quantity supplied by domestic producers after trade
$Q_{BT}$: Quantity sold before trade

In the graph above, because a country's domestic price without trade is lower than world price and the country has price competitiveness with other countries, the country becomes an exporter. The world price is given at $P_{AT}$. The volume of export is ($Q^S_{AT} - Q^D_{AT}$). There is a large change in consumer surplus and producer surplus when a country imports. The detailed changes in market participants' net benefit summarized on the table below. In conclusion, the producers are better off, but the consumers are worse off. The net benefit of the country is area d.

위의 그래프에서 무역이 없을 때 그 나라의 국내가격이 세계가격보다 낮으므로, 그 나라는 수출국이 된다. 세계가격은 $P_{AT}$으로 주어진다. 수출량은($Q^S_{AT} - Q^D_{AT}$)이다. 수입의 경우에 보았듯이 소비자잉여와 생산자잉여에 큰 변화가 나타난다. 시장참가자들의 순편익의 변화에 대한 자세한 사항은 아래 표에 요약되어 있다. 결론적으로 생산자들은 더 좋아졌고, 소비자들은 악화되었다. 국가 전체의 순편익 변화는 d 영역이다.

Domestic gains and losses from free trade(exports)

| Area | Before Trade | After Trade |
|---|---|---|
| consumer surplus(CS) | a + b | a |
| producer surplus(PS) | c | b + c + d |
| total surplus | a + b + c | a + b + c + d |

# free-trade and tariff
## 자유무역과 관세

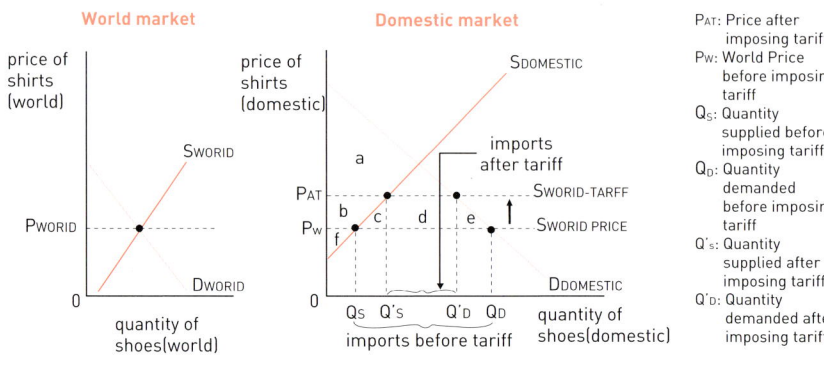

Suppose that a country imports a good. The world price of the good is lower than domestic price of a good. In the graph above, the country imports by the amount of ($Q_D-Q_S$) at Pw. One day, the government made a decision to impose tariff on the imported good. The price rose by the amount of tariff, from Pw to Pw+t. The change in market participants' net benefit occurs. The detailed change in net benefit summarized on the table below. In conclusion, the producer are better off, consumers are worse off, and the government gets tariff revenue. It is important to know that there is deadweight loss of c plus e.

한 나라가 상품을 수입한다고 가정하다. 그 상품의 세계가격은 국내가격보다 낮다. 위의 그래프에서 이 나라는 ($Q_D-Q_S$)만큼 수입한다. 어느 날 정부가 이 제품에 관세를 부과하기로 결정하였다. 가격은 관세만큼 Pw에서 Pw+t로 오른다. 시장참여자들의 순편익에 변화가 생긴다. 자세한 변화 사항은 아래 표에 요약되어 있다. 결론적으로 생산자는 더 좋아지고, 소비자는 악화된다. 정부는 관세수입을 얻는다. 중요한 것은 (c+e)만큼 자중손실, 즉 효율성 상실이 나타난다는 것이다.

- **tariff** 관세

  a tax imposed on imported goods 수입품에 부과한 세금

### Domestic gains and losses from free tariff

| Area | Before Trade | After Trade |
| --- | --- | --- |
| Consumer Surplus(CS) | a + b + c + d + e | a |
| Producer Surplus(PS) | f | b + f |
| Governmen Tariff Revenue | 0 | d |
| Total Surplus(TS) | a + b + c + d + e + f | a + b + d + f |

# Lesson 2: Balance of Payments
## 국제수지

### balance of payments
### 국제수지

The record of receipts and payments of a country's international transactions over a year. Balance of payments is composed of current account balance and financial account balance.

한 나라가 지난 일 년 동안 참여한 국제거래의 수취와 지출의 기록으로 경상수지거래와 자본수지거래로 이루어져 있다.

|  | (credit) Payments from foreigners | (debit) Payments to foreigners | Net |
|---|---|---|---|
| 1 Sale and purchase of goods and services | $2593 | $3064 | −$471 |
| 2 Factor income | 670 | 505 | +165 |
| 3 Transfers | 84 | 220 | −136 |
| Current account (1+2+3) |  |  | −442 |
| 4 Official asset sales and purchases | 181 | 20 | 201 |
| 5 Private sales and purchases of assets | 1288 | 1047 | 241 |
| Financial account (4+5) |  |  | 442 |
| Total | − | − | 0 |

### credit
### 대변(수취)

**Receipts in the international transaction**
국제거래에서 수취한 경우

### debit 차변(지출)

**payments in the international transaction**
국제거래에서 지출한 경우

### current account(CA) 경상수지

**The summary of a country's export and import payments of goods and services to and from the rest of the world, investment income and transfer payments**
한 나라의 상품과 서비스, 투자소득, 이전지출의 지출과 수취

### financial account(FA, capital account) 자본수지

**A record of a country's financial and real asset transactions with the rest of world**
한 나라의 금융자산과 실물자산의 거래 기록

- **Notice that CA plus FA equals zero (CA+ FA =0).**
  경상수지와 자본수지의 합은 영이다.

### foreign direct investment 해외직접투자

**A financial investment that is owned and managed by foreign participants. For example, domestic branch of multinational corporation**
외국경제주체가 소유하여 운영하는 자본투자. 예를 들면, 다국적 기업의 국내 지사

### foreign portfolio investment 해외간접투자

**A financial investment that foreign participants finance but is managed by a domestic entity. For example, stock or corporate bond investment.**
외국경제주체가 자금을 대지만 국내주체가 운영하는 자본투자. 예를 들면, 주식이나 채권 투자

# Lesson 3 | Determining International Value of a Country's Currency 한 나라 통화의 국제가치 결정하기

## foreign exchange market
외환시장

**The market that a country's currency is traded.**
한 나라의 통화가 거래되는 시장

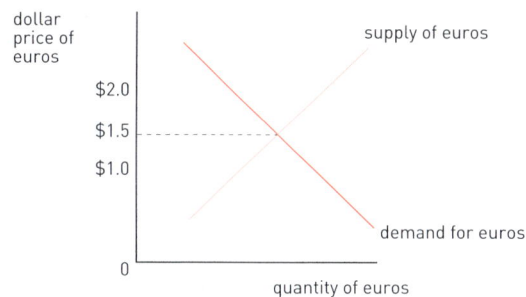

The market for the euros currency

The currency of a country is demanded when people want to buy the country's goods or assets and is supplied when people want to trade the currency to other currency in the order to buy other country's good or assets. Here we will focus on how the international value of euros, the currency of the European Union is determined. The counterpart country is the United States. Demand for and supply of euros is confined to international transactions. In the graph above, the market for euros currency, euros is demanded by US purchase of European goods and assets. On the other hand, euros is supplied by EU purchase of US goods and assets.

한 나라의 통화는 사람들이 그 나라의 재화와 자산을 구하고자 할 때 수요되고, 사람들이 그 통화를 다른 통화와 바꿔서 다른 나라의 재화와 자산을 구매하고자 할 때 공급된다. 여기에서는 유럽연합의 통화인 유로화의 국제가치가 어떻게 결정되는지에 초점을 둘 것이다. 유럽연합의 상대국은 미국이다. 어느 국가의 통화에 대한 수요와 공급은 국제거래에 한정한다. 위의 유로화 시장의 그래프에서 유로는 미국사람들이 유럽의 상품과 자산 구매할 때 수요된다. 다른 한편으로, 유로는 유럽사람들이 미국 상품과 자산을 구매할 때 공급된다.

> **Tip** Demand for the currency of Country A: the demand for the good and service and real and financial assets of Country A
>
> Supply of the currency of Country A: the demand for the good and service and real and financial assets of Country B

## price level and interest rate
물가 수준과 이자율

**Two most important factors determining the international value of a currency**
통화의 국제적 가치를 결정하는 가장 중요한 두 가지 요인

- **Purchasing Power Parity** 구매력평가설(the law of one price 일물일가설)

  the proposition that: the international value of a currency reflects the ratio of the domestic price and foreign price of the same good because the same good must have the same price everywhere.
  같은 상품은 가격이 같아야 하기 때문에 한 통화의 국제가치는 같은 상품의 국내가격과 외국가격의 비율을 반영한다는 주장

- **Interest Rate Parity** 이자율평가설

  The proposition that differences in interest rates on similar bonds in different countries reflect expectations of future changes in international value of a currency
  두 나라의 비슷한 채권의 이자율의 차이가 미래 환율변화에 대한 기대를 반영한다는 주장

## determinants of demand for and supply of a currency 통화의 수요와 공급의 결정요인

**price level**(inflation rate) 가격, **interest rate** 이자율, **preference**(tastes) 선호(취향), **capital flight**(political stability) 자본도피(정치적 불안), **speculation** 투기

❶ **Change in price level or Inflation rate** 가격수준 또는 인플레이션률의 변화

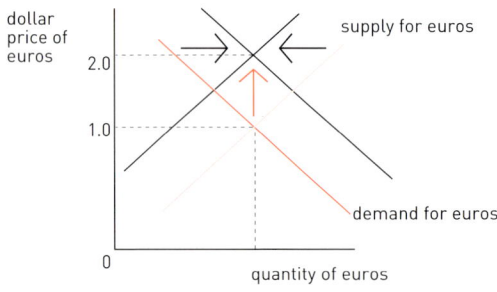

If the inflation rate rises faster in the US than in the EU, EU good becomes relatively cheaper. The demand for the EU good rises, so demand for the euros increases. On the other hand, EU imports less US goods because US goods are relatively expensive. The supply of euros decreases. The international value of euros increases.(Euros appreciates)
미국에서 인플레이션이 더 빠르게 상승한다면 유럽의 상품이 상대적으로 더 싸진다. 유럽의 상품에 대한 수요가 증가하고 따라서 유로에 대한 수요가 증가한다. 반면에 유럽은 미국 상품이 더 비싸기 때문에 미국상품의 수입이 감소될 것이다. 유로화의 공급이 감소한다. 유로화의 국제 가치는 상승한다.

❷ **Change in interest rate** 이자율의 변화

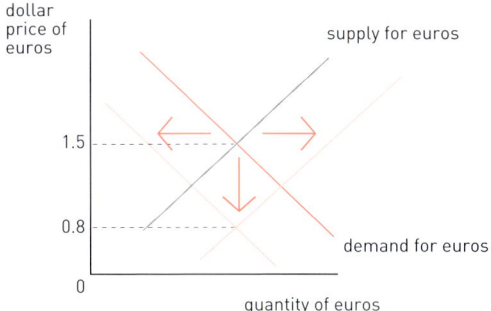

If the interest rate in US rises when the interest rate in EU stays the same, the US financial assets are more attractive. The demand for US financial assets increases. Europeans sell euros to buy dollars, so the supply of euros increases. On the other hand, EU financial assets become less attractive, so the demand for euros decreases. Therefore the international value of euros falls.(Euros depreciates)

유럽의 이자율은 변화가 없는데 미국의 이자율이 상승한다면, 미국의 금융자산이 더 큰 이득을 주게 된다. 미국의 금융자산에 대한 수요가 증가한다. 유럽사람들은 유로를 팔고 달러를 살 것이고 그래서 유로의 공급이 증가한다. 반면에 유럽의 금융자산은 이득이 줄어들게 되어 유로에 대한 수요는 줄어들게 된다. 따라서 유로의 국제 가치는 떨어진다.

❸ **Change in income** 소득의 변화

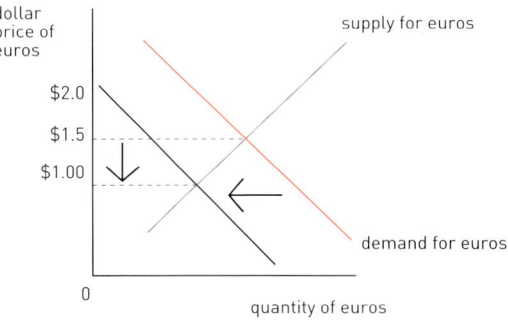

If the US goes in to a recession, income of US households falls. American purchasing power would decline. Americans can not afford to buy EU goods and services as before. So the demand for euros decreases, and euro depreciates.

미국이 경기침체로 들어가면 미국 가구의 소득은 떨어진다. 미국의 구매력이 줄어드는 것이다. 미국인들은 유럽의 재화와 서비스를 이전만큼 구매할 수 없다. 유로에 대한 수요가 줄어들고 유로는 평가절하된다(가치의 하락).

### ❹ Political instability(capital flight) 정치적 불안정(자본도피)

a large-scale and abrupt decrease in the demand for real and financial assets of a country

한 나라의 실물자산과 금융자산에 대한 수요가 대규모로 갑작스럽게 감소하는 것.

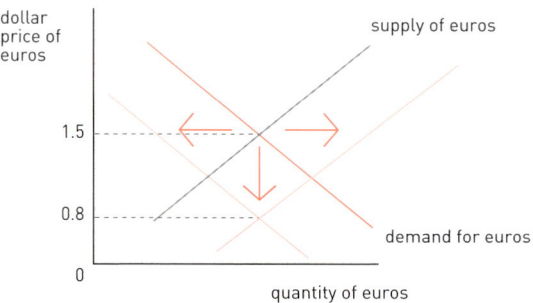

Suppose that Europe is politically unstable. Some countries in Europe are going back to the socialist system. New power leaders are trying to confiscate private property. In such situation, capital flight is likely to begin, because Europe is not a safe place to invest any more. When people who possess euros try to convert euros into dollars, there is a large supply of euros, and simultaneously the demand for euros decreases because EU financial assets is not attractive any more. Therefore, the international value of euros sharply falls. 유럽이 정치적으로 불안정하다고 가정하자. 유럽의 몇몇 국가들이 사회주의체제로 돌아가려고 한다. 새로운 권력자들은 사유재산을 몰수하려고 시도하고 있다. 이런 상황에서는 유럽이 더 이상 투자에 안전한 장소가 아니기 때문에 자본도피가 시작될 것이다. 유로를 가진 사람들은 유로를 다른 안전한 통화나 금융자산으로 바꾸려고 할 것이다. 그래서 유로화의 공급이 증가한다. 동시에 유럽의 금융자산이 더 이상 매력적이지 않기 때문에 유로화에 대한 수요는 감소한다. 그러므로 유로화의 국제가치는 크게 떨어진다.

### ❺ Speculation(Speculative attack) 투기(투기적 공격)

The behavior of engaging in risky financial transactions in an attempt to profit from it

이득을 얻기 위해 위험한 금융거래에 참여하는 행동

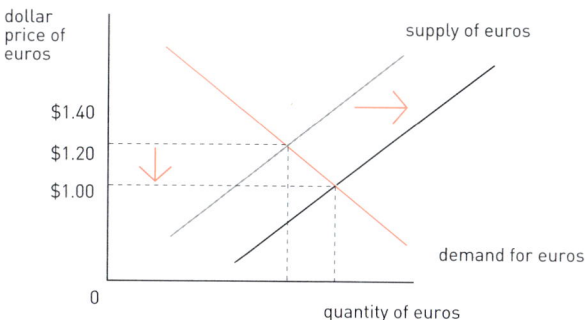

If people expect that the euro will depreciate soon, they will try to sell euros before the price of euros falls. So there would be more supply of euros, shifting the supply curve to the right. Euro depreciates.

❻ **Change in tastes & preference** 취향과 선호의 변화

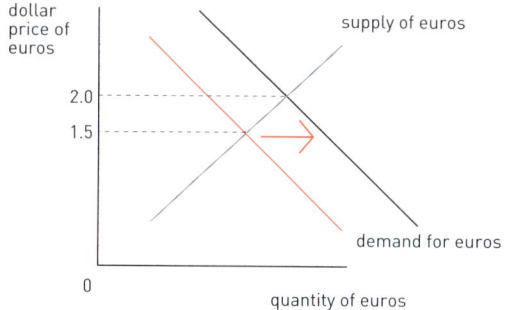

If Americans think that the EU goods are more charming, they import more EU goods. The demand for the euros increases, so the international value of euro rises.
미국인들이 유럽상품이 더 매력적이라고 생각한다면 유럽상품을 더 수입할 것이다. 유로에 대한 수요가 증가하고 유로의 가치가 상승한다.

# Problem Set A — Short Answer Question

Write down a proper word for the definition

**1** a tax imposed on imported goods

**2** the record of receipts and payments of a country's international transactions over a year, It is composed of current account balance and financial account balance

**3** receipts in the international transaction

**4** payments in the international transaction

**5** the summary of country's export and import payments of goods and services to and from the rest of the world

**6** a record of a country's financial and real asset transactions and direct foreign investment with the rest of world

**7** the behavior of engaging in risky financial transactions in an attempt to profit from it

**8** The market that a country's currency is traded

**9** the law that the same good must have the same price everywhere

**10** the proposition that differences in interest rates on similar bonds in different countries reflect expectations of future changes in international value of a currency

**11** the proposition that: the international value of a currency reflect the ratio of the domestic price and foreign price of the same good because the same good must have the same price everywhere

**12** a large-scale and abrupt decrease in the demand for real and financial assets of a country

### Answer

**1** tariff  **2** balance of payments  **3** credit
**4** debit  **5** current account(CA)  **6** financial account(FA, capital account)
**7** speculation  **8** foreign exchange market
**9** law of one price  **10** interest rate parity
**11** purchasing power parity  **12** capital flight

# Problem Set B: multiple questions

**1.** The summary of the receipts and payments of international transactions is called the _____.

A) bank balance sheet
B) Fed balance sheet
C) balance of payments
D) capital account

**2.** The money sent to the orphanage in India from the US is recorded in accounts called the balance of _____ of US and recorded as a _____.

A) official reserves, credit
B) capital account, debit
C) financial account, credit
D) current account, debit

**3.** Which of the following is not correct about a balance of payments account?

A) It has two main components of current account and financial account
B) Current account records the purchase and sale of good and service
C) Capital account records the net investment income
D) Current account plus capital account equals zero

**4** Which one is recorded in the current account?
A) a country's foreign direct investment
B) changes in the official reserves, the government's payments holdings of foreign currency
C) trade, net investment income, net transfers
D) only trade

**5** Which one is recorded in the capital account _____.
A) an interest income earned by possessing foreign corporate bonds
B) changes in the official reserves, the government's payments holdings of foreign currency
C) trade, net investment income, net transfers
D) the money given to people who live overseas

**6** Rupee, the currency of India, will be likely to depreciate if _____.
A) interest rates in India rises relative to those of other countries
B) price level in India falls relative to those of other countries
C) income level in India rises relative to those of other countries
D) speculators expect Rupee to appreciate in the near future

**7** When China exports goods and services to the United States, there is an increase in the _____.

A) supply of Yuans
B) demand for dollars
C) demand for Yuans
D) Chinese financial account balance

**8** One Korean Won exchanged for 1100 Turkey Lira. In the near future the one Korean Won exchanges for 1050 Turkey Lira. The Won will _____ and the Rira will _____.

A) appreciate; appreciate
B) depreciate; appreciate
C) appreciate; depreciate
D) depreciate; depreciate

**9** An increase in the interest rate in EU leads to _____ in the international value of euros because the demand for euros _____.

A) rise; increases
B) rise; decreases
C) fall; increases
D) fall; decreases

**10** An increase in the inflation rate in the U.S. leads to _____ in the international value of dollar because the demand for dollar _____.

A) rise; increases
B) rise; decreases
C) fall; increases
D) fall; decreases

**11** A decrease in the income level of the U.S. leads to _____ in the international value of dollar because the supply of dollar _____.

A) rise; increases
B) rise; decreases
C) fall; decreases
D) fall; increases

**12** When a country imposes a tariff on an imported good, the _____.

A) deadweight loss is not incurred
B) price of the good falls
B) the quantity of the good imported increases
C) quantity of the good produced in the country increases

## 13. After the government imposes a tariff on a imported good, how much money should consumers pay as a price?

A) average total cost + world price
B) tariff + average total cost + world price
C) tariff + license cost
D) world price +tariff

## 14-15

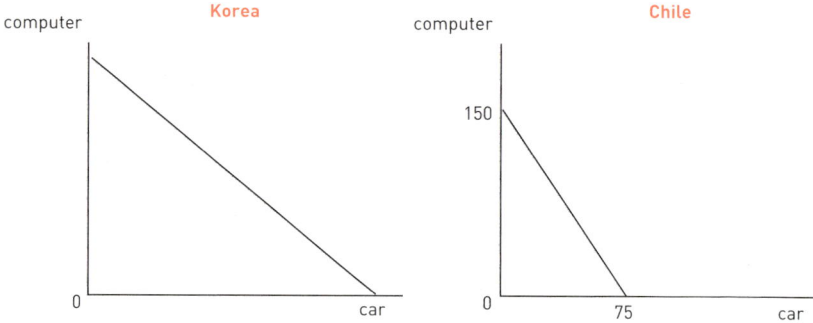

## 14. Which one is correct?

A) Chile has absolute advantage in the production of computer and comparative advantage in the production of computer
B) Korea has absolute advantage in the production of car, and comparative advantage in the production of computer
C) Chile has no absolute advantage in the production but comparative advantage in the production of car
D) Korea has absolute advantage in the production of computer, and comparative advantage in the production of car

**15** Which one is appropriate as the terms of trade?(B=broccoli, C=coffee)

A) 1 B = 1 C
B) 1.5 B = 1 C
C) 1 B = 1.5 C
D) 1 B = 2 C

**16** A limit on the quantity of a good that can be imported is a _____.

A) tariff
B) embargo
C) sanction
D) quota

**A n s w e r**

**1** C  **2** C  **3** C  **4** C  **5** B  **6** C  **7** C  **8** B  **9** A
**10** D  **11** B  **12** D  **13** D  **14** D  **15** C  **16** D

# Practice Exam Macroeconomics
Time: 50 minutes

**1** The asset demand for money is primarily related to money's use as a _____

A) medium of exchange
B) unit of account
C) store of value
D) liquidity preference
E) measure of value

**2** A country's currency will depreciate when _____

A) supply of the currency decreases
B) the country's export increases
C) the country's import decreases
D) the inflation rate in the country rises
E) the interest rate in the country rises

**3** Paul's disposable income is $2000. His monthly consumption is $1600, and his marginal propensity to save(MPS) is 0.3. Suppose that his disposable income rises by $100. Which of the following will be true?

|    | Savings | Consumption |
|----|---------|-------------|
| A) | $450    | $1650       |
| B) | $430    | $1670       |
| C) | $420    | $1650       |
| D) | $400    | $1630       |
| E) | $380    | $1610       |

**4** Which of the following would be most likely to be included in a country's current gross domestic product(GDP)?

A) A famous cook prepares dinner for his family in his home
B) The government increases unemployment benefits to the unemployed in the era of economic downturn
C) A seller with import license reduces the amount of imported clothes
D) A piece of Picaso's painting is sold with some commissions of auction in the New York Sotherby
E) The inventories of a firm produced two years ago start to be sold

**5** The real interest rate is 3 percent and the expected inflation rate is 5 percent. Which of the following is the nominal interest rate.

A) 10 percent
B) 8 percent
C) 6 percent
D) 4 percent
E) -2 percent

**6** Suppose that gross domestic product of a country rises from $10 trillion in 2000 to $15 trillion in 2010 due to a technological advance and there had been no inflation. Which of the following is NOT true?

A) Nominal gross domestic product rises between 2000 and 2010
B) Real income increased between 2000 and 2010
C) Purchasing power increased between 2000 and 2010
D) Nominal income decreased between 2000 and 2010
E) There had been no change in the price level

## 7

Government fiscal policy is primarily composed of government spending and taxation. Which of the following is the necessary combination of government fiscal policy change in order to cool down overheated economy?

|   | Tax | Government spending |
|---|---|---|
| A) | increase | increase |
| B) | decrease | decrease |
| C) | increase | decrease |
| D) | decrease | increase |
| E) | no change | decrease |

## 8

Which of the following would lead to an increase in price level or inflation?

I. A rightward shift of the aggregate demand curve
II. A leftward shift of the aggregate demand curve
III. A rightward shift of the aggregate supply curve
IV. A leftward shift of the aggregate supply curve

A) I only
B) II, IV only
C) I and IV only
D) I, II and III only
E) I, II and IV only

## 9

If real interest rate falls, what will happen to the consumption, investment, and real income?

|   | consumption | investment | real income |
|---|---|---|---|
| A) | decrease | decrease | decrease |
| B) | no change | decrease | decrease |
| C) | increase | increase | increase |
| D) | no change | increase | increase |
| E) | increase | decrease | decrease |

**10** When there is a natural disaster in a country and investment increases, which of the following will definitely occur?

|  | Price level | Real GDP |
|---|---|---|
| A) | increase | uncertain |
| B) | increase | increase |
| C) | decrease | decrease |
| D) | decrease | uncertain |
| E) | increase | decrease |

**11** According to expenditure approach, Gross Domestic Product equals

A) Consumption + Investment + Government Spending + Export
B) Wage + Income + Rent + Profit
C) market value of all final goods and services produced within a country in a period of time
D) Consumption + Investment + Government Spending + Export - Import
E) Wage + Income + Rent + Profit + Business Tax + Depreciation

**12** The table below shows national economic figures of a country in millions of dollars

| components | millions of dollars |
|---|---|
| consumption | 5,800 |
| investment | 1,700 |
| government spending on goods and services | 1,800 |
| export | 400 |
| import | 600 |
| depreciation | 300 |
| sales tax | 500 |

Based on the data on the table above, what is the GDP of the country, in millions of dollars?

A) $9,100
B) $9,900
C) $9,300
D) $8,800
E) $8,300

**question 13-14 refers to the table below.**

|  | Year 2011 | | Year 2012 | |
| --- | --- | --- | --- | --- |
|  | quantity | price | quantity | price |
| tomato | 5 | $3 | 7 | $5 |
| peanut | 7 | $2 | 8 | $3 |

**13** The table above gives the production and prices for a small country that produces only tomatoes and peanuts. The base year is 2011. What is nominal GDP, real GDP, and approximate price index in 2012?

|  | Nominal GDP | Real GDP | Price index in 2012 |
| --- | --- | --- | --- |
| A) | $ 29 | $37 | 63 |
| B) | $ 59 | $59 | 100 |
| C) | $ 46 | $46 | 100 |
| D) | $ 46 | $59 | 78 |
| E) | $ 59 | $37 | 160 |

**14** Compute the Consumer Price Index(CPI) in 2012. Then find the approximate inflation rate between 2011 and 2012. The basket for CPI covers only 3 tomatoes and 3 peanuts. Year 2011 is the base year.

A) 50, -50%
B) 100, 0%
C) 160, 60%
D) 200, 100%
E) 300, 200%

**15** Which of the following explains that national income decreases when government spending and tax decrease by the same amount?

A) Spending multiplier is less than tax multiplier when government spending and tax decrease by the same amount simultaneously
B) People save some portion of tax cuts
C) People have tendency to spend all the tax cuts on consumption
D) People hold money when the economy seems to be in recession
E) Tax cuts have more impact on economy than government spending

**16** John who took the class of AP Macroeconomics last semester, observed that inflations and unemployment rises at the same time. If he has learned macroeconomics well, which of the following will be the most appropriate explanation?

A) Increase in government spending
B) Increase in human capital
C) Increase in export
D) Increase in real GDP
E) Increase in expected inflation

**17** The official unemployment rate tends to underestimate. Choose the proper combinations of the possible reasons.

I. discouraged workers
II. job seekers who has already her job
III. part-time workers
IV. new entrants to job market

A) I, only
B) I. II only
C) I, III only
D) I. II. III, only
E) I. II, III, IV only

**18** An increase in government spending will most likely to _____

A) decrease real income
B) decrease the price level
C) decrease inflationary expectations
D) decrease investment
E) decrease import

## 19

Which of the following tools of monetary policy by the central bank does have the greatest impact on the economy in the period of severe recession?

|  | Open market operations | discount rate | reserve requirements |
|---|---|---|---|
| A) | buy | raise | lower |
| B | buy | lower | raise |
| C) | sell | raise | raise |
| D) | sell | raise | lower |
| E) | buy | lower | lower |

**question 20 and 21 refers to the graph below.**

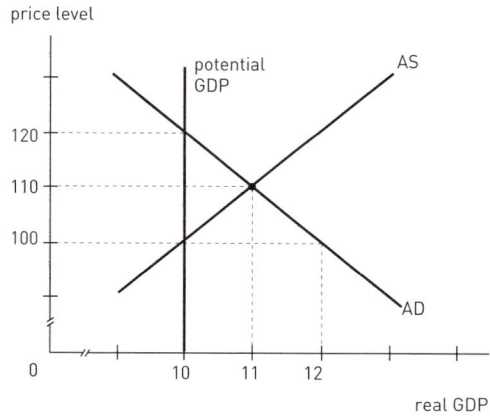

## 20

The economy is in the short-run equilibrium. Which of the following is the long-run real GDP in trillions dollars and the price level?

|  | Price level | Real GDP |
|---|---|---|
| A) | 100 | 10 |
| B) | 110 | 11 |
| C) | 110 | 12 |
| D) | 120 | 10 |
| E) | 120 | 11 |

**21** Suppose that The policy maker tries to implement economic policy to stabilize economies. Which of the following is the price level and real GDP after implementing the policies?

|    | Price level | Real GDP |
|----|-------------|----------|
| A) | 100         | 10       |
| B) | 110         | 11       |
| C) | 110         | 12       |
| D) | 120         | 10       |
| E) | 110         | 10       |

**22** In the injection- leakage model of the economic circulation of income and expenditure, the injection is composed of

(a) Consumption, government spending, saving
(b) Investment, tax
(c) Investment, government spending, and export
(d) Saving, tax, and import
(e) Consumption, imports, taxes

**23** In the injection- leakage model of the economic circulation of income and expenditure, the leakage is composed of

(a) Consumption, government spending saving
(b) Investment, tax
(c) Investment, government spending, and export
(d) Saving, tax, and import
(e) Consumption, imports, taxes

**24** All of the following are the possible explanations why the short-run aggregate supply curve is upward sloping except that

A) Wages are rigid in the short run
B) Producers can have misperceptions what is going on the market
C) Prices are sticky in the short run
D) Input costs are not flexbile in the short run
E) In the long-run all prices become flexible

question 25 and 26 refers to the graph below.

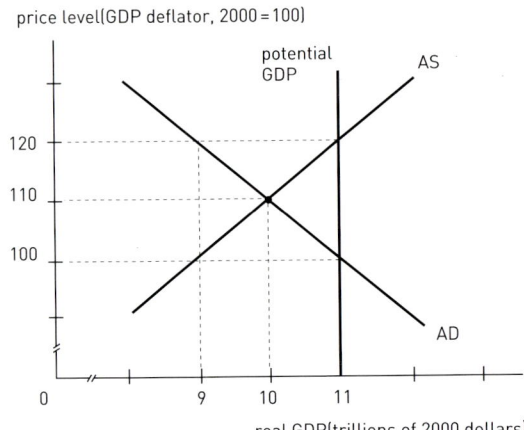

**25** The economy is in the short-run equilibrium. Which of the following is the long-run real GDP in trillions dollars and the price level?

|   | Price level | Real GDP |
|---|---|---|
| A) | 100 | 10 |
| B) | 100 | 11 |
| C) | 110 | 11 |
| D) | 110 | 10 |
| E) | 120 | 9 |

**26** Suppose that The policy maker tries to implement economic policy to stabilize economies. Which of the following is the price level and real GDP after implementing the policies?

|    | Price level | Real GDP |
|----|-------------|----------|
| A) | 100         | 9        |
| B) | 110         | 10       |
| C) | 110         | 11       |
| D) | 120         | 11       |
| E) | 120         | 9        |

**27** Which of the following would lead to the largest decrease in aggregate demand?

|    | Fiscal Policy | Monetary Policy |
|----|---------------|-----------------|
| A) | $100 billion reduction in government spending | $100 billion open market sale of government bond |
| B) | $100 billion increase in tax | $100 billion open market purchase of government bond |
| C) | $100 billion reduction in government spending | $100 billon open market purchase of government bond |
| D) | $100 billon increase in tax | $100 billion open market sale of government bond |
| E) | $100 billon reduction in government spending | No change |

**28** A expansionary monetary policy will cause interest rate, investment, aggregate demand change in which of the following ways in the short run?

|    | interest rate | investment | aggregate demand |
|----|---------------|------------|------------------|
| A) | Decrease | Decrease | Decrease |
| B) | Increase | Increase | Increase |
| C) | Decrease | Inrease  | Decrease |
| D) | Increase | decrease | Increase |
| E) | Decrease | Increase | Increase |

**29** One day, John discovered $100 under his mattress. He deposited the money into the bank. The reserve requirement is 20%. Which of the following is the maximum amount of money that could be created through the banking system in the country?

A) $100
B) $200
C) $300
D) $400
E) $500

**30** Under which of the following economic situation would a expasionary monetary or fiscal policy be most appropriate?

|  | Inflation | Unemployment |
|---|---|---|
| A) | High | High |
| B) | High | Low |
| C) | Low | High |
| D) | Low | Low |
| E) | Low | doesn't depend |

question 31 and 32 refers to the table that shows the balance sheet of a commerical bank.

| assets | | liabilities | |
|---|---|---|---|
| required reserves | $1000 | demand deposits | $5000 |
| excess reserves | $200 | owner's equity | $5000 |
| loans | $5000 | | |
| government securities | $3000 | | |
| build, equipment, and fixtures | $800 | | |

**31** According to the balance sheet of the bank, what is the value of required reserve ratio?

A) 5%
B) 10%
C) 15%
D) 20%
E) 25%

**32** If the bank sells its $1000 government securities, which of the following would occur to the balance sheet of bank?

|   | Assets | Liability |
|---|---|---|
| A) | decrease by $1000 | decrease by $1000 |
| B) | increase by $1000 | increase by $1000 |
| C) | no change | no change |
| D) | decrease by $1000 | increase by $1000 |
| E) | increase by $1000 | decrease by $1000 |

**33** Which of the following ordinarily prevents the banks to create money to its maximum in the fractional reserve banking system?

I. Limited money multiplier
II. People's money holding
III. Banker's excess reserves
IV. Inflationary expectations

A) I only
B) I, II, only
C) I, II, and III, only
D) II, III, only
E) II, III, and IV only

## 34

Suppose that a economy produces equilibrium output, 1,700,000. The full employment output of the economy is 1,800,000. The marginal propensity to save is 0.25. A Keynesian economist will agree with the idea to propose _____

A. Decreasing taxes by $33,333
B. Decreasing taxes by $100,000
C. Decreasing government spending by $25,000
D. Increasing government spending by $33,333
E. Increasing government spending by $100,000

## 35

When the Fed, US central bank, raises the interest rate through contractionary monetary policy, which of the following will occur to the international value of dollars and US imports in the short run?

|   | International value of dollar | US Import |
|---|---|---|
| A) | rise | rise |
| B) | fall | fall |
| C) | rise | fall |
| D) | fall | rise |
| E | rise | no change |

## 36

According to the rational expectation theory, which way will the government spending have impact on the economy if people expect the government to increases its spending while the economy is currently at full-employment output?

|   | Price Level | Output |
|---|---|---|
| A) | rise | rise |
| B) | rise | fall |
| C) | fall | no change |
| D) | no change | no change |
| E) | rise | no change |

**37** Which of the following is NOT true why aggregate demand curve slopes downward?

A) real balance effect
B) interest rate effect
C) wealth effect
D) multiplier effect
E) net-export effect

**38** All of the following represent the ideas or traditions of classical economists except that _____

A) Supply creates its own demand
B) Prices and wages are flexible
C) Short-run AS is vertical at the potential output
D) Philips curve is vertical at the natural rate of unemployment
E) The economy may lose its self-regulating mechanism for a short time

**39** Which of the following groups of people would benefit from unanticipated inflation?

I. net-creditors
II. net-debtors
III. employee with cost of living adjustments(COLAs)

A) I only
B) II, only
C) I, II only
D) II, III, only
E) I, II, and III only

**40** All of the following represent the ideas or traditions of Keynesian economists except that _____

A) Demand creates its own supply
B) The government can intervene the economy when the economy is in recession or overheated situations
C) Input prices are rigid, or sticky in the short run
D) The economy may be in equilibrium less than full employment
E) The economy is always self-correcting to full employment

# Answer Practice Macroeconomics

**1 | C**    The asset demand for money is very closely associated with money's use as a store of value.

**2 | D**    When the inflation rate in a country rises, the good becomes more expensive and the export of the country will decrease. Then the demand for the currency decrease, and the value of the currency falls(depreciate).

**3 | B**    Before his disposable income rises, his consumption is $1600, and his savings is $400. His consumption will increase by $70, and his saving will increase by $30 because his marginal propensity to consume is 0.7 and his marginal propensity to save is 0.3   Remember this equation, MPC + MPS = 1

**4 | D**    The price of Picaso's painting is not included in the current GDP, because it is not produced in the current year, but the commission earned by providing service at the auction market is calculated in the current GDP.

**5 | B**    Remember the Fisher equation, nominal interest rate(i) = real interest rate(r) + expected inflation($\pi$).

**6 | D**    Nominal income increased because the nominal GDP rises.

**7 | C**    To fight against overheated economy, the government should necessarily increase tax and decrease government spending.

**8 | C**    The rightward shift of AD results in demand-pull inflation, and the leftward shift of AS leads to cost-push inflation.

**9 | C**    When real interest falls, consumption will increase because people can borrow money at the lower cost, investment will increase due to fall in opportunity cost of investment, and real income(real GDP) will increase because consumption and investment increases.

**10 | A**    When there is a natural disaster, aggregate supply curve shifts to the left. When investment increases, aggregate demand curve shifts to the right. Obviously, the price level rises, but the change in real GDP is ambiguous.

**11 | D**    Expenditure approach measure the sum of expenditures by households, firms, the government, and foreign consumers.

**12 | A**    In equilibrium, GDP = Consumption + Investment + Government Spending + Net Export. Depreciation and sales tax do not affect GDP.

**13 | E**    Nominal GDP is calculated by multiplying the **current price** and current quantity sold. Real GDP is calculated by multiplying the **base year** price and current quantity sold.

**14 | C**    The cost of basket in 2011 and 2012 is $15, $24 respectively. The CPI in 2011, base year is 100, and the CPI in 2012 is $\frac{24}{15} \times 100 = 160$

**15 | B**    Because people save some portion of tax cut, the whole tax cuts do not impact the economy as the government spending does. Spending multiplier is greater than tax multiplier.

**16 | E**    The question is asking the cause of stagflation. Stagflation is represented by the leftward shift of AS. The leftward shift of AS is caused by the increases in production cost and inflationary expectation

**17 | C**    Discouraged workers and partime workers are the causes of underestimation of official unemployment rate announced by the government.

**18 | D**    An increase in government spending raises the interest rate, reducing private investment. This phenomenon is called 'crowding-out effect'.

**19 | E**    The central bank should buy bonds, lower the discount rate, and lower reserve requirements for the most effectice monetary policy in recession.

**20 | D**

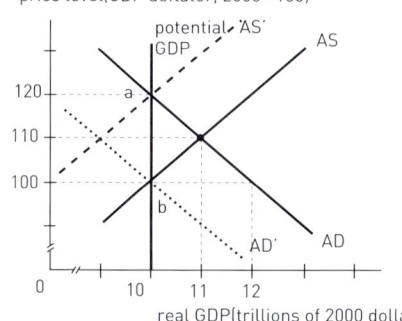

In the long run, the aggregate supply curve shift to the left.
point a: the long-run equilibrium without government policy

**21 | A**    With government contractionary policy the aggregate demand shifts to the left.
point b: the equilibrium with government contractionary policy

**22 | C**    refer to the table below.

**23 | D** refer to the table below
In the injection- leakage model of the economic circulation of income and expenditure, the injection and leakage are as follows according to the definition of economy.

| assets | assets | leakage |
|---|---|---|
| simple private economy | investment | savings |
| closed economy with public sector | investment + government spending | savings + taxes |
| open economy | investment + government spending + export | investment + govermment spending + import |

**24 | E** In the long run, the prices are flexible, but not in the short run.

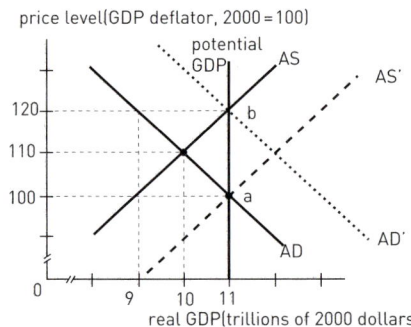

**25 | B** In the long run, the aggregate supply curve shifts to the right, because input cost falls. point a: the long-run equilibrium without government policy.

**26 | D** With government expansionary policy, the aggregate demand shifts to the right.
point b: the equilibrium with government contractionary policy

**27 | A** Because the spending multiplier is greater than tax multiplier, the same amount of change in government spending has greater impacts on the economy than in tax. Open market purchase is one of the expansionary monetary policy.

**28 | E** If money supply increases, interest rate falls. which increases investment. Increase in investment shift AD curve to right because investment is a components of AD.

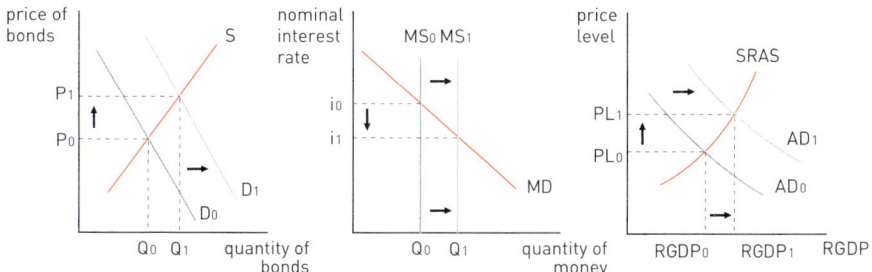

**29 | D**    maximum of money creation = $\frac{1}{R}$ × (Initial excess reserves)
400 = 5 × 80

**30 | C**    Expansionary policy is proper and most effective when inflation is low and unemployment is high.

**31 | D**    required reserve ratio = required reserves ÷ demand deposits × 100
           10%    =      1000      ÷      10000     × 100

**32 | C**    No change in liability and assets. The purchase and sale of government securities by bank change only the inside section of liabilities. In this case of sale of government securities, the government security section decreases by $1000, but the excess reserves increases by $1000 received through the sale.

**33 | D**    People's money holding and bankers' excess reserves are the two reasons for the questions. They are obstacles to the process of making loans, the key to creating money in the economy. Remember these two reasons.

**34 | A**    Decreasing tax by 33,333 or increasing government spending by 25,000 will suffice to recover the economy back to the potential output.

**35 | A**    Higher interest rate is more attractive to foreign investors, so the demand for dollar increases, and the international value of dollar rises(appreciate), The appreciated dollar has more purchasing power, Therefore, imports increase.

**36 | E**    According to the rational expectation, expected government spending will only raise the price level, not output. This is called the government policy ineffectiveness hypothesis.

**37 | D**    Real balance effect or wealth effect, interest rate effect, and net-export effect(exchange rate effect) are the causes of a downward sloping AD.

**38 | E** The classical tradition asserts that the economy is self-correcting to potential output.

**39 | B** Net-debtor benefit from the unanticipated inflation, because the money he should pay back becomes cheaper.

**40 | E** Keynesian economists do not believe that the economy is always self-regulating or self-correcting to full employment. Therefore, they argue that the government should step in the market to stabilize the economy.

# Appendix

### Index

1 ABC순 단어 정리
2 미국경제교육학회가 제시하는
  20가지 경제법칙

# ABC순 정리

- **absolute advantage 절대우위**
  The ability to produce more with the same amount of resources
  같은 양의 생산요소로 더 많은 것을 생산할 수 있는 능력

- **accounting cost 회계비용**
  The direct outlay of money from your wallet or bank account
  지갑이나 은행 계좌에서 직접적인 돈의 지출

- **accounting profit 회계이윤**
  Total revenue minus total explicit cost
  총수입에서 명시적 비용의 차이

- **aggregate-demand curve 총수요곡선**
  The curve that shows the total quantity of final goods and services consumers are willing and able to buy in the economy
  경제 내의 최종재화와 서비스에 대한 소비자들의 총구매욕구를 보여주는 곡선

- **aggregate-supply curve 총공급곡선**
  The curve that shows the total quantity of final goods and services suppliers are willing and able to provide at a given price level

- **allocative efficiency 배분효율성**
  Production level of the combination of goods and services maximizing total net benefit to society. It is accomplished when marginal benefit equals marginal cost, or price equals marginal cost
  사회의 순편익을 극대화하는 재화와 서비스의 생산 수준, 한계

- **animal spirit 야성적 충동**
  The term introduced by Keynes to refer to movements in investment
  투자의 움직임을 언급하려고 케인즈가 소개한 용어

- **appreciation 평가절상**
  An increase in the value of a currency measured in terms of a foreign currency
  외국통화로 측정한 한 통화의 가치 상승

- **arbitrage 차익거래**
  Buying a good at low price in one place and selling it at a higher price somewhere else
  한 곳에서 낮은 가격에 구매하여 다른 곳에서 높은 가격에 판매하는 것

- **automatic stabilizers 자동안정화장치**
  Built-in mechanism that stabilize economy countercyclically without policy makers' extra deliberate action, such as unemployment benefits, progressive tax system

정책결정자가 별도로 행동을 할 필요가 없이 경제를 경기에 반하여 안정화시키는 내부 메커니즘, 실업보험이나 누진세

- **autonomous consumption 기초소비**

    The amount of consumption that does not depend on the level of disposable income, the minimum consumption when a man has no income
    처분가능소득 수준에 관계없는 소비, 소득이 없을 때 하는 최소한의 소비

- **average cost pricing 평균비용가격설정**

    Setting price equal to average total cost
    가격을 총평균비용과 같게 하는 것

- **average fixed cost 평균고정비용**

    Total fixed cost divided by the quantity supplied, fixed cost per unit
    총고정비용을 생산량으로 나눈 값, 단위당 고정비용

- **average revenue 평균수입**

    Total revenue divided by the number of units sold
    총수입을 판매량으로 나눈 값

- **average tax rate 평균조세율**

    Total taxed paid divided by total income
    총세금을 총소득으로 나눈 값

- **average total cost 평균총비용**

    Total cost divided by the output, a per unit cost of production
    총비용을 산출량으로 나눈 값, 단위당 생산비

- **Average variable cost 총가변비용**

    Variable costs divided by output
    가변비용을 산출량으로 나눈 값

- **balance of payment 국제수지표**

    The record of the payments received by a country from foreign countries and the payments sent by the country to foreign countries
    외국으로부터 수취와 외국으로 지급한 거래의 기록

- **balanced budget 균형예산**

    A budget in which tax revenues equals government spending
    조세수입과 정부지출이 크기가 같은 예산

- **balanced budget multiplier 균형재정승수**

    A change in total income when government spending and tax change by $1 in the same direction
    정부지출과 세금이 1달러만큼 같은 방향으로 움직일 때 총소득의 변화분. 균형재정승수는 1이다.

- **balanced trade 무역균형**

    A situation in which exports equal imports
    수출과 수입이 같아지는 상황

- **bank run 뱅크런**

    Simultaneous attempts to withdraw their money from a bank by depositors
    예금자들이 동시에 은행에서 돈을 인출하려는 시도

- **barrier to entry 진입장벽**

    Anything that prevents new firms from entering a market. Ex. Exclusive rights such as patent law, copyright law, core resources, and structure of production cost(natural monopoly)
    새로운 기업이 시장으로 들어가는 것을 막는 것. 특허법, 저작권법 같은 독점권, 핵심생산자원, 생산비용 구조

- **barter system 물물교환제도(바터 시스템)**

    The exchange of goods and services without using money
    화폐 사용 없이 재화와 서비스를 교환하는 행위

- **base year 기준년도**

    The reference year to compare the price level between different years
    서로 다른 연도 사이에서 물가를 비교하기 위한 참조년도

- **benefits principle 편익원칙**

    The idea that people should pay taxes based on the benefits they receive
    사람들이 자신이 받은 편익에 기초하여 세금을 내야한다는 사고

- **bond 채권**

    A certificate of debt
    채무증서

- **budget constraint 예산제약**

    All combinations of goods that can be purchased with an buyer's income
    구매자의 소득으로 구입할 수 있는 모든 재화의 조합

- **budget deficit 예산적자**

    A situation in which governments spending is greater than tax revenues
    정부지출이 조세수입보다 큰 상황

- **budget surplus 예산흑자**

    A situation in which tax revenue is greater than government spending
    조세수입이 정부지출보다 큰 상황

- business cycle 경기변동
  
  Fluctuations in the level of output in the economy
  한 경제 내의 생산수준의 변동

- capital 자본
  
  A good used to produce other goods and services, the equipment, structures, and machinery
  다른 재화와 서비스를 생산하기 위해 사용되는 재화, 장비, 구조물, 설비

- capital account(financial account) 자본계정
  
  A record of a country's asset transactions and direct foreign investment with the rest of world
  한 나라의 자산거래와 외국인직접투자의 기록

- capital accumulation 자본축적
  
  Increase in capital stock
  자본총량의 증가

- cartel 카르텔
  
  A group of firms that explicitly agree to set prices or control production
  명시적으로 가격을 설정하고 수량을 통제하기로 동의한 기업 집단

- ceteris paribus
  
  All else equal, or other things being equal
  다른 것이 모두 일정한 상황

- checkable deposit 당좌예금
  
  Deposits at banks and other financial institutions against which checks can be written
  은행이나 다른 금융기관에 둔 수표사용가능 예금

- circular-flow diagram 경제순환모형
  
  A model that shows how households and Firms circulate goods, services, resources, revenues, and incomes through markets
  가계와 기업의 활동을 통해 재화, 서비스, 생산자원, 수입, 소득이 시장을 통해 순환하는 것을 보여주는 모형

- classical dichotomy 고전적 이분법
  
  The division of real variables and nominal variables by classical school
  고전학파의 이분법으로 실질변수와 명목변수를 분리해서 생각하는 것

- closed economy 폐쇄경제
  
  An economy that does not trade goods and services with other economies
  다른 나라와 재화와 서비스를 거래하지 않는 경제

- **classical school 고전학파**
  
  A group of scholars that believe that the market regulates and corrects itself without any government intervention
  시장이 정부개입 없이 스스로를 규제하고 교정할 수 있다고 믿는 학자 집단

- **Coase theorem 코즈의 정리**
  
  The argument that private parties can solve the problems of externalities on their own without government intervention
  민간경제주체가 정부의 개입 없이 외부성의 문제를 스스로 해결할 수 있다는 주장

- **collusion 담합**
  
  An agreement among firms about price and quantity
  가격과 수량에 대한 기업들 간의 합의

- **commodity money 상품화폐**
  
  Commodity which is used as money
  화폐로 사용되는 상품

- **common resources 공유자원**
  
  A resource, such as air and water, that is freely available to anyone
  공기나 물처럼 누구나 무료로 이용 가능한 자원

- **Comparative advantage 비교우위**
  
  The ability to produce a good with lower opportunity cost
  더 낮은 기회비용으로 생산할 수 있는 능력

- **complements 보완재**
  
  Two goods that tend to be used together, therefore a rise in the price of one leads to a decrease in the demand for the other
  함께 사용되는 두 재화로 한 재화의 가격이 상승하면 다른 재화에 대한 수요가 감소하는 재화

- **constant returns to scale 수확불변**
  
  Tthe property in production process that output is doubled when input is doubled, in other words, long-run average total cost remains the same as the quantity of output changes.
  투입이 두 배로 변할 때 산출이 두 배로 변하는 생산과정에서의 성질. 산출량이 변화할 때 장기평균비용이 변화가 없음

- **consumer confidence index 소비자 신뢰지수**
  
  An index computed monthly that estimates consumer confidence about current and future economic conditions
  매달 계산되는 지표로 현재와 미래의 경제조건에 대한 소비자의 확신, 신뢰를 측정함

- **consumer price index (CPI) 소비자물가지수**
  
  The cost of a typical basket of goods and services bought by consumers
  소비자들이 구매하는 재화와 서비스의 대표적인 상품바구니의 비용

- **consumer surplus 소비자잉여**
  The difference between a consumer's willingness to pay and the amount the consumer actually pays
  소비자의 지불용의금액과 소비자가 실제 내는 금액의 차이

- **consumption 소비**
  The purchase of goods and services by consumers, with exception of spending on new housing(macroeconomics)
  소비자들의 재화와 서비스의 구매, 신축주택구입 제외(거시경제)

- **contraction 수축, 위축**
  A period when output is falling
  생산량이 떨어지는 시기

- **contractionary policy 긴축정책**
  Economic policy to decrease aggregate demand through increasing taxes and decreasing government spending or money supply
  세금을 증가시키거나 정부지출, 또는 통화량을 감소시켜서 총수요를 감소하려는 경제정책

- **cost of living adjustment 생계비조정**
  An annual adjustment to a salary in order to maintain the purchasing power of the income
  구매력 보존을 위해 매년 봉급을 조정하는 행위

- **cross-price elasticity of demand 교차탄력성**
  A measure of how much the quantity demanded of a good X responds to a change in the price of good Y
  Y재화의 가격변동에 X재화의 수량이 변화하는 정도

- **crowding-out effect 구축효과**
  A decrease in investment due to an increase in interest rate when government finances to fund deficit spending
  적자 지출을 위한 정부의 자금조달 시 이자율의 상승으로 인한 투자의 감소현상

- **currency 통화**
  The paper bills and coins in the hands of the public
  사람들이 가지고 있는 지폐와 동전

- **current account 경상수지**
  the summary of payments and receipts of country's exports and imports
  다른 나라와의 수입과 수출의 지출과 수취의 기록

- **cyclical unemployment 경기적 실업**
  The unemployment that occurs due to economic downturn
  경기저하로 발생하는 실업

- **deadweight loss 자중손실**
  The lost total surplus caused by market failures, government intervention, and taxation
  시장실패, 정부개입, 과세로 인한 총잉여의 감소

- **decreasing cost industry 비용저감산업**
  An industry whose long-run supply curve is downward sloping
  장기공급곡선이 우하향하는 산업

- **decreasing returns to scale 수확감소**
  When a doubling of inputs results in increase in output by less than doubling
  투입요소를 두 배로 했을 때 산출량이 두 배가 안 되는 현상

- **deflation 물가하락**
  A decline in the price level, opp inflation
  물가지수의 하락, 인플레이션의 반대말

- **demand curve 수요곡선**
  A curve that shows the relationship between the price of a good and the quantity demanded
  상품의 가격과 수요량의 관계를 보여주는 곡선

- **demand deposits 요구불예금**
  A bank accounts that depositors can write checks or get cash on demand
  예금자가 수표를 쓰거나 현금을 얻을 수 있는 은행예금계좌

- **demand-pull inflation 수요견인인플레이션**
  Inflation that is caused by the increase in total spending.
  총수요의 증가로 발생하는 인플레이션

- **derived demand 파생수요**
  Demand for a factors of production. demand for factors comes from the demand for the goods
  생산요소에 대한 수요, 생산요소에 대한 수요는 생산품에 대한 수요에서 나온다.

- **depreciation 감가상각**
  A decrease in value of a capital asset as it is used over time
  자본이 계속 사용되면서 가치가 떨어지는 현상

- **depression 불황**
  A severe and long-lasting recession
  심각한 장기지속의 경기침체

- **diminishing marginal product 한계생산체감**
  Additional increase in total product declines as the number of inputs increases
  투입을 증가시킬 때 총생산의 추가증가분이 감소하는 성질(다른 표현으로 diminishing returns)

- **discount rate 재할인율**

  The interest rate at which commercial banks borrows from the Federal Reserves(central bank)
  상업은행이 중앙은행으로부터 자금을 빌릴 때 적용되는 이자율

- **discouraged workers 구직포기자**

  Individuals who have given up looking for a job
  일자리를 찾는 것을 포기해 버린 사람

- **diseconomies of scale 규모의 비경제**

  The phenomenon that the long-run average total cost rises as output increases
  생산량이 증가할 때 장기평균총비용이 상승하는 현상

- **disinflation 디스인플레이션**

  A decrease in inflation
  인플레이션의 감소

- **Disposable income 처분가능소득**

  The income a consumer has after paying taxes
  세금을 낸 후 소비자의 소득

- **dominant strategy 우월전략**

  A strategy that is best for a player regardless of what strategy a rival chooses
  상대의 선택전략에 관계없이 한 게임자에게 최선의 전략

- **economic cost 경제적 비용**

  Total opportunity cost
  총기회비용

- **economic growth 경제성장**

  The increase in real GDP or increase in real GDP per capita
  실질 GDP의 증가, 또는 1인당 실질 GDP의 증가

- **economic profit 경제적 이윤**

  Total revenue minus total explicit cost and implicit cost
  총수입에서 명시적 비용과 암묵적 비용을 뺀 값

- **economic rent 경제적 지대**

  The difference between the payments to a factor and the minimum amount that must be spent to get the factor
  생산요소에게 지불된 비용에서 생산요소고용을 위한 최소한의 비용을 뺀 값

- **economics 경제학**
  The study of how society allocates its scarce resources
  사회가 희소한 자원을 어떻게 배분하는가에 대한 연구

- **economies of scale 규모의 경제**
  The phenomenon that the long-run average total cost falls as output increases
  생산량이 증가할 때 장기 총평균비용이 감소하는 현상

- **efficiency wages 효율임금**
  The wage a firm pays to an employee as an incentive to work more productively
  기업이 생산성을 높이려고 고용인에게 지불하는 경제적 유인(인센티브)로서의 임금

- **efficient scale 최소효율규모**
  The quantity of output that minimizes average total cost - unit cost
  평균총비용(단가)을 최소화하는 생산량

- **elasticity 탄력성**
  A measure of responsiveness of one variable to the change in the other variable
  다른 변수의 변화에 대한 한 변수의 반응의 정도

- **equation of exchange 교환방정식**
  The equation says that price level(P) multiplied by real GDP(Q) is equal to the quantity of money(M) multiplied by the circulation of average currency(V)
  물가(P)에 실질 GDP(Y)를 곱하면 통화량(M)과 통화의 평균 순환회수(V)를 곱한 값과 같다는 것을 보여주는 방정식

- **equilibrium 균형**
  A situation in which quantity demanded equals quantity supplied
  수요량과 공급량이 같아지는 상황

- **equilibrium price 균형가격**
  The price that balances supply and demand
  공급과 수요를 균형 시키는 가격

- **euro 유로화**
  The new European currency, which replaced national currencies in 11 countries in 2002
  유럽의 새로운 통화, 2002년에 11개 국가의 국별 통화를 대체

- **european union 유럽연합**
  A political and economic organization of 15 European countries
  유럽 15개 국가의 정치와 경제기구

- **excess capacity 초과설비**
  The difference between the long-term quantity of output and the output at minimum average total cost(the efficient scale)
  장기 생산량과 평균총비용의 최솟값에서의 생산(효율규모)량의 차이

- **excess demand 초과수요**

    Demand that results when the quantity demanded exceeds the quantity supplied
    수요량이 공급량을 초과하는 결과로 발생한 수요

- **excess supply 초과공급**

    The situation that quantity demanded is greater than quantity supplied
    수요량이 공급량보다 많은 상황

- **exchange rate 환율**

    The rate at which one unit of currency A is exchanged for the currency B, the amount of the currency B that one unit of currency A can obtain
    통화 A가 다른 통화 B와 교환될 때의 비율, 통화 A 한 단위가 얻을 수 있는 통화B의 양

- **excise tax 물품세**

    A per unit tax on a specific good, such as tobacco, alcohol
    담배나 술처럼 특정 재화에 단위당 부과하는 세금

- **excludability 배제성**

    The good is excludable when it is possible to prevent a person from using it.
    다른 사람이 사용하는 것을 막을 수 있을 때, 그 재화는 배제성이 있다.

- **expansion 확장**

    A period of the increase in output
    생산이 증가하는 시기

- **expansionary policy 확장정책**

    Economic policy to increase aggregate demand through decreasing taxes, increasing government spending and money supply, either together or separately
    세금 인하, 정부지출증가, 통화량증가를 함께 또는 따로 사용하여 총수요를 증가시키는 경제정책

- **explicit costs 명시적 비용**

    The actual outlay of money by a firm, such as wages, cost of materials, and rental cost. Also referred to as accounting costs.
    임금, 원료비용, 임대료 같이 기업의 실제 지출, 회계비용이라고도 한다.

- **exports 수출**

    Economic activity that goods and services produced domestically and sold abroad
    재화와 서비스를 국내에서 생산하여 해외에서 파는 경제활동

- **externality 외부효과**

    Unintended costs or benefits caused by a producer or consumer to a bystander
    생산자나 소비자가 제3자에게 초래하는 의도치 않은(미리 계산되지 않은) 비용이나 편익

- **factors of production 생산요소**

    Inputs or resources used to produce goods and services

재화와 서비스 생산에 사용되는 투입요소와 자원

- **federal funds rate 연준금리**

  Interest rate on short-term loans between commercial banks in the United States
  미국에서 일반은행들 간 단기대출의 이자율

- **Federal Open Market Committee(FOMC) 공개시장위원회**

  A committee of the Fed that directs the activities relating to open market operations
  공개시장 관련 화동을 지시하는 연방준비은행의 위원회

- **Federal Reserve(Fed) 연방준비제도**

  The central bank of the US
  미국의 중앙은행

- **fiat money 법정화폐**

  Paper and coin money without intrinsic value that is used as money because the government mandates it by law
  내재 가치가 없지만 정부의 법률위임으로 통화로 사용되는 지폐나 동전

- **final good 최종재**

  Goods that is ultimately consumed. On the other hand intermediate good is used in the production of another good.
  최종적으로 소비되는 재화. 반면에 중간재는 다른 재화의 생산에 사용되는 재화이다.

- **financial intermediaries 간접금융기관**

  Financial institution that receives fund and provides it to borrower, such as bank, mutual fund
  자금을 받아서 다른 사람에게 빌려주는 금융기관, 은행이나 뮤추얼 펀드

- **financial market 직접금융시장**

  Markets where financial assets are direclty traded such as stock market, bond market
  주식시장이나 채권시장처럼 금융자산이 직접 거래되는 시장

- **fiscal policy 재정정책**

  Government's action on its spending and tax collection
  정부지출과 조세징수에 관한 정부의 행동

- **Fisher effect 피셔효과**

  The proposition that nominal interest rate and inflation rate increase by the same amount in the long run
  명목이자율과 인플레이션율은 장기적으로 같은 크기만큼 상승한다는 주장

- **first-degree price discrimination(perfect price discrimination) 일급의 가격차별**

  Charging each consumer her willingness to pay for a good
  각 소비자에게 상품에 대한 지불용의금액을 부과하는 것

- **fixed costs 고정비용**

Costs that does not change on the level of production, such as plant maintenance and insurance
생산수준에 따라 변화하지 않는 비용, 설비유지비, 보험비 등

- fixed inputs 고정투입요소

    Factors that cannot be changed in the short run
    단기에 변경되지 않는 생산요소

- flow 유량

    A variable whose value is expressed as a quantity per unit of time
    단위시간당 양으로 그 값이 표현되는 변수

- foreign direct investment 외국인직접투자

    The purchase of incumbent firms or the management of new firms by foreign investors
    외국인투자자들이 기존 기업을 구매하거나 새로운 기업을 경영하는 경제활동

- fractional-reserve banking 부분지급준비금제도

    A banking system in which only a fraction of deposits is held as reserves
    예금의 일정부분만을 준비금으로 보유하는 은행제도

- free entry 진입자유

    A condition that a firm can enter freely market, because there are no barriers to entry
    진입장벽이 없어서 자유롭게 시장으로 들어갈 수 있는 상황

- free rider 무임승차자

    Free rider is a person who consumes a good or service without paying for it
    재화나 서비스에 대한 비용을 지불하지 않고 그것을 소비하는 사람

- frictional unemployment 마찰적 실업

    Frictional unemployment occurs because it takes time for workers to move to another firm, or for new entrants to get a job
    노동자들이 새로운 직장으로 옮기거나 신규 노동시장 진입자가 직장을 얻는데 시간이 걸리기 때문에 발생하는 실업

- full-employment 완전고용

    Full-employment is a condition of an economy when there is no cyclical unemployment
    경기적 실업이 없는 경제 상황

- G-7

    The seven major economic powers in the world: the US, Germany, Japan, France, the United Kingdom, Italy, and Canada
    세계의 주요한 경제 강국, 미국, 독일, 일본, 프랑스, 영국, 이태리, 캐나다

- game theory 게임이론

    Game theory is the study of a person's success is based on the choices of others

다른 사람의 선택에 기초하여 한 사람의 성공을 연구하는 분야

- **GDP deflator GDP디플레이터**
  The ratio of nominal GDP to real GDP, a measure of the average price level in the economy
  실질 GDP에 대한 명목 GDP의 비율, 경제의 평균적 가격수준의 척도

- **Giffen good 기펜재**
  A good that the quantity demanded of the good increases when price rises.
  가격이 상승할 때 그 수요량이 증가하는 재화

- **Gini coefficient 지니계수**
  A measure of income inequality whose value is derived from the Lorenz curve
  소득불평등지수로 그 값은 로렌츠 커브에서 도출되는 지수

- **gold standard 금본위제**
  A monetary system in which money supply of a country is determined by the amount of gold
  금의 양에 의해 통화량이 결정되는 통화제도

- **government securities(government bond) 정부채권**
  A bond issued by a government or a government agency
  정부나 정부기관이 발행하는 채권

- **government debt 정부부채**
  Tthe accumulation of budget deficit
  정부예산적자의 누적

- **government spending 정부지출**
  Spending on goods and services by government
  정부가 재화와 서비스에 지출하는 행위

- **gross domestic product(GDP) 국내총생산**
  The market value of all final good and services produced within a country in a certain period of time
  일정한 기간 동안 한 국가 내에서 생산된 최종재화와 서비스의 시장가치의 합

- **Great Depression 대공황**
  The Great Depression is the most severe and worldwide economic depression from 1929 to the late 1930s
  1929년에서 1930년대 후반까지 있었던 가장 심각하고 세계적인 경제 불황이다.

- **human capital 인적자본**
  The amount of knowledge and skills possessed by an individual worker through

education and training
한 개인이 교육과 훈련을 통해 소유하게 된 지식과 기술의 총합

- **hyperinflation 초인플레이션**

    very rapid and high inflation. Usually 50 percent rise per month
    매우 속도가 빠르고 정도가 높은 인플레이션, 보통 월 50%의 물가상승을 지칭

- **implicit costs 암묵적 비용**

    The cost that a firm must give up without direct payments
    직접 지출 없이 포기해야 하는 비용

- **import quota 수량통제**

    Restrictions on the quantities of goods that can be imported
    수입되는 물건의 양을 제한하는 것

- **imports 수입**

    Economic activity that goods and services produced abroad and sold domestically
    재화와 서비스를 해외에서 생산하여 국내에서 파는 경제활동

- **in-kind transfers 현물공여**

    Good and services that government give to the poor
    정부가 가난한 사람들에게 주는 재화와 서비스

- **income effect 소득효과**

    The change in consumption caused by an change in consumer's purchasing power(real income)
    소비자의 구매력(실질소득)의 변화로 초래되는 소비의 변화

- **income elasticity of demand 소득탄력성**

    A measure of how responsive consumption of a good is to a change in consumer's income
    소득의 변화에 재화의 소비가 얼마나 반응하는지의 정도

- **indexation 물가연동**

    Tthe automatic correction of wage according to the announced inflation rate to keep the purchasing power through law or contracts
    구매력을 유지하기 위해 인플레이션율에 따라 법이나 계약을 통해 임금을 자동으로 조정하는 경제행위

- **indifference curve 동일효용곡선**

    A curve that shows the combinations of two goods that give the consumer the same level of satisfaction
    소비자에게 똑같은 만족감을 주는 두 재화의 조합을 보여주는 곡선(무차별곡선으로 더 많이 불림)

- **inferior good 열등재**

    A good which consumption falls as a consumer's income rises
    소득이 증가할 때 소비가 줄어드는 재화

- **inflation 인플레이션**

An increase in the overall price level
전체적인 물가수준의 상승

- **inflation rate 인플레이션율**

A measure of inflation, at the rate of increase of price index
인플레이션의 측정, 물가지수의 증가율

- **inflation tax 인플레이션세**

The revenue the government raises when the government increase money supply and incur inflation
정부가 통화량을 증가시켜 인플레이션을 초래할 벌어들이는 소득

- **inflationary gap 인플레이션 갭**

The difference between the current real GDP and the full employment output when the former is greater than the latter
현재 실질 GDP가 완전고용 GDP보다 클 때, 그 둘의 차이

- **intermediate good 중간재**

A good that is used in the production of a final good
최종재의 생산에 사용되는 재화

- **internalizing an externality 외부효과의 내부화**

Changing incentives so that people consider the external cost or benefit.
사람들이 외부비용과 편익을 고려할 수 있도록 유인을 바꾸는 것

- **interest rate 이자율**

The price of loan, the rate at which one can borrow or lend money
대출의 가격, 돈을 빌려주거나 빌릴 때의 비율

- **interest rate effect 이자율효과**

The effect of interest rate on investment when price level changes, When price level falls, investment increases because people demand less money, which lowers interest rate. When interest rate falls, investment rises.
물가가 변화 될 때 투자에 미치는 영향, 물가수준이 떨어질 때, 투자는 증가한다. 사람들의 화폐수요가 줄어들어 이자율이 떨어지기 때문이다.

- **inventory investment 재고투자**

The difference between production and sales
생산과 판매의 차이

- **investment 투자**

Purchases of new capital goods(equipment, plants, and machinery) by firms and the purchase of new houses and apartments by people
기업의 새로운 자본재(장비, 설비,기계류)의 구입과 소비자의 신축주택이나 아파트의 구매

- **investment demand 투자수요**

The relationship between the real interest rate and the investment. Investment

Increases as real interest rate falls.
실질이자율과 투자의 관계, 실질이자율이 떨어지면 투자는 증가한다.

- **investment tax credit 투자세액공제**

  Incentives for a firm that make investment
  투자하는 기업에 대한 인센티브

- **junk bond 정크본드**

  Very high risk bond
  매우 위험한 채권

- **job search 구직**

  The process by which workers try to find a job
  노동자가 직장을 구하는 과정

- **Keynesian School 케인즈학파**

  A group of economists that believe the market is not perfect, so it is necessary for government to intervene until the economy come back to full employment.
  시장이 완벽하지 않기 때문에 경제가 완전고용을 회복할 때까지는 정부가 개입할 필요가 있다고 생각하는 경제학자 집단

- **kinked demand curve 굴절수요곡선**

  The demand curve that in oligopoly firms face due to the prices rigidity
  과점에서 가격경직성으로 인해 기업들이 직면하는 수요곡선

- **labor force 경제활동인구**

  The sum of the employed and the unemployed
  취업자와 실업자의 합

- **labor-force participation rate 경제활동참가율**

  The percentage of the adult population that is in the labor force
  노동가능인구 중에 경제활동인의 비중

- **labor productivity 노동생산성**

  The output per worker in a certain period of time
  시간당 노동자당 생산량

- **Laffer curve 래퍼 곡선**

  A curve that shows the relationship between tax size(rate) and tax collection(revenue)
  세율과 조세수입의 관계를 보여주는 곡선

- **law of demand 수요의 법칙**

  The general tendency that the quantity demanded of a good rises as the price of a good falls, other things equal
  다른 것이 일정할 때 가격이 떨어지면 수요량이 증가하는 일정한 경향성

- **law of diminishing marginal utility 한계효용체감의 법칙**

  The additional increase in total satisfaction from a good declines as consumption increases
  소비가 증가할 때 총만족감의 추가적인 증가분이 줄어드는 현상

- **law of diminishing returns 수확체감의 법칙**

  The additional increase in total output falls as a firm use one more unit of a factor
  기업이 생산요소를 한 단위 더 고용할 때 총생산의 추가증가분이 줄어드는 현상

- **law of supply 공급의 법칙**

  The general tendency that the quantity supplied of a good rises as the price rises, other things equal
  다른 것이 일정할 때 가격이 상승하면 공급량이 증가하는 일정한 경향

- **least cost rule 최소비용규칙**

  The cost-minimizing combination of labor and capital for a given production
  주어진 생산량에서 생산비용을 최소화하는 노동과 자본의 조합

- **life cycle 생애주기**

  The regular pattern of income variation over a person's life
  한 개인의 소득이 변화되는 규칙적인 유형

- **liquidity 유동성**

  The property that the asset can be traded easily
  자산이 쉽게 거래되는 성질

- **liquidity trap 유동성위기**

  A situation where monetary policy cannot stimulate an economy because people are extremely reluctant to trade liquid assets
  사람들이 극단적으로 유동성 있는 자산을 거래하지 않으려고 해서 통화정책으로 경제를 부양시키지 못하는 상황

- **lump-sum tax 정액세**

  The same amount of tax for everyone
  모든 사람에게 같은 액수의 세금

- **luxury 사치재**

  A good whose consumption rises more than in proportion to increases in income. Income elasticity of demand is greater than one.
  소비량의 증가율이 소득의 증가율보다 큰 재화. 소득탄력성이 1보다 크다.

- **M1**

  The index of money supply that is made up of currency, demand deposit, and traveler's checks
  현금통화, 요구불예금, 여행자수표 등으로 이루어진 통화량지표

- **M2**

    M1 plus saving deposits, money market mutual funds, time deposit, and etc.
    M1에 정기적립금, 뮤추얼펀드, 정기예금으로 이루어진 통화량지표

- **macroeconomics 거시경제학**

    the study of a country's economy as a whole, such as of national income, inflation, unemployment and exchange rate
    국민소득, 인플레이션, 실업, 환율을 연구하는 분야로 경제가 전체적으로 어떤 방식으로 작동하는가를 연구하는 학문

- **marginal cost 한계비용**

    The additional increase in total cost from producing one more unit of good
    한 단위 생산할 때 총비용의 증가분

- **marginal product 한계생산**

    The additional increase in total output from using one more unit of input
    투입요소 한 단위 추가 시에 총생산의 증가분

- **marginal propensity to consume 한계소비성향**

    The effect on consumption of an additional dollar of disposable income
    처분가능소득 1달러의 증가가 소비에 미치는 영향

- **marginal propensity to save 한계저축성향**

    The effect on savings of an additional dollar of disposable income
    가처분소득 1달러의 증가가 저축에 미치는 영향

- **marginal revenue 한계수입**

    The additional increase in total revenue from one more unit sold
    제품 하나 더 판매 시 총수입의 증가분

- **marginal revenue product 한계수입생산**

    The additional increase in total revenue from one more unit of an input
    투입요소 한 단위를 늘렸을 때 총수입의 증가분

- **marginal social cost 사회적한계비용**

    The sum of marginal cost and marginal external cost
    한계비용과 외부비용의 합

- **marginal tax rate 한계세율**

    The extra taxes paid on an additional dollar of income
    소득 1달러 증가 시 내는 추가세금

- **marginal utility 한계효용**

    The additional satisfaction from consuming one more unit of a good
    한 단위 추가 소비 시 만족의 증가분

- **market 시장**

    A group of buyers and sellers of a good or service

재화와 서비스의 구매자와 판매자의 집단

- **market economy 시장경제**

    An economy system where resources are allocated through market
    시장을 통하여 자원이 배분되는 경제체제

- **market failure 시장실패**

    A situation in which market fails to allocate resources efficiently
    시장이 자원을 효과적으로 배분하지 못하는 상황

- **market for loanable funds 대부자금시장**

    The market in which brings savers who want to supply fund and borrowers who want to demand together
    자금을 공급하려고 하는 저축자들과 자금을 수요하고자 하는 차입자들을 한 곳에 모은 시장

- **market power 시장지배력**

    The ability to influence market outcome, especially price
    특히 가격 등의 시장의 결과에 영향을 미치는 능력

- **markup pricing 비용할증**

    Increasing the price of a good by a certain rate
    일정 비율만큼 상품 가격을 올리는 것

- **medium of exchange 거래수단**

    An asset that people acquire for the purpose of trading rather than for their own consumption
    사람들이 소비보다는 거래의 목적으로 획득하는 자산

- **menu costs 메뉴 비용**

    The cost incurred when raising price due to inflation
    인플레이션으로 인한 가격상승으로 초래되는 비용

- **microeconomics 미시경제학**

    The study of how households and firms allocate resources
    가계와 기업이 자원을 어떻게 분배하는가를 연구하는 분야

- **monetarism 통화주의**

    A group of economist in the 1960s who argued that monetary policy based on rule is effective way to manage economic activities
    1960년대에 규칙에 입각한 통화정책이 경제활동을 조절하는 효과적인 방법이라고 주장하며 나타난 경제학자 집단

- **monetary contraction(monetary tightening) 통화긴축**

    A decrease in money supply
    통화량을 감소시킴

- **monetary expansion 통화확장**

    A increase in money supply

통화량을 증가시킴

- **monetary neutrality 화폐의 중립성**
  The proposition that the increase in money supply has no effect on real output, only increasing price level in the long run
  통화량의 증가가 장기적으로는 실질생산에는 아무런 영향을 미치지 못하고 물가만을 상승시킬 것이라는 주장

- **monetary policy 통화정책**
  The control and regulation on money supply to influence the economy by the central bank
  중앙은행이 경제에 영향을 미치려고 통화량을 통제하고 규제하는 것

- **money 화폐**
  The set of assets that people use in order to buy goods and services
  사람들이 재화와 서비스를 구매하기 위해 사용하는 자산 집합

- **money demand 화폐수요**
  The sum of the transaction demand and the asset demand for money, There is a inverse relationship between nominal interest rate and the quantity of money demanded.
  거래수요와 자산수요의 합으로 명목이자율과 화폐수요량은 역관계이다.

- **money market 화폐시장**
  The market that bring money demand and money supply together
  화폐수요와 화폐공급을 모아주는 시장

- **money multiplier 통화승수**
  The increase in the money supply created by a single dollar increase in excess reserves
  초과지급준비금이 1달러 증가했을 때 창출되는 통화량의 증가

- **money supply 통화공급**
  The total amount of money available in the economy by central bank
  중앙은행에서 공급하는 통화의 총량

- **monopolistic competition 독점적 경쟁**
  A market in which many firms sell differentiated product with easy entry and exit into the market
  진입과 이탈이 용이한 가운데 많은 기업들이 차별화된 상품을 팔고 있는 시장

- **monopoly 독점**
  a market in which one firm is the single seller of a product
  한 기업이 상품의 유일한 판매자인 시장

- **monopsony 수요독점**
  A factor market in which one firm is the single buyer of a resource
  한 기업이 생산요소의 유일한 소비자인 생산요소시장

- **moral hazard 도덕적 해이**
  The danger that one party of a contract change his conduct for profits
  계약의 한 당사자가 이익을 위해서 자신의 행동을 바꾸는 위험

- **multiplier effect 승수효과**
  A increase in a component of aggregate demand creates a greater change in nation's income
  총수요의 한 구성요소의 변화가 국민소득에 큰 영향을 미치는 효과

- **mutual fund 뮤추얼펀드**
  An financial institution that pools money from the public to purchase financial asset
  자금을 모아서 금융자산을 구매하는 간접금융기관

- **Nash equilibrium 내쉬 균형**
  The situation that no single player can be better off by unilaterally changing her strategy
  누구도 일방적으로 자신의 전략을 바꾸어서는 더 상황이 좋아질 수 없는 상황

- **natural monopoly 자연독점**
  A monopoly that arises economies scale are so remarkable that a single firm can provide goods to the entire market
  규모의 경제가 매우 현저하게 나타나서 한 기업이 시장전체에 상품을 공급할 수 있기 때문에 발생하는 독점

- **natural-rate hypothesis 자연실업률가설**
  The hypothesis argued by Milton Friedman that there is no trade-off between inflation and unemployment in the long run and the long-run philips curve is vertical at the natural rate of unemployment.
  밀턴프리드먼의 주장으로 인플레이션과 실업 사이에는 장기에는 아무런 상충관계가 없으며, 필립스 커브는 장기에 자연실업률에서 수직이라는 가설

- **natural rate of unemployment 자연실업률**
  The unemployment rate at which full employment is achieved
  완전고용이 달성되었을 때의 실업률

- **natural resources 천연자원**
  The resources provided by nature, such as land, water, and mineral
  땅, 물, 미네랄처럼 자연이 공급해주는 자원

- **necessity 필수재**
  A good whose consumption rises less than in proportion to increases in income. Income elasticity of demand is less than one
  소비량의 증가율이 소득의 증가율보다 작은 재화. 소득탄력성이 1보다 작음

- **negative externality 부정적 외부효과**

The cost to a bystander caused by market activity
시장 활동으로 제3자에게 비용을 발생시키는 것

- **negative income tax 부(負)의 소득세제**

  A tax system that impose tax on high income households and gives transfers to low-income households
  고소득자들에게 세금을 거두어 들여 저소득자들에게 이전지출하는 조세체제

- **net exports 순수출**

  exports minus imports
  수출에서 수입을 뺀 값

- **nominal GDP 명목GDP**

  GDP in current dollars
  현재 달러로 측정한 GDP

- **nominal variables 명목변수**

  Variables measured in monetary units
  통화단위로 측정한 변수

- **normal good 정상재**

  A good for which demand increases with an increase in consumer income
  소득 증가 시 수요가 증가하는 재화

- **normal profit 정상이윤**

  The opportunity cost of a person's talents, time and energy. If a firm is making normal profit, it is earning zero economic profit.
  한 개인의 재능, 시간, 에너지의 기회비용, 기업이 정상이윤을 벌고 있다면 경제적 이윤이 영이다.

- **normative statements 규범적 진술(처방적 분석)**

  Analysis that attempt to recommend or prescribe how the world ought to be
  세계가 어떻게 해야 하는가에 대해 조언하고 처방하려는 목적의 분석

- **not in the labor force 비경제활동인구**

  Number of people who do not belong to the employed nor the unemployed among adult population. They have no willingness to work.
  성인인구 중에 취업자나 실업자가 아닌 사람들, 일할 의사가 없는 사람이다.

- **official reserve account 공적 준비자금 계정**

  Foreign currency deposits and bonds held by central banks and monetary authorities
  중앙은행이나 통화당국이 보유한 외환이나 외국채권

- **Okun's law 오쿤의 법칙**

  The inverse relationship between GDP growth and unemployment. Simply put, as output falls, unemployment rises GDP.
  성장과 실업간의 역 관계, 간단하게 말하면 생산이 떨어지면 실업은 증가한다.

- **oligopoly 과점**

  A market with a few mutually interdependent sellers who are providing similar goods with a considerable barrier to entry
  소수의 상호간에 의존하고 있는 판매자들이 상당한 진입장벽 하에 유사한 상품을 팔고 있는 시장

- **open-market operations 공개시장조작**

  The purchase or sale of government bonds by the central bank
  중앙은행이 정부채권을 구매하고 판매하는 행위

- **opportunity cost 기회비용**

  The cost of any choice measured in terms of the value of the best alternative that is foregone.
  지나가버린 최상의 대안의 가치를 기준으로 측정한 선택의 비용

- **paradox of saving 저축의 역설**

  The situation that if everyone try to save more money in recession, total spending will fall, so will total income, which in turn will decrease total savings
  경기침체 시에 누구나 저축을 더 하려고 한다면 총지출의 감소로 인해 소득이 줄어들고 그로 인해 총저축이 줄어드는 역설적인 상황

- **perfect competition 완전경쟁**

  A market in which no firm can influence market outcome with no barriers to entry and exit
  진입장벽이 없는, 기업의 영향이 없는 시장

- **Phillips curve 필립스 곡선**

  The relationship between inflation and unemployment
  인플레이션과 실업의 관계

- **physical capital 실물자본**

  Equipment, machinery, and structures that are used to produce goods and services
  재화와 서비스의 생산에 사용되는 장비, 기계류, 구조물

- **Pigovian tax 피구세**

  A tax enacted to correct the effects of a negative externality
  부정적 외부효과를 교정하기 위해 실시하는 세금

- **positive statements 실증적 진술**

  Claims that attempt to describe the world as it is
  세계가 어떠한 모습인가를 서술하려는 주장

- **poverty line 빈곤선**

  An specified level of income below which a household is regarded to be in poverty

그 선 아래에 사는 가구는 빈곤한 상태에 있는 것으로 간주되는 특정한 소득수준

- **poverty rate 빈곤율**
  The percentage of the population whose households income falls below the poverty line
  빈곤선 아래에 해당하는 가구의 전체인구에서의 비중

- **predatory Pricing 약탈적 가격덤핑**
  The business practice that an oligopolistic firm slash its price in order to drive its competitors out of market and then regain its monopoly power and raise prices
  과점적 기업이 가격을 크게 내려서 경쟁자들을 시장에서 내쫓은 후 다시 독점력을 얻어 가격을 올리는 사업관행

- **price ceiling 가격상한제**
  Maximum price charged for a product by government (for the protection of consumers)
  정부가 부과한 한 상품의 최고가격(소비자 보호 목적)

- **price discrimination 가격차별**
  Business practice of charging different prices to different customers for the same good or service
  동일한 상품이나 서비스를 다른 소비자에게 다른 가격을 부과하는 기업관행

- **price elasticity of demand 수요의 가격탄력성**
  A measure of how responsive the quantity demanded of a good is to a change in the price of that good
  가격이 변화할 때 수요량의 변화 정도

- **price elasticity of supply 공급의 가격탄력성**
  A measure of how responsive the quantity supplied of a good is to a change in the price of that good
  가격이 변화할 때 공급량의 변화정도

- **price floor 가격하한제**
  minimum price charged for a product by government (for the protection of consumers)
  정부가 부과한 한 상품의 최소가격(생산자 보호 목적)

- **price level 물가 수준**
  Average level of prices in an economy
  한 경제 내의 가격의 평균적 수준

- **price support 가격지지**
  A policy by which the government sets the price of a good, usually an agricultural product, above the free-market level and buys up whatever output is needed to maintain that price
  보통 농산물시장에서 정부가 시장균형 이상으로 가격을 정하여 그 가격을 유지하기에 필요한 생산량만큼 사들이는 정책

- **price taker 가격수용자**

    A firm which act according to the price determined in market. It has no power to influence price.
    시장에서 결정되는 가격에 따라 행동하는 기업, 가격에 영향을 미칠 힘이 전혀 없다.

- **principal-agent problem 주인-대리인문제**

    The problem that arises when managers(agents) pursue their own profits, even if that entails lower profits for the owners of the firm(the principals)
    경영자(대리인)가 기업의 소유자(주인)에게 낮은 이익을 가져올 수도 있지만 자기 자신의 이익을 추구할 때 발생하는 문제

- **prisoners' dilemma 죄수의 딜레마**

    A situation that shows why two individuals might not cooperate, even if appears mutually profitable
    두 개인이 협력하는 것이 상호간에 이익이 됨에도 불구하고 서로 협력하지 못하는 상황

- **producer price index 생산자가격지수**

    A price index measuring the cost of a bundle of goods and services purchased by firms
    기업이 구매하는 재화와 서비스의 묶음 비용을 측정하는 가격지수

- **producer surplus 생산자잉여**

    The difference between price and the seller's cost 가격과 판매자의 비용의 차이

- **production function 생산함수**

    The relationship between inputs and total outputs
    투입요소와 총산출의 관계

- **Production possibilities curve(production possibilities frontier) 생산가능곡선**

    A diagram showing the maximum combinations of output of two goods given the available resources and technology
    주어진 자원과 기술 하에 두 재화의 최대생산조합을 보여주는 도표

- **productivity 생산성**

    The amount of output per unit of input in a given time period
    주어진 시간에 투입요소당 산출량

- **profit 이윤**

    Total revenue minus total cost
    총수입과 총비용의 차이

- **profit maximization 이윤극대화**

    Maximizing the difference between total revenue and total cost, which is the goal of a firm and achieved at MR=MC.
    총수입과 총비용의 차이를 극대화하는 것이고 기업의 목표이며 MR=MC에서 달성된다.

- **progressive tax 누진세**

    A tax by which tax rate increase as income increases
    소득이 상승할 때 세율도 올라가는 세금

- **proportional tax 비례세**

    A tax by which tax rate stay the same as income increases
    소득이 증가할 때 세율은 변함이 없는 세금

- **public goods 공공재**

    Non-rival and non-exclusive good
    비경합적이고 비배제적인 재화

- **purchasing power 구매력**

    Income in terms of goods how much quantities of good can be bought with the income given, in other sense, real income.
    주어진 소득으로 얼마나 많은 재화를 구매할 수 있는가를 재화기준에서 본 소득, 실질소득이라고도 한다.

- **purchasing Power Parity 구매력평가설**

    The proposition that the international value of a currency reflect the ratio of the domestic price and foreign price of the same good because the same good must have the same price everywhere.
    같은 상품은 가격이 같아야하기 때문에 한 통화의 국제가치는 같은 상품의 국내가격과 외국가격의 비율을 반영한다는 주장

- **quantity demanded 수요량**

    The quantity of a good which is demanded at any given price
    주어진 가격에서 수요 되는 재화의 수량

- **quantity supplied 공급량**

    The quantity of a good which is supplied at any given price
    주어진 가격에서 공급되는 재화의 수량

- **quantity theory of money 화폐수량설**

    A theory asserting that the quantity of money available determines the price level and that the growth rate in the quantity of money available determines the inflation rate
    통화공급량이 물가수준을 결정하고 통화공급량의 증가율이 인플레이션율을 결정한다는 이론

- **quota 수량제한**

    Restrictions on the quantities of goods that can be imported
    수입될 수 있는 재화의 수량을 제한하는 것

- **rational expectations 합리적 기대**

    According to rational expectation, people forecast the future using all the optimal information available to them.
    사람들은 가용한 모든 최적의 정보를 사용하여 미래를 예측한다는 것

- **real exchange rate 실질환율**

  The relative price of foreign goods in terms of domestic goods
  국내재화를 기준으로 외국재화의 상대적 가격

- **real GDP 실질GDP**

  The total production of goods and services using base year price, GDP in constant dollars, GDP adjusted for inflation
  기준년도를 사용한 재화와 서비스의 총생산. 변함없는 달러로 계산한 GDP, 인플레이션 조정을 한 값이다.

- **real interest rate 실질이자율**

  The interest rate adjusted for inflation, the interest rate in terms of goods
  인플레이션 조정을 한 이자율. 실물의 관점에서 본 이자율

- **real variables 실질변수**

  Variables measured in physical units
  실물단위로 측정한 변수

- **recession 경기침체**

  A period of negative GDP growth
  GDP성장이 마이너스인 기간

- **regressive tax 역진세**

  A tax by which tax rate decrease as income increases
  소득이 증가할 때 세율이 감소하는 세금

- **required reserves 법정지급준비금**

  The minimum amount of deposits that bank should hold as reserves
  은행이 지급준비금으로 보유해야 할 최소한의 예금

- **required reserve ratio(reserve requirements) 법정지급준비율**

  The fraction of total deposits that bank must hold as reserves
  은행이 법률상 준비금으로 보유해야 할 총예금의 비율

- **rivalry in consumption 소비의 경합성**

  Property of a good whose consumption by one consumer diminishes the possibility of consumption by other consumers
  한 소비자의 소비가 다른 사람의 소비가능성을 줄일 수 있는 재화의 성질

- **sacrifice ratio 희생률**

  The number of percentage points of annual output lost in the process of reducing inflation by 1 percentage point
  인플레이션을 1퍼센트 줄이는 과정에서 상실되는 연간 산출량의 퍼센트

- **scarcity 희소성**
  The fundamental economic situation in which men have unlimited wants and needs in a world of limited resources
  무한한 욕구와 유한한 자원의 세계에서 살고 있는 근본적인 경제 상황

- **shoe-leather costs 구두창비용**
  The cost of time and efforts that people spend trying to hold less cash
  현금을 적게 보유하려는 가운데 발생하는 시간과 노력의 비용

- **shortage 부족**
  A situation in which quantity demanded is greater than quantity supplied. Excess demand
  수요량이 공급량보다 많은 상황, 초과수요

- **short-run 단기**
  The time span in which there exist fixed costs, which does not vary with the quantity of output
  생산량의 변화에 따라 달라지지 않는 고정비용이 존재하는 시간

- **specialization 전문화(특화)**
  Production of the goods with comparative advantage
  비교우위를 가진 재화를 생산하는 것

- **spending multiplier 지출승수**
  The amount by which real GDP change when spending changes by $1
  지출이 1달러 증가할 때 실질 GDP가 변화하는 크기

- **spill-over benefit(positive externality) 파급편익**
  Unintended benefit to the bystander through the market activity, such as research and development
  연구 개발과 같은 것으로 시장 활동을 통해 발생하는 제3자에게 의도없이(계산되지 않은) 주는 편익

- **spill-over cost(negative externality) 파급비용**
  Unintended cost to the bystander through the market activity, such as pollution
  공해 같은 것으로 시장활동을 통해 제 3자에게 주는 의도 없는(계산되지 않은) 비용

- **stagflation 스태그플레이션**
  The phenomenon in which stagnation(recession) and inflation occurs together
  경기침체와 인플레이션이 동시에 발생하는 현상

- **sticky prices(price rigidity) 가격경직성**
  The property that price level does not change
  물가가 변화되지 않는 성질

- **stock 주식**
  A financial asset that its owner has a claim to partial ownership in a firm
  소유자가 회사의 부분적인 소유권을 주장할 수 있는 금융자산

- **store of value 가치저장**

  A function of an item which people can use to transfer purchasing power from the present to the future
  사람들이 어떤 품목을 통해 구매력을 현재에서 미래로 이전시킬 수 있는 기능

- **strike 파업**

  The organized refusal of working by a union
  노동조합에 의해 조직화된 근무거부

- **structural unemployment 구조적 실업**

  unemployment that persists because people lack the skills necessary for available jobs.
  취업 가능한 직장에 필요한 기술이 부족해서 지속되고 있는 실업

- **subsidy 보조금**

  a government transfer, either to consumers or producers, on the consumption or production of a good
  재화의 소비와 생산에 있어서 소비자나 생산자에게 주는 정부의 이전지출

- **substitutes 대체제**

  Goods that can be replaced by each other because they give the similar satisfaction to the consumer. If the price of one good rises, the demand for the substitutes will also rises.
  소비자에게 유사한 만족감을 주기 때문에 대신 사용할 수 있는 재화. 어느 재화의 가격이 올라갔을 때, 대체재에 대한 수요가 증가한다.

- **substitution effect 대체효과**

  The change in consumption causes by an change in its price because the good has become relatively cheaper or more expensive.
  소비자가 상대적으로 싸졌거나 비싸졌기 때문에 변화하는 소비량의 크기를 말한다.

- **sunk cost 매몰비용**

  A cost that cannot be recovered. This cost should not be considered when making a decision.
  복구할 수 없는 비용. 의사결정을 할 때 이 비용을 고려해서는 안된다.

- **supply curve 공급곡선**

  A graph showing the relationship between the price of a good and the quantity supplied
  재화의 가격과 공급량의 관계를 보여주는 그래프

- **supply shock 공급충격**

  An unexpected shock to economy that affects costs of production and shift aggregate supply curve.
  생산비용에 영향을 미쳐서 총공급곡선을 이동시키는 예기치 않게 경제에 오는 충격

- **supply side economists 공급주의경제학자**

  a group of economist who believe that tax cut would eventually increase tax revenue by encouraging economic activity
  세금인하가 경제활동을 고취시켜 결국에는 조세수입을 증가시킬 것이라고 믿는 경제학자 집단

- **surplus 초과공급**

  excess supply, a situation in which quantity supplied exceeds quantity demanded
  공급량이 수요량을 초과하는 상황

- **tariff 관세**

  a tax imposed on imported goods
  수입제품에 부과하는 세금

- **tax incidence 조세의 귀착**

  the study of who bears the burden of taxation
  누가 조세부담을 짊어지는가에 대한 연구

- **tax multiplier 조세승수**

  The magnitude of the effect that a change in lump-sum taxes by $1 has on real GDP
  정액세 1달러의 변화가 실질 GDP에 미치는 영향의 크기

- **technology 기술**

  A society's scientific knowledge about techniques of production, operation of equipment, and natural resources
  생산기술, 장비운용, 자연자원에 대한 사회의 과학 지식

- **theory of liquidity preference 유동성선호이론**

  Keynes's theory that the interest rate adjusts to bring the money market into balance
  이자율이 화폐공급과 화폐수요를 균형으로 가져다준다는 케인스의 이론

- **total cost 총비용**

  Total fixed cost and total variable cost
  총고정비용과 총가변비용의 합

- **total revenue (for a firm) 총수입**

  Price multiplied by quantity sold, the amount a firm receives for the sale of its output
  가격에 판매량을 곱한 값, 기업이 생산물을 판매하고 받은 금액

- **trade balance 무역균형**

  The difference between exports and imports, net exports
  수출과 수입의 차이, 순수출

- **trade deficit 무역적자**

  The situation that import is greater than export

수입이 수출보다 큰 상황

- **trade-offs 상충관계**

   The situation that one thing has to be given up in order to get another thing
   한 가지가 포기되어야 다른 한 가지를 얻을 수 있는 상황

- **trade surplus 무역흑자**

   The situation that export is greater than import
   수출이 수입보다 큰 상황

- **tragedy of the commons 공유지의 비극**

   the situation in which multiple individuals who behave independently and rationally try to maximize their own self-interest, will ultimately use the common resources excessively
   독립적이고 합리적으로 행동하는 다수의 개인들이 자기이익을 극대화하기 위해 공유자원을 과도하게 사용하게 되는 현상

- **transaction costs 거래비용**

   The costs that are involved in the process of bargaining
   거래의 과정에 수반되는 비용

- **twin deficits 쌍둥이 적자**

   budget deficit and trade deficit
   예산적자와 무역적자

- **tying(bundling) 묶어 팔기**

   Business practice that a firm requires the buyer of a product to also purchase a second product together
   기업이 물건 하나를 사는 사람에게 다른 물건도 함께 구매하도록 요구하는 사업관행

- **underground economy 지하경제**

   Unreported and illegal part of a country's economic activity that is not measured in official statistics due to unlawful activity or tax avoidance
   불법적인 행동이나 세금포탈로 인해 공식통계에 잡히지 않는 한 국가의 경제활동으로 보고되지 않고 불법적인 부분

- **unemployment insurance 실업보험**

   A government transfer that partially protects workers' incomes when they become unemployed
   노동자들의 실직 시에 노동자들의 소득을 부분적으로 보호하기 위한 정부의 이전지출

- **unemployment rate 실업률**

   The ratio of the number of unemployed to the labor force
   경제활동인구에 대한 실업자 수의 비율

- **unit of account 회계단위**

    The measure used to report prices and record debts
    가격을 보고하고 부채를 기록하는 데 사용되는 척도

- **utilitarianism 공리주의**

    The philosophy that utility maximization of the whole society is the most important criteria in government redistribution policy
    사회의 효용극대화 정부의 재분배정책의 가장 중요한 기준이라고 주장하는 철학

- **utility 효용**

    The level of satisfaction, happiness, pleasure, enjoyment that a person gets from consuming goods and services
    재화와 서비스의 소비를 통해서 얻는 만족감, 행복감, 기쁨, 즐거움의 수준

- **utility maximizing rule 효용극대화 원칙**

    means equalizing marginal utility of each good per dollar
    각 재화의 달러당 한계효용을 같게 할 때 효용이 최대화된다는 법칙

- **value of the marginal product 한계생산가치**

    P × MPL, VMPL 가격×한계생산

- **variable costs 가변비용**

    Costs that change with the quantity of output
    생산량이 변할 때 변하는 비용

- **willingness to pay 지불용의금액**

    The maximum amount of money that a buyer will pay for a good
    구매자가 물건을 살 때 지불하고자 하는 최대금액

# 미국경제교육학회 National Council on Economic Education 가 제시하는 20가지 경제법칙

## STANDARD 1
Productive resources are limited. Therefore, people can not have all the goods and services they want, as a result, they must choose some things and give up others.
생산요소는 제한되어 있다. 따라서 사람들은 원하는 재화와 서비스를 모두 누릴 수는 없다. 그 결과로 사람들은 어떤 것은 선택해야 하고 어떤 것은 포기해야 한다.

### Content Keyword
scarcity, choice, goods, services, wants, opportunity cost, consumers, productive resources, natural resources, human resources, capital resources, human capital, entrepreneurs, producers

## STANDARD 2
Effective decision making requires comparing the additional costs of alternatives with the additional benefits. Most choices involve doing a little more or a little less of something: few choices are 'all or nothing' decisions.
효율적인 의사결정을 위해서는 대안의 추가적 비용과 편익을 비교해야 한다. 선택은 대부분 어떤 것을 조금 더 할 것인가 아니면 덜 할 것인가에 대한 것이다. '전부 아니면 전무' 식의 결정을 해야 하는 경우는 거의 없다.

### Content Keyword
decision making, marginal analysis, cost, benefit, profit maximization

## STANDARD 3
Different methods can be used to allocate goods and services. People acting individually or collectively through government, must choose which methods to use to allocate different kinds of goods and services.
재화와 서비스를 배분하기 위해 여러 가지 방법이 사용될 수 있다. 개인적으로 행동하든지 정부를 통해 집단적으로 행동하든지 여러 재화와 서비스를 어떤 방식으로 배분할 것인지를 선택해야 한다.

### Content Keyword
economic systems, market economy, command economy, traditional economy, What? How? For Whom?

## STANDARD 4
People respond predictably to positive and negative incentives.
사람들은 긍정적인 유인과 부정적인 유인에 반응할 것으로 예상된다.

### Content Keyword
incentives, choice

## STANDARD 5
Voluntary exchange occurs only when all participating parties expect to gain. This is true for trade among individuals or organizations within a nation, and usually among individuals or organizations in different nations.

자발적인 교환은 모든 참가자가 이득을 얻을 것으로 예상하는 경우에만 일어난다. 이 사실은 국내든지 국가 간이든지 개인과 집단 사이의 교역에서도 마찬가지이다.

### Content Keyword
exchange, barter, voluntary exchange, barriers to trade, imports, exports

## STANDARD 6
When individuals, regions, and nations specialize in what they can produce at the lowest cost and then trade with others, both production and consumption increase.

개인이나 지역, 또는 국가가 자신이 최저비용으로 생산할 수 있는 제품을 전문화해서 서로 교역하면 생산과 소비가 둘 다 증가한다.

### Content Keyword
specialization, gains from trade, comparative advantage, absolute advantage, investment in human capital, division of labor, productivity, interdependence, relative prices, productive resources, transaction costs, factor endowments

## STANDARD 7
Markets exist when buyers and sellers interact. This interaction determines market prices and thereby allocates scarce goods and services.

시장은 구매자와 판매자가 서로 거래할 때 생겨난다. 이 거래를 통해 시장 가격이 결정되고 희소한 자원과 서비스를 배분된다.

### Content Keyword
markets, prices, producers, consumers, relative prices, equilibrium price, quantity demanded, quantity supplied, exchange rate, shortage, surplus

## STANDARD 8
Prices send signals and provide incentives to buyers and sellers. When supply or demand changes, market prices adjust, affecting incentives.

가격은 구매자와 판매자에게 신호를 보내고 인센티브를 제공한다. 수요와 공급이 변할 때, 시장 가격은 변화되고 인센티브에 영향을 준다.

### Content Keyword
prices, law of demand, law of supply, substitute goods, determinants of demand,

determinants of supply, price ceilings, price floors

## STANDARD 9
Competition among sellers lowers costs and prices, and encourages producers to produce more of what consumers are willing and able to buy. Competition among buyers increases prices and allocates goods and services to those people who are willing and able to pay the most for them.

판매자 간 경쟁으로 비용과 가격이 내려가고 생산자들은 소비자들의 구매의사와 능력이 있는 제품을 더 많이 생산하게 된다. 구매자 간 경쟁으로 가격은 올라가고 가장 높은 가격으로 구매할 의사와 능력이 있는 사람에게 재화와 서비스가 배분된다.

### Content Keyword
competition, levels of competition

## STANDARD 10
Institutions evolve in market economies to help individuals and groups accomplish their goals. Banks, labor unions, corporations, legal systems, and not-for-profit organizations are examples of important institutions. A different kind of institution, clearly defined and enforced property rights, is essential to a market economy.

시장경제에서 제도는 개인과 집단이 각자의 목표 달성에 도움이 되는 방향으로 발전한다. 은행, 노동조합, 주식회사, 법률 체계, 비영리단체의 경우가 중요한 제도의 예이다. 다른 종류의 제도인 재산권은 명확하게 정의되고 강화된다면 시장 경제에 필수적이다.

### Content Keyword
economic institutions, banking, saving, interest, savers, borrowers, labor unions, non-profit organizations, property rights, legal foundations of a market economy, legal forms of business

## STANDARD 11
Money makes it easier to trade, borrow, save, invest, and compare the value of goods and services.

화폐는 교역, 대부, 저축, 투자, 재화와 서비스의 가치비교를 쉽게 할 수 있도록 해준다.

### Content Keyword
role and function of money, money, definition of money, exchange, currency, money supply

## STANDARD 12
Interest rates, adjusted for inflation, rise and fall to balance the amount saved with the amount borrowed, which affects the allocation of scarce resources between present and future uses.

이자율은 물가상승률에 조정되어 오르고 내리면서 저축과 대부의 균형을 맞춘다. 그래서 희소한 자원이 현재와 미래 사이에서 배분되는 일에 영향을 준다.

### Content Keyword
interest rate, real vs. nominal, risk, monetary policy

# STANDARD 13
Income for most people is determined by the market value of the productive resources they sell. What workers earn depends, primarily, on the market value of what they produce and how productive they are.

대부분 소득은 그들이 판매하는 생산요소의 시장 가치에 따라 결정된다. 노동자들의 소득은 주로 그들이 생산하는 제품의 시장가치와 그들의 생산성에 달려 있다.

### Content Keyword
labor, human resources, marginal resource product, wage, investment in human capital, labor market, prices of inputs, derived demand, personal distribution of income, functional distribution of income

# STANDARD 14
Entrepreneurs are people who take the risks of organizing productive resources to make goods and services. Profit is an important incentive that leads entrepreneurs to accept the risks of business failure.

기업가들은 재화와 서비스를 생산을 위해 생산요소의 관리 시 발생하는 위험을 감수하는 사람들이다. 기업가들이 사업실패의 위험을 감수하게 하는 중요한 유인은 이윤이다.

### Content Keyword
entrepreneurship, invention, innovation, benefit, cost, risk, profit, costs of production, taxes

# STANDARD 15
Investment in factories, machinery, new technology, and in the health, education, and training of people can raise future standards of living.

공장·기계·신기술에 대한 투자(물적 투자), 건강·교육·직업훈련에 대한 투자(인적 투자)는 미래의 생활수준을 향상시킨다.

### Content Keyword
investment, human capital, physical capital, standard of living, productivity, technological change, economic growth, intensive growth, opportunity cost, risk, trade-off, interest rates, incentives

# STANDARD 16
There is an economic role for government in a market economy whenever the benefits of a government policy outweigh its costs. Governments often provide for national defense, address environmental concerns, define and protect property rights, and attempt to make markets more competitive. Most government policies also redistribute income.

정부 정책의 편익이 그 비용보다 큰 경우에는 언제든지 정부의 경제적 역할이 시장경제에서도 있는 것이다. 정부는 국방을 제공하고 환경문제를 해결하며 재산권을 확정하고 정의하며, 시장이 보다 더 경쟁적이도록 한다. 정부 정책의 대부분은 소득을 재분배한다.

**Content Keyword**
role of government, distribution of income, taxes, bonds, public goods, externalities, maintain competition, regulation, income tax, transfer payments, non-clearing markets, monopolies, property rights

# STANDARD 17
Costs of government policies sometimes exceed benefits. This may occur because of incentives facing voters, government officials, and government employees, because of actions by special interest groups that can impose costs on the general public, or because social goals other than economic efficiency are being pursued.

정부 정책의 비용이 편익을 초과하기도 한다. 이런 현상은 유권자, 정부관료, 정부고용인 등이 직면하는 유인 때문에 발생하기도 하고 일반 대중에게 비용을 부과하는 특별 이익단체의 행동 때문이거나 경제적 효율성보다는 사회적 목표를 추구하기 때문에 발생하기도 한다.

**Content Keyword**
cost, benefit, barriers to trade, special interest groups

# STANDARD 18
A nation's overall levels of income, employment, and prices are determined by the interaction of spending and production decisions made by all households, firms, government agencies, and others in the economy.

일국의 전반적인 소득, 고용, 가격의 수준은 경제 내의 가계, 기업, 정부기관, 다른 경제주체들이 내리는 지출과 생산의 상호작용에 의해 결정된다.

**Content Keyword**
macroeconomic indicators, GDP, circular flow, potential GDP, per capita GDP, nominal and real GDP

# STANDARD 19
Unemployment imposes costs on individuals and nations. Unexpected inflation imposes costs on many people and benefits some others because it arbitrarily redistributes purchasing power. Inflation can reduce the rate of growth of national living standards because individuals and organizations use resources to protect themselves against the

uncertainty of future prices.
실업으로 개인과 국가에 비용이 발생한다. 예상치 않은 인플레이션은 자의적으로 구매력을 재분배하기 때문에 많은 사람들에게 비용을 부과하면서도 어떤 사람들에게는 이득을 주기도 한다. 인플레이션은 국가의 생활수준의 성장률을 감소시키는데, 이는 개인과 집단이 미래 가격의 불확실성에 대비하여 자신들을 보호하기 위해 생산요소를 사용하기 때문이다.

### Content Keyword
inflation, unemployment, labor force, unemployment rate, types of unemployment, CPI

# STANDARD 20
Federal government budgetary policy and the Federal Reserve System's monetary policy influence the overall levels of employment, output, and prices.
연방정부의 예산정책과 연방 준비제도(미국의 중앙은행)의 통화정책은 전반적인 고용, 생산, 가격 수준에 영향을 미친다.

### Content Keyword
federal budget, fiscal policy, monetary policy, budget deficit, budget surplus, national debt, causes of inflation, tools of the Federal Reserve, open market operations, discount rate, reserve requirements

# Notes

### different types of tax
1) Paul Krugman, Krugman's Economics, chapter 7, PPT 자료 인용
   http://bcs.worthpublishers.com/krugmanwells_econ2/

### production function
2) www.wikipedia.org

### information asymmetry
3) Paul Krugman, Chapter 21

### information asymmetry
3) Paul Krugman, Chapter 21

### 학파에 대한 설명
4) 20세기 경제사, 경제학에 대한 이해는 미국의 공영방송인 PBS에서 제작한 Commanding Heights: Episode1-Battle of Ideas를 강력 추천합니다. youtube에서 검색하면 바로 나옵니다.

### Tip. The limitation of GDP as an index of well-being
5) 로버트 케네디가 GDP의 문제점을 웅변적으로 지적하고 있다.

[Gross domestic product] does not allow for the health of our children, the quality of their education, or the joy of their play. It does not include the beauty of our poetry or the strength of our marriages, the intelligence of our public debate or the integrity of our public officials. It measures neither our courage nor wisdom, nor our devotion to our country. It measures everything, in short, except that which makes life worthwhile, and it can tell us everything about America except why we are proud that we are Americans. — Senator Robert Kennedy from Mankiw, Principles of Economics, 5th. p.520

### paradox of thrift
6) Paul Krugman, chapter 22. PPT 자료 인용

해외 유학생을 위한
# 익혀먹는 레알 AP 경제 용어사전

**1판 1쇄 인쇄** 2013년 8월 1일
**1판 1쇄 발행** 2013년 8월 5일

**지은이** 임해용
**발행인** 이미옥
**발행처** 아이생각
**정　가** 17,000원
**등록일** 2003년 3월 10일
**등록번호** 220-90-18139
**주　소** (143-849)서울 광진구 능동 253-21
**새 주 소** (143-849)서울 광진구 능동로 32길 159
**전화번호** (02)447-3157~8
**팩스번호** (02)447-3159

저자 합의
인지 생략

ISBN 978-89-97466-08-5 (13740)　　　I-13-05
Copyright ⓒ 2013 ithinkbook Publishing Co., Ltd

# 우리는 지금 연수하러 간다!

개성있는 저자들이 들려주는 생생한 연수 이야기!
좌충우돌, 어디로 뛸지 모르는 저자들의 연수 경험과 현지에서 겪어야만 알 수 있는
특별한 이야기 및 노하우가 독자 여러분을 자극합니다.
톡톡 튀는 특별한 연수를 계획해 보세요!
보다 재미있고, 보다 효과적으로, 보다 의욕 충만하도록 다채로운 국가별 연수, 한번 떠나볼까요?

 성공어학연수 1번 미국

**성공어학연수 가이드**
**미국 맞짱뜨기**
이재혁 저 / 정가 12,000원

영어하면 생각나는 그곳은? 당연히 미국이지!
미국 연수생활에 꼭 필요한 정보만 모았다!

 성공어학연수 2번 필리핀

**성공어학연수 가이드**
**필리핀 맞짱뜨기**
박미경 저 / 정가 12,000원

1:1 수업으로 고급 영어를 배우려면? 필리핀으로 가자!
저자가 들려주는 유쾌상쾌통쾌 알짜 필리핀 현지 연수 이야기로
수준 있는 필리핀 연수를 시작한다!

 성공어학연수 3번 캐나다

**성공어학연수 가이드 캐나다 맞짱뜨기**
**우리는 지금 캐나다로 간다!**
양우영 저 / 정가 12,000원

연수생들이 꼭 필요한 것이 무엇인지를 아는 핵심 정보만 모였다!
군더더기 없는 정보와 친절한 가이드로 연수생들의 체계적이고
성공적인 연수를 위해 탄생한 Best of best!

성공어학연수 4번 토론토&밴쿠버

성공어학연수 가이드 - 토론토 & 밴쿠버
캐나다 맞짱뜨기
손영준/박기혁 저 / 정가 13,000원

토론토와 밴쿠버 연수생의 필독서!
캐나다 연수 핵심지의 액기스 정보들을 모아 엮은
토론토&밴쿠버 연수 지침서!

 성공어학연수 5번 중국

성공어학연수 가이드
키스 더 드래곤의 중국 맞짱뜨기
최원철 저 / 정가 13,000원

남다른 열정과 순발력, 유머가 가득한 저자의 연수 경험과 정보는
중국 연수 희망자들을 위한 중국 연수의 이정표가 된다!
남과 다른 CHINA는 중국 연수를 하고 싶다면 무조건 펼쳐라!

 성공어학연수 6번 영국

성공어학연수 가이드 영국 맞짱뜨기
우리는 지금 영국으로 간다
양건희 저 / 정가 15,000원

독자를 매료시킬 준비는 되어있다!
수년간 영국 현지에서 살아온 저자의 연수 노하우가 끊임없이
독자 여러분을 영국으로 인도한다! 여기에 저자가 들려주는
영국문화 이야기와 영국 영어 이야기는 덤!

성공어학연수 7번 뉴질랜드

### 성공어학연수 가이드 - 뉴질랜드 맞짱뜨기
### 우리는 지금 뉴질랜드로 간다
장신영 저 / 정가 15,000원

지상 최고의 낙원이자 레포츠의 천국, 뉴질랜드에서
남다른 연수 경험을 쌓기를 원하는 분께 추천!
본 도서에는 뉴질랜드 연수 전문가의 현지 생활 적응부터 연수 및
워킹홀리데이까지 뉴질랜드로 떠나는 분들을 위한
알찬 정보만을 구성해 엮은 뉴질랜드 연수의 기본서!

 성공어학연수 8번 호주

### 성공어학연수 가이드 - 호주 맞짱뜨기
### 우리는 지금 호주로 간다
김세윤 저 / 정가 15,000원

깨끗하고 청정한 자연 속에서 집중적으로 영어공부를 하고 싶다면?
호주를 빼놓을 수 없다! 호주 연수 및 워킹홀리데이에서 꼭 필요한
정보만 군더더기 없이 골라모아 독자들에게 소개하는 호주 연수와
현지생활 가이드 최고의 지침서!

 성공어학연수 9번 일본

### 성공어학연수 가이드 - 일본 맞짱뜨기
### 우리는 지금 일본으로 간다
이수희 저 / 정가 15,000원

전통과 현대가 공존하는 가깝고도 먼 나라 일본에서의
특별한 연수를 시작하는 분께 추천하는 필독서!
다양한 볼거리와 다양한 먹거리는 물론 제2외국어 선택율로
학생들의 든든한 지지를 받는 일본에서 성공적인 어학연수생활로
이어지는 저자의 현지생활과 연수 이야기를 저자의 노하우와
경험담으로 재미있고 유쾌하게 소개한다.